War, Culture and Society, 1750–1850

Series Editor

Rafe Blaufarb
Florida State University
Tallahassee, USA

Alan Forrest
University of York
York, UK

Karen Hagemann
Netherlands Institute for Advanced Study
Wassenaar, The Netherlands

The century from 1750 to 1850 was a period of seminal change in world history, when the political landscape was transformed by a series of revolutions fought in the name of liberty. These ideas spread far beyond Europe and the United States: they were carried to the furthest outposts of empire, to Egypt, India and the Caribbean, and they would continue to inspire anti-colonial and liberation movements in Central and Latin America throughout the first half of the nineteenth century. The Age of Revolutions was a world movement which cries out to be studied in its global dimension. But it was not only social and political institutions that were transformed by revolution in this period. So, too, was warfare. During the quarter-century of the French Revolutionary and Napoleonic wars in particular, Europe was faced with the prospect of 'total' warfare with mass mobilization on a scale that was unequalled until the Great Wars of the twentieth century. Those who lived through the period shared formative experiences that would do much to shape their ambitions and forge their identities. The volumes published in this series seek to address these issues by: - discussing war across Europe and throughout the Atlantic world, thereby contributing to a global history of war in this period; - integrating political, social, cultural and military history and art history, thus developing a multidisciplinary approach to the analysis of war; - analysing the construction of identities and power relations with reference to various categories of difference, notably class, gender, religion, generational difference, race and ethnicity; - examining elements of comparison and transfer, so as to tease out the complexities of national, regional and global history; - crossing traditional borders between early modern and modern history since this is a period which integrates aspects of old and new, traditional and modern.

More information about this series at
http://www.springer.com/series/14390

Sharon Murphy

The British Soldier and his Libraries, c. 1822–1901

palgrave
macmillan

Sharon Murphy
Dublin City University,
Dublin 9, Ireland

War, Culture and Society, 1750–1850
ISBN 978-1-137-55082-8 (hardcover)   ISBN 978-1-137-55083-5 (eBook)
ISBN 978-1-349-71559-6 (softcover)
DOI 10.1057/978-1-137-55083-5

Library of Congress Control Number: 2016940258

This Palgrave Macmillan imprint is published by SpringerNature
The registered company is Macmillan Publishers Ltd. London.

NOTE ON STYLE

The East India Company maintained a military force in each of the three Presidencies in India: the Bengal army, the Madras army, and the Bombay army. The three armies, however, were often referred to collectively as either the East India Company army or as the army of "John Company," and I follow this practice for the purposes of convenience (except where I am referring to particular regiments). Similarly, men who served in the British army in the nineteenth century might have described themselves as serving in the army of the Crown. I have chosen, however, to discuss the Regular Army (wherever the making of such a distinction is necessary). Names of some of the (surviving) regiments in the British army have been changed since the period under discussion in this book, but I retain the nineteenth-century nomenclature wherever I mention such a regiment.

Any discussion of the East India Company and nineteenth-century India necessarily requires some mention of 1857, the year that transformed the Company's—and Britain's—relationship to the subcontinent. Most of the soldiers with whom this book is concerned would have described the events of that year as the "Indian Mutiny," or as the "Sepoy Mutiny" or the "Sepoy Revolt," but I refer to them as the Indian Rebellion (except where I am quoting from contemporary sources). In doing so, though, I recognize that many would point out that what I am describing actually represents the first manifestation of the movement that eventually secured India's independence from British rule.

Finally, Mumbai was Bombay in the nineteenth century, and Kannur was Cannanore (at least, to Europeans). I have chosen to retain nineteenth-century usage of Indian place names throughout, and this is sometimes reflective of the fact that the spelling of these was not standardized during that period.

Acknowledgements

Thank you, firstly, to the librarians, curators, archivists, and other support staff who have facilitated my research in the following places over the years: the Asian and Africa Studies reading room, the Rare Books and Music reading room, and the Manuscripts reading room in the British Library in London; the National Army Museum in London; the London Metropolitan Archive (which facilitated my reading of NAM material when it closed for the purposes of refurbishment); the different libraries of Trinity College, Dublin, most especially the Official Publications section in the Berkeley Library, and Early Printed Books (where I am particularly grateful to Simon Lang, Helen McGinley, and Shane Mawe); the National Library of Ireland, Dublin; Dublin City University Library; and the Cregan Library, St. Patrick's Campus, DCU.

Quotations from material held at the following shelfmarks in the British Library's Oriental and India Office Collections are copyright the British Library Board, and I am extremely grateful to the Board for granting me permission to use them for the purposes of this study: L/Mil/3/1162; L/Mil/3/1331; L/Mil/3/1457; L/Mil/3/1506; L/Mil/3/1555; L/Mil/5/384; F/4/1243/40911; F/4/1272/51087; F/4/1428/56391; F/4/1486/58611; F/4/1701/68730; F4/1949/84727; E/4/753; E/4/759; E/4/764; E/4/765; E/4/839; E/4/851; E/4/943; Mss Eur D900; Photo Eur 257; Photo Eur C332, 96; and Ms. Add 59876. Similarly, quotations from British newspapers are copyright The British Library Board and, again, thank you to the Board for granting me permission to use them. Quotations from materials in the National Army Museum's collections are courtesy of the Council of the National Army

Museum, and I am very grateful to the council for granting me permission to use them. Part of Chap. 2 was previously published in an earlier form in *Book History* (vol. 12, 2009, pp. 74–100), and is reproduced here with the permission of the editors. Similarly, part of Chap. 3 first appeared in an earlier form in the *Journal of the Royal Asiatic Society* (third series, vol. 21, Oct. 2011, pp. 459–467), and is reproduced by permission of the editors. Part of the material in Chap. 4 appeared in an earlier form, and is adapted by permission of the Publishers from "'Quite incapable of appreciating books written for educated readers': the mid-nineteenth-century British Soldier," in *A Return to the Common Reader* eds. Beth Palmer and Adelene Buckland (Farnham: Ashgate, 2011), pp. 121–32 Copyright © 2011. Thank you to Jackie Brown and Jovita Callueng, Alistair Massie, Jonathon Rose, Charlotte Du Blois, and Keith Towndrow for helping me to arrange the respective permissions outlined above.

St. Patrick's College, Drumcondra, has been going through huge changes during the time that I have been working on the completion of this volume, and I therefore would like to take the opportunity to express my sincere gratitude to that institution for all of its support over the years. I would also like to express my particular gratitude to the College Research Committee for providing financial assistance in relation to the preparation of an index for this study, and Marie-Pierre Evans for so efficiently producing same. I also wish to record here my sincere thanks to the School of English, Trinity College, Dublin, for appointing me in 2005 to the post-doctoral research fellowship that helped me to finance the early part of my research on this project. I would also like to express here my gratitude to all those colleagues and fellow scholars who offered helpful comments and advice over the years, especially Archie Dick, Fionnuala Dillane, Nicholas Grene, Peter Hoare, James Kelly, Caitriona Kennedy, Máire Kennedy, Jarlath Killeen, Esko Laine, Tuija Laine, K.A. Manley, Ian Campbell Ross, Jill Shefrin, and Mark Towsey. I would also like to thank all those readers who read different parts of my research when I submitted it with a view to publication (sometimes successfully, sometimes unsuccessfully); I appreciated the care with which everybody read my work, and thank one and all for their helpful suggestions. I am hugely indebted to all of my colleagues—past and present—in what is still at the time of writing the English Department, St. Patrick's Campus, Dublin City University; most especially, thank you to Noreen Doody and Derek Hand, who offered practical support during the final stages of the composition of this book, and to Louise Callinan, whose generosity as a colleague enabled me to step down from two of my administrative roles within the department for a semester. Thank you, too, to Pauric Travers, Dáire Keogh, Darryl Jones, Declan Kiberd, Margaret Kelleher, and PJ Mathews, who had reason to consider my work in their various official capacities over the years, and who offered generous advice and encouragement.

The writing of a book is a hugely personal as well as professional endeavor, and I am particularly mindful of my late parents as I write this. I therefore would like to pause here and remember Mum and Dad with love; I would also like to acknowledge that I am able to write and teach primarily because they worked so hard to give my brother and myself the opportunities that they never had. Thank you, too, most sincerely, to my brother, David Murphy, for his generous support and advice over the years; to Georgina Laragy, my sister-in-law, for the cheerful way in which she puts up with the other Murphy "twin"; and to my newly minted niece, Ellie, for being so patient with her learner aunt. I would also like to thank my friends for their support, especially Rosanne Roe Florence and Patricia O'Reilly; Jacqueline Belanger and Jeff Nossbaum; Edwina Keown and Carol Taaffe; James McGuire; Patricia Camilleri; Gerry, Noeleen, and Natasha O'Reilly; Victor Bennett, Tricia McCaffrey, Peta Taaffe, and Susan and Neil Comer.

Authors need publishers, and I felt very fortunate indeed when Palgrave Macmillan accepted my book proposal. I therefore wish to extend my sincere gratitude to Jenny McCall, Angharad Bishop, Emily Russell, Rowan Milligan, Ganesh Ekambaram, and the entire production team, who guided me with great good humor and efficiency through the various stages of the publication process. I would also like to thank my "Reader" for the tremendous care that he or she clearly brought to the reading of my work; it was wonderful to receive criticism that was as helpful as it was encouraging. Finally, I wish to thank Aileen Douglas for offering ongoing support when a strand of my doctoral research on Maria Edgeworth eventually took me in a direction that neither of us could have expected. As a very small gesture of my gratitude to Aileen, I am dedicating this book to her.

CONTENTS

CHAPTER 1

Introduction

In 1824, Joseph Donaldson published his recollections of his "eventful" life, which until then he had spent "chiefly" as a soldier. The only son of a father who was employed by a mercantile house in Glasgow, as a young man he seemed to have a promising future before him, but unfortunately he made a number of decisions that were to affect the course of his life adversely. Donaldson made the first of these in 1807, when he decided that he would run away to sea with a school companion. The voyage that the pair eventually made, to the West Indies, cured him of his ambition to become a sailor and, tragically, cost his friend his life. Upon returning home after this ill-fated adventure, Donaldson resumed his education at his father's urging, but in 1809 he decided to run away again. This time, he chose to enlist in the army, a step he noted in his memoir as "the source of constant and unavailing regret"; this was because his experiences in the army exposed him to the harsh realities of a soldier's existence in the early nineteenth century, and convinced him that everything about military life at that time "conspired to sink [men] to that point where they became best fitted for *tractable beasts of burden*." All things considered, he wrote, "if there is one method better than another, to make a man an abject slave to the will of his superiors, without a conscience or a judgement of his own, one calculated to smother every generous and noble feeling,

© The Editor(s) (if applicable) and The Author(s) 2016
S. Murphy, *The British Soldier and his Libraries, c. 1822–1901*,
DOI 10.1057/978-1-137-55083-5_1

to destroy his morals and his constitution, there could not have been a better school chosen than the army, in the state it was in at that time."[1]

Donaldson's memoir is valuable for several reasons, including the fact that it reveals what he believed was the ultimate cause of his decision to enlist. As he put it, it was his early love of reading that distracted him from his education, encouraging him, firstly, to run away to sea and, eventually, take the king's shilling. *Robinson Crusoe* (1719), he declares, was "a great favourite," presumably in one of the cheaper reprints that ensured the continuing popularity of early eighteenth-century fiction well into the 1800s.[2] "I would have suffered shipwreck willingly, to be cast on an island like his," he remarks. "I have often played truant from school to wander into the fields, and read my favourite books; and, when I was not reading, my mind was perfectly bewildered with the romantic notions I had formed."[3] Here, of course, we find the commonly held view of reading at the time that Donaldson was writing; and, indeed, it was one that took on increasing currency during the Victorian period: namely, the belief that it was an activity that worked "through the subjectivity of the reader, transforming the individual from within" and that, as a result, readers had to be carefully supervised to control the possible consequences of this process.[4] The sentiments that Donaldson expresses can be found again and again in the educational treatises and literature of the late 1700s and early 1800s—in particular, in the arguments of those writers who insisted that the reading of young men was of paramount importance for their future development. Writing some 26 years before Donaldson, for example, the Irish writer Maria Edgeworth (1768–1849) had subjected the reading of males to scrutiny in *Practical Education* (1798), and one of her conclusions was that works like Defoe's novel were a dangerous distraction for certain boys and young men. Works like *Robinson Crusoe*, she observed, should "not early be chosen for boys of an enterprising temper,

---

[1] "A Soldier" [Joseph Donaldson], *Recollections of an eventful Life: chiefly passed in the Army* (Glasgow: W.R. McPhun, 1824), pp. 69 and 86–87. Henceforth "Donaldson, *Recollections*."

[2] On how the sale and reprinting of out-of-copyright texts in general were affected by the House of Lord's 1774 decision that perpetual copyright had been illegal since 1710, see William St. Clair's *The Reading Nation in the Romantic Period* (Cambridge: Cambridge University Press, 2004), p. 54, and on how this affected *Robinson Crusoe* in particular, see pp. 507–8.

[3] Donaldson, *Recollections*, p. 3.

[4] Gary Kelly, *Women, Writing, and Revolution, 1790–1827* (Oxford: Clarendon Press, 1993), p. 184.

unless they are intended for a seafaring life, or for the army. The taste for adventure is absolutely incompatible with the sober perseverance necessary to success in any other liberal professions."[5] Donaldson's tragedy, in Edgeworth's terms, was that he was not intended by his father to become either a soldier or a sailor, but the works he read as a boy and young man inappropriately inflamed his imagination and thwarted his father's ambition to place him in his own profession.

Donaldson is not the only nineteenth-century British soldier to have left evidence of his reading habits or preferences, or to have suggested that the works he read—or that were read aloud to him—affected the development of his character or his choice of profession. Sergeant Gowing, for instance, served with the Royal Fusiliers in both the Crimea and India, and revealed that he deliberately selected this regiment as a consequence of "its noble deeds of valour under Lord Wellington, in the Peninsula."[6] He was keen to stress, though, that Wellington was not his only inspiration: "I had read Nelson's exploits from childhood, studied all his principal battles, and learned how he forced our old enemies the French to tremble before him till his glorious deeds made the nation love and adore him."[7] Scotsman John Pindar came from a family that earned its living working in the mines and, at the age of ten, he was put to "driving a pony in a coalmine for sixpence a day." Pindar, however, was of "a studious nature," and so embraced every opportunity for self-improvement that came his way. As his "mind became enlightened by the few books [he] managed to buy or borrow," however, he became increasingly dissatisfied with his "monotonous life." "I had now managed," he notes, "to wander

---

[5] Maria Edgeworth and Richard Lovell Edgeworth, *Practical Education*, 2 vols. (London: J. Johnson, 1798), volume 1, p. 336. Edgeworth wrote of the composition of this work, "In [this] work ... the principles of education were peculiarly his [that is, her father's] ... all the general ideas originated with him, the illustrating and manufacturing them [*sic*], if I may use the expression, was mine." See Richard Lovell Edgeworth and Maria Edgeworth, *Memoirs of Richard Lovell Edgeworth, Esq. Begun by himself and concluded by his Daughter, Maria Edgeworth*, 2 vols. (London: R. Hunter, 1820), vol. 2, p. 190.

[6] Timothy Gowing, A *Soldier's Experience; or, Things not generally known, showing the Price of War in Blood and Treasure* (Colchester: Benham & Co., 1883), p. 2.

[7] Thomas Gowing, *Voice from the Ranks: A Personal Narrative of the Crimean Campaign by a Sergeant of the Royal Fusiliers*, edited by Kenneth Fenwick (London: Folio Society, 1954), p. 1. Fenwick notes that Gowing had this text "privately printed" by a Nottingham printer (p. vii), and the old soldier certainly seems to have published or arranged for the printing of his military experiences in several editions/variations. This was no doubt to encourage sales, and may also help to explain the variation of his first name.

through nearly all the works of the British poets, finding they all therein spoke proudly of the British Soldier, and sang his praise in soul-stirring strains. ... Indeed all the poets I had read ... had some encouraging word to say in favour of a soldier's life." Pindar declared himself finally uncertain as to the extent to which reading poetry influenced his decision to join the army, but it is clear that it crucially informed his determination "to look around ... for some occupation more congenial ... than that of a miner.... Professions requiring education were closed against me, and I began to perceive I had no prospect of being able to maintain myself in a respectable position above ground unless I enlisted for a soldier."[8] John Fraser also came from humble origins and was keen to stress that literacy was something that had been prized by his parents. When he came to publish his memoirs, he therefore drew his readers' attention to the fact that certain books had enjoyed pride of place among his family's possessions, and emphasized that the effects of his father's reading aloud of the Bible to him and his siblings each evening had stayed with him throughout the course of his life: "the great copy of the *Pilgrim's Progress* with its crocheted back lying with the equally large Bible and the copy of Burns' poems on the table by the window, the china dogs on the mantelpiece, and the old sofa with its curved back. ... [M]uch of the reading passed into us and became as much a part of us as do most things learned in childhood."[9]

Most soldiers, though, were more like William Lawrence, who was present at some of the "bloodiest and most famous actions" of the Napoleonic Wars. Urged by his friends in later life to record his experiences as a soldier in the early nineteenth century, he had to draw upon the services of an amanuensis because of his illiteracy.[10] The majority of the men who became soldiers resembled Lawrence and came from homes where access to reading material was either limited or nonexistent. For many of these men, it is clear, enlistment in either the East India Company's army or the Regular Army opened up a whole new world in terms of educational opportunities, and access to books and/or libraries was something that they treasured. John Green, for example, published an account of his

---

[8] John Pindar, *Autobiography of a Private Soldier* (Cupar-Fife: Printed in the "Fife News" Office, 1878), pp. 2–3.

[9] John Fraser, *Sixty Years in Uniform* (London: Stanley Paul, 1939), p. 23.

[10] Eileen Hathaway, introduction to *A Dorset Soldier: the Autobiography of Sergeant William Lawrence*, ed. Eileen Hathaway (Tunbridge Wells: Spellmount, 1993), p. ii. Lawrence refers on two respective occasions to letters that he "wrote" or "sent" to his parents during his career in the army; presumably he drew upon the service of an amanuensis here as well (pp. 101, 124).

time in the 68th Durham Light Infantry in the early nineteenth century, wherein he stressed both that he was quickly reckoned "the first scholar" in the school that was set up in the regiment around 1810, and "only regret[ted] that [it] did not commence sooner." He also recorded his gratitude to a Major Thompson, who gave him "liberty to read the books of the circulating library: even when he was on leave of absence, I had the same privilege allowed me."[11] One private, a Richard Perkes, declared in a letter to his brother in 1841 that he was happier than at any point in his life following his enlistment in John Company's army because he now had the opportunity of going to school and there were lots of books to read.[12]

Other men, such as Joseph Hinton, clearly responded in a more compli cated fashion to the military environment in which they found themselves, and decided to learn to read in a manner that preserved their independence. Remembering that "every other night [he] had to sit up to turn the gas out in the barracks," he recalled: "I had been seriously thinking over my ignorance, and one evening I said to my wife, who was living in the barracks with me, 'My dear, I'm going to teach myself to read and write.' She said, 'You'll never learn at your time of life.' 'Won't I?' says I. 'I will, and, what's more, I'll teach you too.' So next morning I went into the town and bought a few schoolbooks, and we stuck to it till I was made lance-sergeant."[13] Hinton was not alone in trying to encourage a loved one to read, and many men like him used their letters to try to convince friends or relatives of the importance of seizing every possible opportunity for self-improvement. Writing to his sister from Salford Barracks in 1854, for example, Sergeant Jowett thanked her for deciding "on a Dictionary as a birthday present for me; a book is always a suitable present, and I am very fond of a book and like to be reading; I find great improvement therefrom, and should advise you to read as much as you can."[14]

[11] John Green, *The Vicissitudes of a Soldier's Life, or a Series of Occurrences from 1806 to 1815; together with an introductory and concluding Chapter: the whole containing, with some other matters, a concise Account of the War in the Peninsula, from its commencement to its final close* (Louth and London: J. & J. Jackson; Simpkin Marshall, 1827), p. 53–54.

[12] See Richard Holmes, *Sahib: The British Soldier in India, 1750–1914* (London: HarperCollins, 2005), p. 94.

[13] E. Milton Small (ed), *Told from the Ranks: Recollections of Service during the Queen's Reign by Privates and Non-Commissioned Officers of the British Army* (London: Andrew Melrose, 1897), pp. 159–60. Hinton was a corporal when he began his studies.

[14] Jowett, W. *Memoir and Diary of Sergeant W. Jowett, Seventh Royal Fusiliers* (London and Beeston, Nottinghamshire: W. Kent & Co. and B. Porter, 1856), p. ix.

These are but very brief glimpses of some of the evidence that exists in relation to the reading of the nineteenth-century British soldier, and we shall see below that other sources are represented by army reports and regulations and testimony given to various committees during the 1800s. Despite the existence of such fascinating material, however, the subject of the nineteenth-century reading soldier has received only limited attention from literary critics and historians, with individuals such as Peter Stanley, Jonathan Rose, and Linda Colley leading the way in this regard.[15] This critical oversight is a remarkable one, especially as scholars have devoted increasing attention to the history of reading, the book, and libraries in recent years, drawing upon the methodologies of their different disciplines. Historians of the book, for instance, have traced what has been described as the communications circuit that runs between author, publisher, printer, shipper, bookseller, and reader, tracing how the book as a material object makes its way into the world.[16] Scholars concerned with reading have moved from the notion of the "common reader" to the significance of individual readers, examining to what extent it is possible to identify "what," "where," and "how" they read.[17] Library historians for

---

[15] See, for examples, K.A. Manley, "Engines of Literature: Libraries in an Era of Expansion and Transition," in Giles Mandelbrote and K.A. Manley (eds), *The Cambridge History of Libraries in Britain and Ireland, Vol. II, 1640–1850* (Cambridge: Cambridge University Press, 2006), pp. 509–528; Holmes, *Sahib*, especially p. 159; Peter Stanley, *White Mutiny: British Military Culture in India, 1825–1875* (London: Hurst & Company, 1998), especially pp. 43–45; Linda Colley, *Captives* (New York: Pantheon Books, 2002), pp. 277–287; and Jonathan Rose, *The Intellectual Life of the British Working Classes* (New Haven and London: Yale University Press, 2001), passim. The only detailed work that has been done to date on the provision of books to soldiers in India is represented by Dora Lockyer's "The Provision of Books and Libraries by the East India Company in India, 1611–1858," Thesis submitted for Fellowship of the Library Association, 1977.

[16] Examples here might include Robert Darnton, *The Kiss of Lamourette: Reflections in Cultural History* (London and Boston: Faber and Faber, 1990), especially pp. 107–35; Simon Eliot and Jonathan Rose (eds), *A Companion to the History of the Book* (Malden, Massachusetts; Oxford, England; and Carlton, Australia: Blackwell, 2007); and Adrian Johns, *The Nature of the Book: Print and Knowledge in the Making* (Chicago and London: University of Chicago Press, 1998).

[17] The seminal work here, of course, is represented by Richard D. Altick's ground-breaking *The English Common Reader: A Social History of the Mass Reading Public, 1800–1900* (1957; Columbus: Ohio State University Press, 1998). Other examples include Louis James, *Fiction for the Working Man, 1830–1850: A Study of the Literature produced for the Working Classes in early Victorian Urban England* (London, New York, and Toronto: Oxford University Press, 1963); Jon P. Klancher, *The Making of English Reading Audiences, 1790–1832* (Madison, Wisconsin and London: University of Wisconsin, 1987); and James Raven, Helen

their part have traced how different types of libraries came into being and, in the case of public libraries in Britain, have explored how ideas about the function, holdings, and operation of these institutions were shaped by debates raging outside their walls.[18] Literary theorists, too, have built upon the efforts of pioneers such as Richard D. Altick, Stanley Fish, and Wolfgang Iser, to name but three examples, and explored how placing the act of reading at the heart of criticism affects their discipline.[19] What they have increasingly recognized is that empirical research in relation to the act of reading has significant implications for literary theorists, and may pose considerable challenges to their long-held convictions about the "meanings" of texts and how they "work."[20]

This study has its origins in a desire to begin to facilitate the testing of one such conviction: namely, the perceived link between the reading of Britons in the late eighteenth and nineteenth centuries, and Britain's emergence at this time as a dominant imperial and global power. As scholars have pointed out, Britain enjoyed unparalleled overseas expansion in the years between 1780 and 1830, consolidating her rule over India and parts of Canada, and developing or adding greatly to her colonial possessions in Australia, South Africa, and the Caribbean.[21] During this same

Small and Naomi Tadmor (eds), *The Practice and Representation of Reading in England* (Cambridge: Cambridge University Press, 1996).

[18] See Alistair Black and Peter Hoare, "Libraries and the Modern World," in Alistair Black and Peter Hoare (eds), *The Cambridge History of Libraries in Britain and Ireland, Vol. III, 1850–2000* (Cambridge: Cambridge University Press, 2006), pp. 7–18; Chris Baggs, "Radical Reading? Working-Class Libraries in the Nineteenth and early Twentieth Centuries," in Black and Hoare (eds), *The Cambridge History of Libraries in Britain and Ireland, Vol. III*, pp. 169–179; Joanna Innes, "Libraries in Context: Social, Cultural, and Intellectual Background," in Giles Mandelbrote and K.A. Manley (eds), *The Cambridge History of Libraries in Britain and Ireland, Vol. II*, pp. 285–300; and Robert Snape, *Leisure and the Rise of the Public Library* (London: Library Association Publishing, 1995) and "Libraries for Leisure Time," in Black and Hoare (eds), *The Cambridge History of Libraries in Britain and Ireland, Vol. III*, pp. 40–55.

[19] Altick, *Common Reader*; Stanley Fish, *Is there a Text in this Class? The Authority of Interpretive Communities* (Cambridge, Massachusetts, and London: Harvard University Press, 1980); Wolfgang Iser, *The Implied Reader: Patterns of Communication in Prose Fiction from Bunyan to Beckett* (Baltimore, Maryland and London: Johns Hopkins, 1974) and *The Act of Reading: A Theory of Aesthetic Response* (Baltimore, Maryland and London: Johns Hopkins, 1978).

[20] Influential works here are represented by Rose's *The Intellectual Life of the British Working Classes* and St. Clair's *The Reading Nation in the Romantic Period*.

[21] Alan Richardson and Sonia Hofkosh, introduction to *Romanticism, Race, and Imperial Culture, 1780–1834*, ed. Alan Richardson and Sonia Hofkosh (Bloomington and Indianapolis, Indiana University Press, 1996), p. 3.

period, "a new cultural and social phenomenon known as 'the rise of the reading public'" emerged, with readers manifesting a particular desire for the prose fiction that rolled off the nation's printing presses.[22] That this prose fiction, in particular, the novel, crucially facilitated the spread of empire has been persuasively argued by theorists and critics, who suggest that the form worked in complex ways to prepare readers to imagine and, hence, "accommodate" the circumstances of Britain's imperial expansion. Through their writing of works such as *Robinson Crusoe* (1719) and *Mansfield Park* (1814), it has been suggested, eighteenth- and nineteenth-century British novelists contributed to the naturalization of a sense of England's cultural and military power, and facilitated the creation of notions of racial identity that made a British Empire seem both inevitable and necessary to the reading public. This is not to say that writers like Daniel Defoe or Jane Austen self-consciously set out to promote imperial ideology in their writing, but rather that their works illuminated "the far from accidental convergence between the patterns of narrative authority constitutive of the novel on the one hand, and, on the other, a complex ideological configuration underlying the tendency to imperialism."[23]

Despite all of the attention that has been paid to the link between the novel and empire, though, literary critics have seemed largely uninterested in empirical research—that is to say, in identifying the types of fiction that may have been read by actual soldiers or sailors, who were, after all, the British Empire's most immediate agents. In part, this may be related to an issue that was highlighted by Colley in 2002, when she remarked that "Historians of Britain" were slower "than some of their Continental European counterparts to integrate men of the sword into broad cultural and intellectual history." "Military and naval historians," she argued, tended to "concentrate on their subjects' administrative, social and warlike roles," while "historians of literature and ideas" often wrote "as if in tacit agreement with Aldous Huxley's view that military intelligence is a contradiction in terms."[24] The situation, of course, has changed considerably since Colley made her comments, and scholars in recent years have devoted increasing attention to previously neglected aspects of British

---

[22] Gary Kelly, "Romantic Fiction," in *The Cambridge Companion to British Romanticism*, ed. Stuart Curran (Cambridge: Cambridge University Press, 1993), p. 197.

[23] Edward Said, *Culture and Imperialism* (London: Chatto and Windus Ltd., 1993), p. 82. See also Suvendrini Perera, *Reaches of Empire: The English Novel from Edgeworth to Dickens* (New York: Columbia University Press, 1991), p. 7.

[24] Colley, *Captives*, p. 278.

soldiers' experiences. The fact remains, though, that most of the work that has been done on soldiers' reading concentrates on twentieth-century soldiers and twentieth-century wars.[25]

Another reason for the scholarly oversight, however, may have been the tendency of most critics to take it for granted that the reading public under discussion was composed of readers living and working in the British isles and, thus, to overlook the men who directly facilitated Britain's securing of her hegemony in far-flung places. Even Gauri Viswanathan's pioneering study of the way in which the introduction of English literature in nineteenth-century India worked to facilitate imperial ideology in the subcontinent focused on the colonized subject, rather than the colonizer, for example, and its analysis of "the Englishman actively participating in the cruder realities of conquest, commercial aggrandizement, and disciplinary management of natives" was predicated on the notion of this Englishman as the "*producer*" rather than the *consumer* of the type of "knowledge that empowers him to conquer, appropriate, and manage" other lands.[26] A crucial issue thus far largely unaddressed by critics is what happened to an English text when it was read by English, Scottish, Welsh, or Irish men in places such as nineteenth-century India—that is, by individuals whose presence on the subcontinent was typically linked to facilitating and sustaining Britain's imperial presence? Did the text in such cases continue to function "as a surrogate Englishman in his highest and most perfect state, [becoming] a mask for economic exploitation," as Viswanathan contends of the English text that was read by Indian readers; or was this ideological effect in some way diluted, erased, or reversed when English,

---

[25] See, for examples, Edmund G.C. King, "E.W. Hornung's Unpublished 'Diary,' the YMCA, and the Reading Soldier in the First World War," *English Literature in Transition*, vol. 57, no. 3 (2014): 361–87, and, "'Books are more to me than Food': British Prisoners of War as Readers, 1914–1918" *Book History*, vol. 16 (2013): 246–71; Amanda Laugesen "*Boredom is the Enemy*": *The Intellectual and Imaginative Lives of Australian Soldiers in the Great War and Beyond* (Farnham: Ashgate, 2012); Molly Guptill Manning, *When Books went to War. The Stories that helped us win World War II* (Boston and New York: Houghton Mifflin Harcourt, 2014); and Donald Mesham, "A Forgotten Book Collection: The Army Standard Unit Library," *Publishing History*, vol. 69 (2011): 85–111. The following work is forthcoming at the time of writing: Shafquat Towheed and Edmund King (eds), *Reading and the First World War: Readers, Texts, Archives*, New Directions in Book History series (Houndsmills, Basingstoke: Palgrave Macmillan, 2015).

[26] Gauri Viswanathan, *Masks of Conquest: Literary Study and British Rule in India* (1989; London: Faber and Faber, 1990), p. 20.

Scots, Welsh, or Irish were the consumers?[27] A further issue that arises here, of course, is whether those responsible for overseeing "the imperial mission of educating and civilizing colonial subjects in the literature and thought of England" in places such as India realized that this mission could or should be extended to British soldiers; whether there was a recognition that this, too, might "in the long run [serve] to strengthen Western cultural hegemony in enormously complex ways."[28]

These questions are, of course, significant ones, and probably beyond the scope of any single study. The ambition of the present volume is to begin to illuminate them by exploring one very particular aspect of the history of the reading of British soldiers in the nineteenth century: the garrison libraries that the East India Company and Regular Army established for them at different points during the 1800s. As we shall see, the materials that exist in relation to these libraries provide real insights into the motivations and responses of those who established, operated, and/or used them, as well as into holdings and borrowing patterns at some of the institutions. In so doing, they also begin to open up two exciting opportunities for scholars, the first of these being another way of exploring conflicting responses to literacy and fiction without falling afoul of what has been called "the receptive fallacy": that is, the way in which much literary criticism tries "to discern the messages a text transmits to an audience by examining the text rather than the audience."[29] Rather than simply speculating upon possible links between the novel and empire, for example, we can identify works of fiction that were actually supplied to soldiers stationed in places such as India, and thereby facilitate the exploration of the ideological messages these texts may have imparted to their audience. What did they have to say about the rights and wrongs of using military force to appropriate the wealth of other lands, for instance, or about viewing India primarily as a place where (British) fortunes could be amassed? Was there, indeed, a contemporary perception that a "recognizable correspondence" might exist between the reading of works such as *Robinson Crusoe* and the "consequent mentalities" of those men most directly implicated in facilitating Britain's emergence as an imperial power?[30]

---

[27] Viswanathan, *Masks of Conquest*, p. 20.
[28] Viswanathan, *Masks of Conquest*, p. 2.
[29] Rose, *Intellectual Life*, p. 4.
[30] St. Clair, *Reading Nation*, p. 433.

Studying the libraries that the East India Company and Regular Army established for soldiers affords the scholar a further opportunity, which is to view the history of nineteenth-century attitudes to working-class reading—*and* leisure—through another lens. What we shall see in the first instance is that key differences existed between the East India Company's and the Regular Army's attitudes to reading soldiers, differences that can be explained at least in part in terms of the different nature and history of the two forces. Most obviously, for example, the East India Company army was the private army of an organization that was originally set up in the seventeenth century to exploit trade opportunities in India and other parts of Asia.[31] For a number of reasons that even it found surprising, the Company came to wield increasing political influence, and eventually found itself governing India on Britain's behalf until 1857.[32] The Regular Army was (and remains) Britain's national army; the primary reason for its existence was to defend Britain and Britons, and to protect and further British overseas interests.[33] One of the points of comparison that existed between the two armies, though, was the fact that both forces drew the majority of their rank-and-file troops from among the working classes; in other words, from that very section of the population whose reading and leisure habits in general caused such anxiety during the 1800s. We have already noted, for instance, that there was increasing concern about how the reading process affected the subjectivity of the reader from at least the late eighteenth century, and that this was accompanied by a

[31] Useful works on the history of the East India Company Army include Gerald James Bryant, "The East India Company and its Army, 1660–1778," Ph.D. Thesis submitted to the University of London, 1975; Raymond Callahan, *The East India Company and Army Reform, 1783–1798* (Cambridge, Massachusetts: Harvard University Press, 1972); and Alan J. Guy and Peter B. Boyden (eds), assisted by Marion Harding, *Soldiers of the Raj: The Indian Army, 1600–1947* (London: National Army Museum, 1997). See also T.A. Heathcote's *The Indian Army: The Garrison of British Imperial India, 1822–1922* (Newton Abbot, Devon: David & Charles (Holdings) Ltd., 1974).

[32] The East India Company's commercial and political power was increasingly checked from the late 1700s onward. On the history of the Company, see Lawrence James, *Raj: The Making and Unmaking of British India* (1997; London: Abacus, 1998); John Keay, *The Honourable Company: A History of the English East India Company* (London: HarperCollins, 1991); and Philip Lawson, *The East India Company: A History* (London and New York: Longman, 1993).

[33] Useful texts here include Barnett Correlli, *Britain and her Army, 1509–1970: Military, Political and Social Survey* (Harmondsworth: Penguin, 1970), and Richard Holmes, *Redcoat: The British Soldier in the Age of Horse and Musket* (Hammersmith: HarperCollins, 2001).

growing conviction that the ideological consequences of reading had to be controlled. This attitude, however, had a further outcome: it meant that "women, children, the lower classes, and the peoples Britain seemed destined to protect and 'civilize'" were often "treated in the same way or made figures for each other as intellectual inferiors, social dependents, and moral wards of a professional middle class figured as a professional European or British man."[34] One of the things the following chapters will show is that the individuals who were responsible for the establishment and/or oversight of soldiers' libraries in the nineteenth century expertly illustrate this argument, for they were largely drawn from the middle or upper classes, and clearly felt a duty to supervise and improve the reading habits of the men who were their inferior dependents. Recognition of this latter fact is obviously crucial, because it reminds us that the establishment of the libraries for soldiers by the East India Company and Regular Army had origins and motivations other than purely military ones, and must be contextualized in terms of the wider concern with working-class reading—particularly of fiction—in both the Romantic and Victorian periods. What we shall see is that many of those most nearly concerned with the provision and/or operation of the soldiers' libraries manifested anxiety in relation to what has been termed "the Janus faces of literacy"; namely, the fact that the newly literate sometimes read material that their "superiors" never intended.[35]

This leads us to our next point, which is that that the reasons advanced for the establishment of the soldiers' libraries—to help combat drunkenness among the troops, for instance, or to provide the men with something beneficial to do in their spare time—also must be contextualized in terms of growing anxiety in relation to working-class leisure during the nineteenth century. As historians have demonstrated, concern about "public leisure" grew in Britain after industrialization, and contemporaries increasingly became convinced that the paucity of recreational facilities available to the general population went a long way toward explaining the "disorder, drunkenness, violence, and immorality" associated with the "popular leisure" of the working classes.[36] It was in this context that

---

[34] Kelly, *Women, Writing, and Revolution*, p. 183.

[35] Carl F. Kaestle, "Studying the History of Literacy," in Shafquat Towheed, Rosalind Crone, and Katie Halsey (eds), *The History of Reading*, Routledge Literature Readers (London and New York: Routledge, 2011) p. 175.

[36] Snape, *Leisure and the Rise of the Public Library*, p. 15.

both the *Report from the Select Committee on Public Walks* (1833) and the *Report from the Select Committee on Inquiry into Drunkenness* (1834) "pointed out that a major cause of the problem [with public leisure] was the shortage of recreational facilities other than licensed premises," for example; and it was also why both the 1834 report on drunkenness and James Silk Buckingham's *Public Institutions Bill* (1835) recommended the provision of institutions such as libraries as one means of ameliorating the conditions of working-class life. In the event, the *Public Libraries Act* was not passed until 1850, but by this time there was a growing conviction that libraries as well as museums and parks should be provided to the working-class population in order to contribute to their well-being and, arguably, facilitate greater social control.[37] Authorities also hoped that the provision of facilities like libraries would help to save the state money, lessening what had to be spent "on controlling and containing immoral behaviour, including criminality."[38] What the following chapters will show is that many of those involved with the provision and/or operation of soldiers' libraries entertained similar ambitions in relation to these institutions, and became increasingly convinced of their ability to regulate soldiers' attitudes *and* behavior. This means that study of the history of the soldiers' libraries contributes not only to our understanding of how attitudes to military discipline evolved in the nineteenth century, but also to our appreciation of the history of leisure (broadly conceived).

There are, then, several motivations at play in the chapters that follow, and they draw upon a wide range of material—including archival sources, official reports and regulations, memoirs and other writings published by soldiers, contemporary journals, newspapers, and letters—to facilitate both the illumination of the nineteenth-century military library and reader, and the drawing of fruitful comparisons between other types of libraries and readers during the 1800s. The utilization of official reports and regulations, it should be noted, provides valuable insights into both the soldiers' libraries and the attitudes and responses of the men who used them, but

---

[37] Snape, *Leisure and the Rise of the Public Library*, pp. 17–19. Snape refers to P. Bailey's arguments in relation to this in his *Leisure and Class in Victorian England: Rational Recreation and the Contest for Control, 1830–1885* (London: Routledge and Kegan Paul, 1978).

[38] Alistair Black, "The People's University: Models of Public Library History," in Black and Hoare (eds), *The Cambridge History of Libraries in Britain and Ireland, Vol. III*, p. 29. On the "*public* function" of libraries, see Joanna Innes, "Libraries in Context," in Mandelbrote and Manley (eds), *The Cambridge History of Libraries in Britain and Ireland, Vol. II*, p. 285.

it is important to sound a note of caution here in relation to this material. As Alan Ramsay Skelley points out, official reports can be misleading as they are sometimes conflicting and/or inaccurate, and army regulations may not always reflect reality as it existed on the ground: "Regulations said one thing, but how they were applied by the officers on the spot and to what extent official policy was out of touch with particular conditions is another question." In order to "strike a fair balance," Skelley suggests, we therefore need to turn to the "pertinent observations made to committees of enquiry, particularly by serving officers," as well as to "the accounts of men who served in the ranks."[39] We have already had a glimpse of the usefulness of the latter resource, but, again, it is important to recognize that the soldiers who produced and/or published journals, memoirs, or other works that purported to offer glimpses of military life were not typical of the vast majority of the rank-and-file, whose opinions—on anything—largely went unrecorded. As one Private Wheeler put it in relation to the fuss that inevitably accompanied reports of the wounding or killing of a general or colonel: "[W]ho shall record the glorious deeds of the soldier whose lot is numbered with the thousands in the ranks who live and die and fight in obscurity."[40]

Wheeler, it must be noted, made his remark in 1813, and so it predates that moment when military memoirs began to achieve critical and commercial success as a genre. In his recent study of Peninsular Wars memoirs, Neil Ramsey suggests that this happened particularly in the years between 1825 and 1835, when "the military author emerged from this body of writing to assume a recognized and prestigious position in British letters."[41] That said, however, private soldiers were "denied recognition as authors. Their work remained outside of [efforts to commemorate the wars], continuing on as a form of writing that could be associated with anti-war sentiments and radicalism." As the years went by, the memoirs that such men produced were "increasingly marginalized as a form of military writing," not least because their veracity or authenticity was often questioned.[42] It is for this reason, then, that it is important to recognize that

---

[39] Alan Ramsay Skelley, *The Victorian Army at Home: The Recruitment and Terms and Conditions of the British Regular, 1859–1899* (London: Croom Helm, 1977), pp. 19–20.

[40] Quoted in Roy Palmer, *The Rambling Soldier: Life in the Lower Ranks, 1750–1900, through Soldiers' Songs and Writings* (Gloucester: Alan Sutton Publications, 1985), p. 1.

[41] Neil Ramsey, *The Military Memoir and Romantic Literary Culture, 1780–1835* (Farnham: Ashgate, 2011), p. 2.

[42] Ramsey, *The Military Memoir*, pp. 51–52, 72.

the private soldiers who produced memoirs of their experiences frequently did so with the explicit intention of securing eventual publication and, as such, often manifested an acute awareness of both the features typically associated with the tradition in which they were writing and, linked to this, the expectations of their audience.[43] John Shipp's *The Military Bijou; or, The Contents of a Soldier's Knapsack: Being the Gleanings of Thirty-Three Years Active Service* (1831), for example, is an odd compendium of a work that offers readers a selection of narratives and opinions purportedly inspired by his military experience. It is significant, though, for several reasons, including the fact that its preface not only reveals that he obviously had very particular readers in mind when he penned it, but also implies that these can trust to the essential veracity of his work:

> ... I have been induced to lay this work before my military readers, not only for the purpose of getting some return for my labour, but also in the humble hope that the compilation will be found both entertaining and instructive, as the narratives are generally founded on facts. Many an old veteran will read them with feelings of deep interest, as faithful portraitures of the vicissitudes of war; and when dull ennui steals a march upon the mind robbed of its best energies by the toils of war, and there is no counter-marching from its gloomy influence, I hope he will be able to make a good retreat by a peep into the Military Bijou.
>
> To the young aspirant the volumes may prove a source of amusement and instruction, and a stimulus to emulating exertion; and as they were more especially written and compiled for their edification, I feel myself warranted in claiming their special patronage.[44]

Implicit here, we might think, is proof of Ramsey's statement that memoirs published by other than the officer class required "a particularly clear defence of the text's propriety, usefulness and authenticity,"[45] but so, too, is evidence of the fact that soldiers were frequently hugely invested in their works in a financial sense. As Kenneth Fenwick points out, for instance, Sergeant Gowing "kept a large stock of *A Voice from the Ranks* in his

---

[43] Carolyn Steedman also makes this point in her introduction to *The Radical Soldier's Tale* (London and New York: Routledge, 1988), pp. 38–39.

[44] Shipp, John. *The Military Bijou; or, The Contents of a Soldiers' Knapsack: Being the Gleanings of Thirty-Three-Years Active Service* (London: Whitakker, Treacher, and Co., 1831), p. vii.

[45] Ramsey, *Military Memoir*, p. 115.

house and used to set forth most mornings with a bag filled with copies, travelling around the industrial areas of Lancashire selling them to the workers in offices and factories. This and his pension seem to have been his only sources of income in the closing years of his life."[46]

Before we turn to our consideration of the history of the garrison libraries, we have to consider a number of points in particular, and the first of these concerns the literacy of British soldiers during the 1800s. This issue was of great concern to both the East India Company and the Regular Army, especially as commanding officers, army inspectors, and chaplains often indicated that the number of literate soldiers could vary greatly both between and within different corps and regiments. There are, clearly, several factors that must be borne in mind when contemplating the literacy of British soldiers in the nineteenth century, and the first of these is that, until after the Indian Rebellion of 1857, we are talking about two forces. The "differing purposes" for which the two armies were intended meant that they had different attitudes to literacy, and this in turn affected the type of men that that they attracted and recruited.[47] The East India Company, as we have already noted, for example, was like the Regular Army in that it drew the majority of its rank-and-file soldiers from the English, Scottish, Welsh, and Irish working classes,[48] but it was unlike the King's and then the Queen's army in that it actively sought out literate recruits, and placed a premium on promoting literacy among its soldiers. In relation to the former point, it has been argued both that "there is a strong case for suggesting that the Company attracted a better-quality recruit [than the Regular Army], and not simply men faced with the stark alternatives of serving or starving,"[49] and that the "bulk" of the Company's officers in the early nineteenth century seem to have come "from the middling sort out to improve their lot";[50] in other words, from that class of society that was increasingly associated with the book-reading public during the period under discussion. Also significant is the fact that, "Over decades the Directors managed their patronage so dispassionately that poverty was actually a recommendation to their benevolence; consequently the writerships and cadetships in their gift were populated by the

---

[46] Fenwick, introduction to *Voice from the Ranks*, p. xiv.

[47] Stanley, *White Mutiny*, p. 43.

[48] Holmes, *Sahib*, pp. 233–34.

[49] Holmes, *Sahib*, p. 236.

[50] Lawson, *East India Company*, p. 132.

offspring of commerce and trade, and the genteel and literate poor."[51] Thomas Quinney, whom we shall meet again in Chap. 3, provided a particularly powerful insight into the social composition of the East India Company's army when he described the types of men to be encountered in the service. "[Y]ou may find men," he wrote, "who have been connected with almost every trade or profession, from the mason's labourer up to those who have been intended for the study of medicine, law, and even divinity." These "intended professional men," he remarked,

> may be divided into three classes, namely, those who have been compelled to enlist through their own imprudence, in recklessly squandering away the means they may have possessed; secondly, those whom adversity may have deprived of means, without any imprudence on their own parts; and lastly, (by far the smallest number), those who are led to embrace a military life from mere inclination, or from their parents attempting to force professions upon them for which they had no desire, or saw clearly they could not follow out with comfort or credit to themselves.[52]

The Regular Army had the reputation of attracting a very different class of recruit into its rank-and-file, and was viewed by many as the last refuge of the criminal, the feckless, and the desperate. This perception of the army lasted well into the nineteenth century and, even in the early 1900s, many families still viewed a son going for a soldier as a mark of disgrace. The fact that the Regular Army drew so many of its recruits from the most deprived parts of the population might be expected to have significant consequences for the literacy of its soldiers because, as Roger S. Schofield points out, "occupational hierarchy is one of the most consistent features of illiteracy in the past."[53] Charles Henry Smith, who joined the 7th Royal Fusiliers in 1852, for example, clearly appreciated the link that existed between the deprived nature of most soldiers' to indicate possession backgrounds and their level of education, and also recognized that this was

[51] Alan J. Guy, "People who will stick at nothing to make money?: Officers, Income, and Expectations in the Service of John Company, 1750–1840," in Guy and Boyden (eds), assisted by Harding, *Soldiers of the Raj*, p. 50.

[52] Thomas Quinney, *Sketches of A Soldier's Life in India by Staff Sergeant Thomas Quinney, Honorable East India Company's Service* (Glasgow: David Robertson and Edinburgh: Oliver & Boyd, 1853), pp. 10–11.

[53] Roger S. Schofield, "Dimensions of Illiteracy in England, 1740–1850," in Towheed, Crone, and Halsey (eds), *History of Reading*, p. 157.

something many of the men would never be able to overcome. "A share of schooling comes to each Soldier, after Enlisting," he wrote,

> ... If I were to go on, to say that Soldiers had the best of Education[,] it would be Derogatory on my Part—Some have A good [if?] passable education coming with the service[;] others are quite A Dunce. Why is it so, its because there [sic] Respective friends have to send their children to Work instead of sending them to school. In fact the Poor People in England can't afford to send their Children to School to give them A good Education. For there [sic] means will not allow them.[54]

Notwithstanding the several differences that existed between the East India Company and the Regular Army, however, it is important to recognize that *both* forces attracted men who realized that their literacy would be advantageous to them following enlistment. This is very clearly demonstrated by the recollections of Alexander Somerville, which reveal not only that he enlisted in the Regular Army primarily because of the dire economic circumstances of the early 1830s, but also that his consciousness of his superior level of education nearly affected his choice of regiment: "I had heard enough from old soldiers to be convinced that having a fair education in writing and account-keeping I would have a much better chance of promotion in a regiment of English [or] Irish, where there were few men who could write, than in an exclusively Scottish regiment, where almost every man was a writer or accountant." Despite this, however, he was unable to resist "the charm of the Greys being Scottish, with their fame for deeds of gallantry."[55] John Ramsbottom, who was from Sheffield, enlisted in the East India Company's army in the early 1850s, and was for his part delighted when he discovered that his literacy would lead to rapid promotion: "when I have been in the regiment 2 months if I behave myself being a desant [sic] scholar I shall be made corporal. I ham [sic] as happy as a king."[56]

Recognition of the fact that both forces attracted literate men, particularly in times of economic hardship, invites speculation that literacy rates between the two may not have differed all that greatly, and that the only

---

[54] MS Private Charles Henry Smith, NAM 2004-01-39, pp. 46–47.

[55] Alexander Somerville, *The Autobiography of a Working Man, By "One Who Whistled at the Plough"* (London: Charles Gilpin, 1848), p. 188.

[56] Sergeant John Ramsbottom to William, letter undated [November 1854?], Ms Add 59876.

difference between them may have been that the Company attracted men of slightly better ability. This is a point that Peter Stanley makes in his study of British military culture in India between 1825 and 1875, where he observes: "Relative levels of literacy in the two services are difficult to determine definitively. ... The Company enjoyed no clear superiority: the distinction was probably one of quality rather than quantity." Stanley suggests that up to 60 % of both forces may have been functionally literate, but, while this figure is useful, it is important to recognize that it may not provide a complete picture of the number of reading soldiers during the period with which we are concerned. In the first place, Stanley arrived at his figure for the East India Company troops by examining soldier's wills between 1851 and 1852, discovering that "at least" 60 % of these were signed by the men themselves.[57] The ability to sign, of course, has long been viewed by scholars as a meaningful measure of literacy, but these have also increasingly recognized that it may exclude a considerable number of people with reading skills. Significantly, this has become particularly evident in research that has been done in relation to literacy in the early nineteenth century, which suggests that "the proportion of the population claiming a basic level of reading ability may have been half as much again as the proportion able to sign, and that the proportion able to sign corresponded roughly with the proportion able to read fluently."[58] To put this another way, more people than were previously thought may have learned to read—but not sign or write—during the course of their limited schooling, and thus would not be reflected in an estimation of literacy based on the survey of signed documents such as wills. The only formal education that William Jowett received, for instance, was at Sunday school; he was set to work at the age of seven and, in his spare time, read the weekly paper that his master purchased, "or such books as his limited means could procure." Unable to write when he joined the 7th Royal Fusiliers, he seems to have taken every opportunity to rectify this deficiency, and within a few years "became so proficient in the art of penmanship as to write a beautiful neat hand, and in 1852 he was appointed to the office of assistant schoolmaster."[59]

[57] Stanley, *White Mischief*, p. 43.

[58] Schofield, "Dimensions of Illiteracy in England," in Towheed, Crone, and Halsey (eds), *History of Reading*, p. 154.

[59] William Jowett, *Memoir and Diary of Sergeant W. Jowett, Seventh Royal Fusiliers* (London and Beeston, Nottinghamshire: W. Kent & Co. and B. Porter, 1856), pp. vii-viii.

Stanley predicates his argument in relation to the functional literacy of the men in the Regular Army upon his consideration of, firstly, Henry Marshall's *Military Miscellany* (1846), which gives him his basis for the earlier period, and, secondly, Alan Ramsay Skelley's analysis of the army's own figures, which brings him up until 1875. Again, Marshall's observation that he was "disposed to believe that from 30 to 50 %. of the men who enlist[ed] [were] unable to read with profit and satisfaction, or, at any rate, without much difficulty" was based, in part, on analysis of the Registrar General's Returns and, as such, may not have taken account of those who had limited reading skills but were unable to sign their names in marriage registers. In the interest of fairness, though, it must be acknowledged that Marshall drew on a number of other sources before arriving at his "conjecture," including figures for literacy among those charged with offenses in England for the 4 years between 1836 and 1839. These suggested that roughly 50 % of those charged with offenses in these years could read and write "imperfectly" and roughly 10 % could read and write "well."[60] In this context, the 60 % figure advanced by Stanley seems a reasonable one, not least because it represents the mid-point of Marshall's figures.

The second part of Stanley's argument, that the "proportion" of functionally literate men in the Regular Army "appears to have remained roughly consistent" during the period with which he is concerned, is obviously informed by his appreciation of Skelley's suggestion that the army's figures for the second half of the nineteenth century must be treated with great caution.[61] On the one hand, literacy in the army definitely appears to have risen from the late 1850s/early 1860s, which would be in line with improvements in literacy rates in general during this period. On the other hand, though, the individuals who were responsible for compiling the army's figures were hugely invested in what the force was attempting, and clearly tried to paint as positive a picture as possible of its educational achievements. The army thus declared that only 20.5 % of the men were unable either to read or write in 1858; by 1876, 1 year after the period with which Stanley is concerned, this was supposedly true of only 4.95 %

---

[60] Henry Marshall, *Military Miscellany, Comprehending A History of the Recruiting of the Army, Military Punishments*, &c. &c. (London: John Murray, 1846), pp. 94–95. According to Marshall, 52 % of the individuals in this category were able to read and write "imperfectly" in 1836 and 1837, while the figure rose slightly to 53 % for each of the following two years. The percentage of those able to read and write "well" also varied slightly across the four years: 10 % in 1836, 9 % for both 1837 and 1838, and back to 10 % again in 1839.

[61] Stanley, *White Mutiny*, Endnote 38, p. 60.

of the men. The remaining 96.5 % of the soldiers in 1876 were classified as being able to read but not write (4.41 %); able to both read and write (45.68 %); and as having achieved a superior level of literacy (44.95 %).[62] The 60 % figure that Stanley suggests, then, may be erring on the side of caution, but is clearly informed by recognition of the dangers of accepting the army's own assessment of its achievements. The army was finally struck by the "absurdity" of the way in which it was assessing men in 1889, as Skelley points out, and so "army statistics [from 1890 onwards] began to represent more accurately the state of education in the forces." This meant that literacy rates were adjusted sharply downwards in the last decade of the century and, in 1899, the army was suggesting that, "nearly thirty years after the passage of Forster's 1870 Education Act and the 1872 Scottish Education Act, fewer than 40 % of the rank and file ... had gone beyond the barest level of literacy, and the standard reached by the majority of those in the ranks was elementary at best."[63]

There is a further point that must be made here, though, and this is that the figure of 40 % itself may be reflective of nothing so much as the cynical manipulations of soldiers themselves. According to John Pindar, the introduction of compulsory school attendance in the army in the 1870s had a very particular outcome: it resulted in more "gifted" men being compelled to do extra duties for their comrades, as school-going soldiers pointed out every time that an exam came around "what a fool they would be to [pass it], and thus become available for parades and fatigues." All that such men had do to avoid compulsory attendance at school, Pindar observed, was to reach "the *lowest* standard of reading, the *lowest* standard in writing, and the four simple rules in arithmetic; and yet I have known some of them commence attending immediately on their joining, and be still in attendance when their 6 years were completed, never having been able to master these simple studies."[64] The 40 % literacy rate that the army attributed to the men in the last decade of the nineteenth century therefore cannot be viewed with total confidence, as it is unclear to what extent it may have been affected by some soldiers' determination to remain in school and, thus, avoid duties that they found unappealing.

---

[62] *First Report by the Council of Military Education on Army Schools* (London: HMSO, 1862), p. iii, and *Third Report by the Director General of Military Education on Army Schools and Libraries* (London: HMSO, 1877), p xii.

[63] Ramsay Skelley, *The Late Victorian Army*, p. 90.

[64] Pindar, *Autobiography of a Private Soldier*, pp. 165–66.

There is, of course, another issue that must be acknowledged here, and this is that literacy rates for nineteenth-century soldiers—however arrived at—probably provide only a partial picture of the number of men who enjoyed the libraries that the East India Company and Regular Army respectively provided. This is because both forces drew the majority of their rank-and-file from the English, Scottish, Welsh, and Irish working classes; in other words, from those very sections of the population where there were "always more people seeking access to the contents of books and documents than were able to own or decipher them."[65] One result of this circumstance was that many of these individuals inevitably encountered books—or other types of reading material—by listening to them being read aloud by the more literate members of their communities; another was that those who could read (and write) were accustomed to sharing the benefits of their superior level of education with those less fortunate than themselves. Both of these points are beautifully illustrated by Alexander Somerville's recollection of an incident in his life before he joined the army, where he describes how he shared the fruits of his reading while working as a farm laborer:

> When the afternoon work began, I related to the other workers what I had read; and even the grieve began to take an interest in the story. And this interest increased in him and in every one else until they all brought their dinners afield, so that they might remain under the shadows of the trees and hear me read. In the evenings at home I continued the reading, and next day at work put them in possession of the events which I knew in advance of them.[66]

Somerville's recollection of this moment in the fields of Scotland reveals several things about the nature of reading at this time, including the fact that it was often a public performance rather than a private practice. This, we shall see, struck those responsible for the day-to-day operation of soldiers' libraries more forcibly as the years went by, and resulted in a modification of attitudes relating to both the "where" of soldiers' reading and the design of their reading environment. Put simply, authorities increasingly recognized that soldiers were used to pooling their resources, and so the design and operation of army libraries and reading rooms ought to take account of the fact that books and newspapers would (or could) be

[65] David Vincent, "Reading and Writing," in Towheed, Crone, and Halsey (eds), *History of Reading*, p. 164.
[66] Somerville, *Autobiography of a Working Man*, p. 92.

read aloud. This latter circumstance, of course, had one great advantage: it meant that even illiterate soldiers could benefit from the reading material that was provided.

One final point must be considered before we turn to our second chapter, and this relates to the huge importance that India came to assume for nineteenth-century Britain and her soldiers. The significance of India to British fortunes grew at a tremendous rate in the first decades of the nineteenth century, which meant that a curiously close relationship came to exist between British soldiers and the subcontinent. As Correlli Barnett puts it: "By 1850 India had become the greatest formative influence on the life, language and legend of the British army, for most British soldiers could expect to serve there, and for a long time. India, with its heat, stinks and noise, its enveloping dust, its glamour and poverty, became the British army's second home—perhaps its first."[67] Proof of this fact increasingly made itself felt in the literature of the late 1800s, and Kipling's works in particular fixed many readers' views of both the subcontinent and the soldiers who served there. To quote Barnett again: "In Rudyard Kipling the army found a poet to express its own private values and record its way of life in India, the country that marked it so deeply."[68] That said, it must be recognized that some soldiers began to write about India themselves from the moment when they first began to arrive there, and recorded their impressions and experiences of the subcontinent in their memoirs and letters. John Corneille, for instance, arrived in India in 1754, and revealed that it was a place for which he was ultimately ill-prepared. "Man's mind naturally, from reading and verbal accounts," he wrote,

> forms notions of places and things, but such ideas ought not to be depended upon, being often erroneous either through the misrepresentations of their author or prejudice of the reader, generally contracted from a very limited view of things. At least so it was with me. The idea I had of this part of the world I found to be very different from reality. I expected nothing but a scorching sun, a parched country inhabited by a set of savage idolaters, sickness and death in abundance, and life gloomy, sad and melancholy. On experience the phantom vanished and I was agreeably disappointed, for bountiful nature has not here been sparing of her blessings.[69]

[67] Barnett, *Britain and her Army*, p. 278.
[68] Barnett, *Britain and her Army*, p. 314.
[69] John Corneille, *Journal of My Service in India* (ed), with an introduction by Michael Edwardes (London: The Folio Society, 1966), p. 70.

Corneille's musings in the first instance remind us once again of the dangers of making generalized assumptions about the way in which reading or texts "work," but they also underline the crucial role that India played in the lives of many British soldiers from at least the mid-1700s. It is for this reason, then, that India features so strongly in the chapters that follow, and why some Regular Army soldiers make appearances in both "parts" of the book.

Chapter 2, appropriately, takes us to India, and examines both the somewhat ad hoc evolution of the libraries that the East India Company began to establish for soldiers on the subcontinent from the early 1820s, and the competing motivations that underpinned their establishment. On the one hand, it will show, the Company's decision to establish the libraries may be interpreted as a benevolent and/or pragmatic gesture, one reflective of the overwhelmingly positive—or tolerant or realistic—attitude that it seems to have adopted in relation to the literacy of its forces. On the other hand, though, the East India Company's decision to establish the libraries was plainly informed by a further factor: namely, the notion that such institutions could play a vital role in regulating the behavior—and, potentially, the attitudes—of the readers by whom they were frequented. Making careful use of the lists of books and reports that were generated in relation to the libraries, this chapter advances a dual argument: that deliberate efforts were made to shape the soldier readers through the books that were provided, but that the libraries developed in response to the demands of the men themselves.

Chapter 3 is concerned with the way in which the East India Company's libraries evolved over the years, and so it explores in the first instance how attitudes to the "where" of soldiers' reading were gradually modified to take account of the realities of military service. In the very early days of the libraries, it is clear, the East India Company attempted to regulate reading at their stations in India, by issuing a series of rules that stressed the privileged nature of the institutions. Although the Company does not appear to have directed explicitly that books could not be removed from the libraries, this seems to have been the initial conclusion—or conviction—of those responsible for the operation of the institutions, who dictated that men should only read in rooms that were under the supervision of persons such as chaplains, schoolmasters, or librarians. The impractical nature of this policy evidently became increasingly apparent as the years went by, and those responsible for the libraries appear to have become convinced that it did not take sufficient account of the peculiar nature of military life on the subcontinent. This realization in due course caused chaplains and commanding officers to modify their attitude in relation to the removal of books to barracks, and, as a result, the reading experiences of soldiers—and their illiterate comrades—were transformed. To put all of this another way, this chapter is peculiarly concerned with scenes of reading and readers in India, and so it will draw on soldiers' letters as well as on official records in an attempt to illustrate "where," "how," and "why" men read on the subcontinent.

Some individual regiments in the Regular Army began to establish libraries for themselves in the late eighteenth century, with probably the earliest and most famous of these being the garrison library that was founded at Gibraltar in 1793. This was moved in the early 1800s to a building that was "specially erected by government," which prompted one individual to remark wryly in 1831 that this was "the only instance in which Mr. Pitt publicly patronised literature."[70] Another celebrated library for soldiers was the one that was set up in Malta in 1825 by the 80th Regiment of Foot; this contained 1000 volumes by 1833, and was always taken by the regiment when it moved.[71] The Regular Army, though, entertained reservations about the *official* provision of books and libraries to rank-and-file soldiers well into the nineteenth century, believing it was for a number of reasons dangerous to promote literacy among such troops. Chapter 4 explores both why this should have been the case, and the motivations behind the government's eventual decision to grant funds toward the setting up of garrison libraries in the late 1830s; it also examines the reasons why military authorities became increasingly convinced that more should be done to facilitate the recreational reading of troops, particularly in light of growing public concern about the welfare of soldiers both during and after the Crimean War. In tracing the history of the garrison libraries, this chapter demonstrates the link that supporters of the institutions increasingly made between the peculiar circumstances of military life and the subsequent (mis)behavior of soldiers, and also illustrates the different strategies that were employed in an attempt to regulate the reading preferences and habits of the Her Majesty's forces.

---

[70] "Letters from Gibraltar." No. VII [October 26th]. By the Author of "The Military Sketch Book," in *The United Service Journal and Naval and Military Magazine*, 1831 (Part I), p. 45.

[71] See T.A. Bowyer-Bower, "The Development of Educational Ideas and Curricula in the Army during the Eighteenth and Nineteenth Centuries," Thesis submitted to the University of Nottingham for the Degree of Master of Education, May, 1954, p. 70, and Manley, "Engines of Literature," in Mandelbrote and Manley (eds), *The Cambridge History of Libraries in Britain and Ireland, Vol. II*, p. 523.

Chapter 5 traces the way in which the soldiers' libraries evolved in the Regular Army, focusing in particular on the increasing emphasis that was placed on the men's reading environment. During the early days, it is clear, the accommodation of the majority of the libraries and reading rooms was unfit for the purpose, and authorities came to recognize this was a major reason why they were underused by the men. Concerted efforts were subsequently made to improve every aspect of the physical environment of the libraries and reading rooms, and the strategies adopted in this regard shed crucial light on the link contemporaries made between physical spaces and subsequent attitudes and behavior. The recommendations that were made in relation to improving the physical accommodation of the libraries and reading rooms are significant for a further reason, however, and this is that they provide a fascinating insight into the nature of the reading that was carried on within the institutions; specifically, it demonstrates not only that the quality of reading plainly varied in accordance with prevailing circumstances at the different garrisons and stations, but also that the activity was for many men simply another aspect of their wider social—or recreational—life. Once again, then, we will hear from soldiers themselves in this chapter and, thereby, hopefully shed further light on the "where," "how," and "why" of the reading of Her Majesty's forces.

Taken together, the six chapters of this study help situate the nineteenth-century soldiers' libraries in terms of wider—and evolving—debates relating to books, libraries, and reading during the 1800s, and provide a way of thinking about issues such the "Great Fiction Question," for example, from a perspective different to that commonly pursued by literary critics and historians. This question, Robert Snape points out, was a "contentious issue" for both librarians and wider society in the years between 1850 and 1914, and revolved around "the proper place of leisure [or recreational reading] in the public library service."[72] Alistair Black puts it this way in his consideration of public libraries as sites of "contested culture":

> The tension between the public library's educational and recreational roles has been an enduring feature of provision. Under the influence of its utilitarian pioneers, the dominant aim at the outset of the public library movement was to dispense only "useful" culture, which meant a heavy emphasis on non-fiction reading. However, to retain any credibility as popular institu-

[72] Snape, "Libraries for Leisure Time," in Black and Hoare (eds), *The Cambridge History of Libraries in Britain and Ireland, Vol. III*, p. 40.

tions, public libraries were forced to accommodate public demand and make available large amounts of imaginative literature.[73]

There were crucial differences between the libraries that were set up for soldiers and the free public libraries, of course, and not the least of these - as we shall see - is the fact that they were established at an earlier point (or points) in the 1800s. What we shall also see, though, is that the "tension" that Black describes in relation to the provision of fiction or imaginative literature in free public libraries is also to be traced throughout the history of the soldiers' libraries, and their educational and recreational roles—and holdings—were debated from the very first. One ambition of the chapters that follow, then, is to begin to fill what is a significant gap in both library and military history; others are to provide further insight into nineteenth-century attitudes to working-class literacy and recreational pursuits and, thereby, open up avenues for further research. At the heart of every chapter, though, is a desire to throw into sharper relief the working-class soldiers who made up the bulk of the rank-and-file in both the East India Company and Regular armies—specifically, to shed light on how the men's reading choices and experiences were affected by the libraries that were set up especially for them during the course of the 1800s. The Honourable Company led the way in setting up libraries for the men with whom we are concerned and, as John Mercier MacMullen's recollection of his time in India makes clear, they were "invaluable" to the soldier: "It is almost impossible for one who has not been to India, to imagine how difficult it was to exist at this period, in what is considered the hottest part of the world. ... Those who could not read were ... almost destitute of amusement."[74] It is to this world, and these libraries, that we will turn in our next chapter.

[73] Black, "The People's University," in Black and Hoare (eds), *The Cambridge History of Libraries in Britain and Ireland*, Vol. III, p. 35.
[74] "A Late Staff Sergeant of the 13th Light Infantry" [John Mercier MacMullen or McMullen], *Camp and Barrack Room; or, The British Army as it is* (London: Chapman and Hall, 1846), pp. 154–55.

CHAPTER 2

The East India Company's Libraries

Going for a soldier in nineteenth-century India could be a fatal decision, which explains the reaction of John Fraser's mother to news of his immi-nent posting to the subcontinent: "It's absolute lunacy … You might as well go and commit suicide straight away."[1] Firstly, there were the difficul-ties and dangers attendant on the long voyage out to India; then there were the realities of trying to adjust to a climate and environment that were particularly challenging for Europeans. "The climate is dreadfully hot, and the monsoons fall very heavy," as Sergeant William Hall put it. "Few Europeans like to go out in the day, and the soldiers are confined to their barracks from ten in the morning to four in the afternoon, and all field days and parades are performed before the sun is up. … A soldier has very little to do in quarters, but attend to his duty, as there are natives employed to cook, wash, sweep, and clean the barracks."[2] Men who joined the Honourable Company's army in the early nineteenth century often did so in the pursuit of adventure and riches, or, at the very least, in the hopes of finding lives there that were better than those that they left

---

[1] John Fraser, *Sixty Years in Uniform* (London: Stanley Paul, 1939), p. 75.

[2] Hall, William. *The Diary of Sergeant William Hall, of Penzance, Cornwall, Late of Her Majesty's Forty-First Regiment: Containing the Incidents connected with Two Years' Campaign in Scinde and Affghanistan During the Late War: to which is Also Added the Sermon Preached to the Troops on the Sunday After the Battle by the Rev. J.N. Allen, B.A. … Also the Particulars of Numerous Shooting Excursions in India After Game of All Descriptions, Including the Lion and Other Wild Beast of the Jungle.* (Penryn, printed for the author: n.d. [1848?]), pp. 13–14.

© The Editor(s) (if applicable) and The Author(s) 2016
S. Murphy, *The British Soldier and his Libraries, c. 1822–1901*,
DOI 10.1057/978-1-137-55083-5_2

behind them. What they frequently found in India, instead, were long, hot, boring days spent on cantonments that were miles from anywhere, and a growing awareness, or fear, that they might never see home again. It was plainly in the latter context, for example, that Gunner William Hurd Eggleston wrote a poignant letter to his sister in August of 1846, telling her he had "no chance of ever seeing you anymore unless I have the good luck to get a leg or an arm broke and then I should be discharged." The young soldier's letter proved painfully prophetic, for he died of dysentery within a year of sending it (he was aged either 25 or 26 years).[3] Staff-Sergeant Bancroft for his part revealed the speed with which Europeans could lose their lives in India, when he described the toll that an outbreak of cholera took on the inhabitants of a station on the upper plains. "The mortality was so great," he wrote, "that coffins could not be provided for the dead, many of whom had to be buried in their quilts."[4] It is not too surprising, then, that many soldiers turned to drink, gambling, or other forms of "vice" in a desperate attempt to escape temporarily the harsh reality of their day-to-day lives, especially as such a considerable difference existed between their living conditions and those of their officers. As one Private Douglas observed: "an officer's life in India is quite endurable. But far different to this is the life of John Private: in his bungalow there is no *punkah* to cool him, no sofa to lie upon, no jilmils (Venetian blinds) to keep out the blazing sun."[5]

The East India Company became increasingly aware of the challenges faced by rank-and-file soldiers in early nineteenth-century India and, we shall see below, this partly informed their decision to establish soldiers' libraries on the subcontinent. It is important to point out, though, that the Company already had a tradition of providing reading for its servants in India, and had long recognized that the provision of books could play a valuable role on the subcontinent. As Dora Lockyer observes, "Books were originally sent on the early voyages with the intention that they be left in India with the Company's employees, so as to provide them with some form of recreation," and "Concern over the spiritual and moral welfare of its servants [in the late seventeenth and early eighteenth centuries]

---

[3] Gunner William Hurd Eggleston, Letter dated 10 August 1846, Photo. Eur. 257.

[4] N.W. Bancroft, *From Recruit to Staff Sergeant*, facsimile of 2nd edition of 1900 (Hornchurch, I. Henry: 1979), p. 27.

[5] William Douglas, Private, 10th Royal Hussars, *Soldiering in Sunshine and Storm* (Edinburgh: Adam and Charles Black, 1865), p. 3.

prompted the Company to send liberal supplies of Bibles, prayer books, catechisms, and books of sermons to the different factory libraries that it established."[6] The Company's interest in these factory libraries declined from the mid-1700s, on the one hand because the commercial importation of books into India began to rise and, on the other, because circulating and subscription libraries were gradually established on the subcontinent. The value of printed books exported from Britain to the East Indies rose from £8,725 in 1791 to £66,180 in 1810, for example,[7] and a spirited defense of Calcutta's libraries in the *Government [Calcutta] Gazette* for December 20, 1830, gives an indication of the range of institutions that were available to readers by this period:

> Besides, the Library of the Asiatic Society [in Calcutta] ... There is an excellent classical library in the College of Fort William, which is also rich in Oriental M.S.S. and there is a very extensive collection of Standard Works, and all the new publications of the day belonging to the Calcutta Library Society, which has been established more than 12 years ago. There is an excellent English Library of the Standard Works of Literature and Science in the Hindoo College, for the use of the Students—and I apprehend that any person subscribing to the Hurkaru Circulating Library and Reading Rooms will find much larger collection of modern literature at his command, with all the Periodicals and newspapers, etc. [sic], than the Bombay General Library will accumulate for many years.[8]

Recognition of the growth of both libraries in and book imports to India is obviously important because it reminds us that soldiers at the Company's stations potentially could draw their reading material from a variety of sources. In the first place, soldiers, particularly officers, frequently brought a selection of books with them to India, and often gave these away or sold them when they were faced with the difficulties of transporting their belongings home or to a new posting. When contemplating the fitting out of his brother for India, for example, George Purvis recalled the expense of a John Leman. The final figure for this gentleman, he remarked, included "To the Bookseller £13.15s.6d, (but remember

[6] Dora Lockyer, "The Provision of Books and Libraries by the East India Company in India, 1611–1858," Thesis submitted for Fellowship of the Library Association, 1977, p. 4.
[7] Lockyer, "Provision of Books and Libraries," p. 188.
[8] Anil Chandra Das Gupta (ed), *The Days of John Company: Selections from Calcutta Gazette, 1824–1832* (Calcutta: Government Printing, 1959), p. 596.

in this article was included what I think rather an unnecessary article, a Persian dictionary of about 16 guineas but some of his friends thought otherwise)." Richard Purvis later commented on the practical difficulties of owning books in India: "I have not a book to look into; I left them all at Cawnpore on account of the enormous expense, the carriage of them is, for we have no such things as Baggage Waggons in this country, we keep our own camels, bullocks etc. and at this rate I thought it best to leave them behind as they would have required an additional camel."[9] Albert Hervey obviously shared Purvis' opinion of the expenses of transporting books in India, describing how he sold his effects in 1835 before he left Mangalore for a new posting: "I think I got some seventy and odd rupees, and I had sofas, chairs, tables, pictures, glass and crockery, books and other things, all of the best description."[10] A Major Thompson for his part advertised his belongings for sale in the *Delhi Gazette* in 1837, and among the items he hoped to dispose of because he was "gone to the Hills" were ten volumes of Scott's poetical works, the first and second series of both *Chronicles of the Cannon Gate* and *Tales of My Grandfather*, as well as six volumes of Byron's poetry.[11]

Soldiers also bought books at the public auctions that disposed of the effects of deceased men, and often left their own books and other belongings to their comrades. Peter Stanley's examination of soldiers' wills, for instance, revealed that "More than half named comrades as beneficiaries, often as 'my friend and comrade.'"[12] Men also supplemented their personal reading material through subscription, as at Chunar, where "the 350 invalids ... (notoriously the most 'dissipated' of the Company's old soldiers) purchased 801 works between 1839 and 1843, most 'novels, tales [and] romances.'"[13] Similarly, one commanding officer informed the East India Company in 1832 that the men he commanded had never had access to station libraries, but maintained "a small collection of Books purchased and kept up by Monthly subscriptions from their pay."Any "Addition or

[9] Iain Gordon (ed), *Soldier of the Raj: The Life of Richard Purvis, 1789-1868. Soldier, Sailor, and Parson* (Barnsley: Leo Cooper, 2001), pp. 42, 67.

[10] Hervey, Captain Albert, *A Soldier of the Company: Life of an Indian Ensign*, ed. by Charles Allen (London: Michael Joseph, 1988), p. 113.

[11] *The Delhi Gazette*, 9 August 1837.

[12] Peter Stanley, *White Mutiny: British Military Culture in India, 1825–1875* (London: Hurst & Company, 1998), p. 65. See also Lockyer, "Provision of Books and Libraries," pp. 177–78.

[13] Stanley, *White Mutiny*, pp. 43–44.

Assistance" that might be provided in this regard, he observed, "would be most gratefully received, and attended with much benefit both to the morals and comfort of the men."[14] Soldiers, too, of course, were able to supplement their reading by joining the circulating libraries, library societies, or reading rooms that were so prevalent in India at this period, and newspaper and journal advertisements for these institutions often revealed an acute awareness of the different types of potential patrons that existed and emphasized that their rates were carefully tailored in this regard. An 1822 advertisement in relation to the "Terms of Subscription to the Hurkaru Circulating Library" in Calcutta, for example, stressed that the institution catered for three different classes of subscribers: "First Class," which paid eight rupees per month, and second and third class, which paid six and four rupees, respectively. The difference between these different classes of subscribers manifested itself in the number of books that each could take out every month, as well as in the range of material that was available to them. First-class readers were entitled to "three or more sets of Books, not exceeding eight volumes at a time; also to all the New Novels, Plays, Pamphlets, and Periodical Publications, *immediately* on their arrival." Third-class subscribers were "entitled equally with Subscribers in the First and Second Classes, to all the Books in the Library published before 1st January 1821; in the proportion of one set, or not more than four volumes at a time," but not to the "New" works.[15]

Booksellers also provided a further source of reading material, advertising their wares in periodicals and newspapers. The *Delhi Gazette*, for instance, frequently carried full-page advertisements for "Books for Sale at Delhi," listing a huge variety of works. By 1837, these advertisements were carrying a pointed addendum: "*Terms–Cash:* and to avoid misunderstanding it is particularly notified that, no application will be attended to, unless accompanied by references for payment: it is also requested that, all orders from out-stations may include a moderate sum for packing &c [sic] along with the price of the *books* required."[16] Booksellers, it must be remarked, advertised both "new" books imported from Britain as well as works that were published—or reprinted—in India. An advertisement in

---

[14] "Report upon the Soldiers Libraries, and recommendation that they should be formed into Regimental, instead of Station, Libraries, and that the number of Books be increased," F/4/1486/58,611, Collection No. 4, pp. 58–59. Hereafter "Report upon the Soldiers Libraries."

[15] *Bengal Hurkuru*, 1 August 1822.

[16] *Delhi Gazette*, 1 February 1837.

the *Government [Calcutta] Gazette* for November 27, 1826, for example, observed that the Government Gazette press would publish "by subscription a reprint of that excellent little work (not procurable in Calcutta) The Christian on the Man of the World[,] or, the Advantages of a Life of Early Piety to a Life of Fashionable Dissipation by Major-General Burn[,] Fourth Edition—London 1818." An advertisement for May 17, 1830, advised "Gentlemen in the Civil and Military Services" in particular, as well as "the Community at large," that "a Branch of the Asiatic Lithographic Company's Establishment, has this day commenced operations" at Cawnpore: "The various useful English, Nagree, Arabic, Persian and Hindoostanee Works, that have been printed and published at the Calcutta Press, are procurable at the Cawnpore Branch at the original prices."[17] Richard Hardcastle, who went to India with the Royal Horse Artillery in the mid-1850s, plainly procured books from some or all of these sources and consequently had difficulty putting money by on the subcontinent. As he explained in one of his letters to his parents: "Certainly I spend part money [sic] on books[,] in fact this is my chief medium of expenditure but in lieu of my money I am vain enough to say that I get golden fruit; more tangible than wealth and in my opinion of more utility."[18]

Missionary and tract societies in India were also keen to reach the reading soldier, particularly once the passing of the India Bill of 1813 compelled the Company to admit missionaries to its territories and, 20 years later, when its right to license missionaries was removed. Prior to this, the Company adopted a remarkably even-handed approach to native religions in India, and tried to limit the influence of missionary and tract societies within its territories. Once the Company's abilities in this regard were weakened, missionary and tract societies took full advantage, and poured increasing resources into the subcontinent. Among their other activities, they provided Bibles, tracts, prayer books, and other edifying works to soldiers; and, as we shall see below, the Society for Promoting Christian Knowledge actually anticipated the Company in providing libraries for soldiers at some of the stations.[19] At the other end of the scale, we might presume, pornographers in India probably were just as keen to

---

[17] Das Gupta (ed), *Days of John Company*, pp. 179, 603.

[18] Richard Hardcastle, Letter of 24 August 1860, Photo Eur C332, p. 174.

[19] See Lawrence James, *Raj: The Making and Unmaking of British India* (1997; London: Abacus, 1998), pp.223–24, and Lockyer, "Provision of Books and Libraries," pp. 152–62.

reach soldiers as were their counterparts in Britain, where "Prosecutions made by the Society for the Suppression of Vice suggest [pornographic publications] were mostly peddled around to army barracks and boarding schools."[20] Frank Richards' much later recollection of his experiences as a private in India in the early part of the twentieth century certainly suggests a reason why pornographers would have been anxious to target the men who served on the subcontinent, as Jonathan Rose observes:

> Abroad, in Indian bazaars, where there were no Ten Commandments, soldiers could buy the semi-pornographic Paul de Kock and *Droll Stories of Balzac.* "As for the *Decameron of Boccaccio,* in my time every soldier of the British forces in India who could read had read this volume from cover to cover," according to [Richards]. "It was considered very hot stuff; but the Prayer-Wallah used to say that in this respect it did not come within shouting distance of certain passages in the Old Testament, once you got the hang of the Biblical language."[21]

The East India Company's renewed interest in the reading of soldiers in the late 1810s and early 1820s, however, seems to have represented a response to an increased awareness of the need to ameliorate the condition of soldiers in India, which, contemporary newspapers suggest, was of growing concern at this period. In a letter to the *Bengal Hurkuru* in November 1822, for instance, one writer noted he had "the pleasure of reading several letters in the public papers on the irregular conduct of European Soldiers," observing—

> many have been so void of common feeling as to make the most insulting remarks touching [soldiers'] characters, and to aver, that *none possessing any abilities, but depraved and abandoned,* could be found in the *situation of Private Soldiers;* and that even some had sought this Country, *as a place of refuge,* to evade the *execution of the law,* which *they had offended;* with such foul aspersions cast, without proof, on the unfortunate.

---

[20] Louis James, *Fiction for the Working Man, 1830–1850: A Study of the Literature produced for the Working Classes in early Victorian Urban England* (London, New York, and Toronto: Oxford University Press, 1963), p. 23.

[21] Jonathan Rose, *The Intellectual Life of the British Working Classes* (New Haven and London: Yale University Press, 2001), p. 209. Rose is quoting from Frank Richards, *Old Soldier Sahib* (1936). Richards was stationed in India between 1901 and 1909.

The writer, who signs himself "Veteran," mounts a spirited defense of private soldiers, emphasizing both that "men of abilities, and of a pure and spotless reputation are to be found, in the humble and neglected walk of a private soldier," and that the reason why there are "so many unfortu-nates" in the Honourable Company's army is largely to do with its own recruiting practices: "*It is a well known fact,*" says one of the advertise-ments inviting Recruits in England, "*that several young men, who entered the service as private soldiers, rose to the highest rank, accumulated immense fortunes, and returned home surrounded with wealth and honors.*" Such grandiose claims, the writer points out, inevitably appealed to ardent and gullible young men, who were appalled when they learned the truth upon their arrival in India: "They are told, that after an elapse [sic] of eight, or ten years, they may attain the progressive rank of Serjeant! That neither talent, conduct, nor any earthly acquirement will bring them one step farther forward, than those possessing neither intellectual nor common place knowledge; and when arrived at that rank, the utmost reward (with few exceptions) for an Indian Soldiers [sic], they must for ever half [sic]." It is hardly surprising, he thus declares, that many men react negatively to this discovery and, "in too many instances, [develop] a determination to indulge in every excess."[22] Another letter in the *Bengal Hurkuru* in August that same year praised the efforts that were being made "to ame-liorate the condition of the Common Soldier" in India, but suggested that the provision of facilities such as libraries was not sufficient: "I am fully aware that there are many men in a Barrack-room, who will gladly avail themselves of the 'Feast of Reason' supplied for them, yet there are others, who, if a motive or incentive be not given, if there be no 'Parent to direct their Flight,' will still remain in pristine ignorance."[23]

The fact that the Company had high hopes in relation to the provision of libraries is expertly illustrated by an extract from a military letter from Bombay on January 29, 1823, wherein it is noted that Sir Charles Colville, the Commander-in-Chief, believed their establishment—

> to be a measure likely to prove of much benefit to the European Soldiers in this country, to have the use of a set of well selected Books, as while they would afford rational amusement to the Soldiers in their leisure hours, they would likewise tend to improve their minds and to lessen licentious

---

[22] *Bengal Hurkuru*, 8 November 1822.
[23] *Bengal Hurkuru*, 22 August 1822.

propensities often induced by mere mischief and want of something to occupy their attention. Such libraries when once established would add greatly to the Comforts and recreations desirable from the Canteen system introduced last year, and which under good regulations and a watchful superintendence, will, it may be confidently hoped, lessen the inclination to vice and induce to better principles and greater regularity of habits among the European soldiery.[24]

The sentiments expressed in this passage are to be found again and again in records relating to the establishment and, eventually, the operation of lending libraries—and savings banks and five courts[25]—for soldiers in the East India Company's three presidencies, and so it is necessary to make a

---

[24] Military letter from Bombay [extract], 29 January 1823, L/MIL/5/384, Collection 85A, p. 274. K.A. Manley appears to attribute the sentiments contained in this extract to the Marquess of Hastings, who was appointed as Governor-General of India in October 1812 (although he did not arrive on the subcontinent until October of the following year). I would suggest that the fact that letter speaks of the Commander-in-Chief in the present tense—he "considers it to be"—means the remarks are unlikely to be those of Hastings, as he had been recalled to England and sailed from India on 1 January 1823 (i.e., before the letter was written). Further, the overall sense of the extracted letter, together with other material in the collection, leads me to believe it is the opinion of those in command in *Bombay* that is at stake, and that the remarks should be attributed to either Mountstuart Elphinstone, who served as Governor of Bombay between 1819 and 1827, or to Colville, who was appointed as Commander-in-Chief of Bombay in 1819 and served in that capacity until 1825. Again, the overall sense of the extract, together with other material in the collection, prompts me to attribute the remarks to Colville (although, of course, I could be mistaken). See K.A. Manley, "Engines of Literature: Libraries in an Era of Expansion and Transition," in Giles Mandelbrote and K.A. Manley (eds), *The Cambridge History of Libraries in Britain and Ireland, Vol. II, 1640–1850* (Cambridge: Cambridge University Press, 2006), p. 523; C.A. Bayly, "Elphinstone, Mountstuart (1779–1859)," *Oxford Dictionary of National Biography*, Oxford University Press, 2004; online edn, Jan 2008 [http://www.oxforddnb.com.remote.library.dcu.ie/view/article/8752, accessed 17 Oct 2015]; John F. Riddick, *Who Was Who in British India* (Westport, Connecticut, and London: Greenwood Press, 1998), pp. 3, 81, and 118; H.M. Stephens, "Colville, Sir Charles (1770–1843)," rev. Roger T. Stearn, *Oxford Dictionary of National Biography*, Oxford University Press, 2004 [http://www.oxforddnb.com.remote.library.dcu.ie/view/article/6008, accessed 17 Oct 2015]; and Roland Thorne, "Hastings, Francis Rawdon, first marquess of Hastings and second earl of Moira (1754–1826)," *Oxford Dictionary of National Biography*, Oxford University Press, 2004; online edn, Jan. 2008 [http://www.oxforddnb.com.remote.library.dcu.ie/view/article/12568, accessed 13 Oct. 2015].

[25] "Fives" is a ball game played by two or four players in a court enclosed on three or four sides. See *"fives, n.2,"* *OED Online*, Oxford University Press, December 2015, http://www.oed.com.dcu.idm.oclc.org/view/Entry/70809, (accessed 20 Oct 2015).

number of observations here.[26] Firstly, Colville's remarks were informed by the recognition that facilities like libraries were particularly necessary for soldiers in India, given the harsh nature of military service on the subcontinent. He clearly hoped that the provision of the libraries would provide a vital outlet for bored and restless men and, in this context, the East India Company's decision to establish the institutions may be interpreted as a benevolent and/or pragmatic gesture—one, moreover, that may be related more broadly to how it conducted its business practices. As Margaret Makepeace points out in her study of the East India Company's management of its warehouse workers, for example, "benevolence formed an integral part of [its] domestic business practices," and there is much evidence to support the argument that it was an enlightened employer. That said, the model of business that the Company adopted was clearly tinged with a healthy dose of pragmatism, and the "directors and senior company officials actively sought to project an image of paternal benevolence both in India and at home to counteract any public criticism of their general *modus operandi*."[27] In the case of soldiers, this included placing a recruiting notice in *The Public Advertiser* in December 1785, which stated, "It is well known that the Honourable Company takes Care and are Tender of all Men who are sick or lame in their Service, by supplying them with every Necessary of Life." It also included the establishment in the late eighteenth century of "a programme of land grants in northern India for native soldiers, both to the young who were wounded and to those who were no longer fit to serve because of age or infirmity."[28]

The Company's decision to establish libraries for soldiers therefore may be seen as either an enlightened or pragmatic gesture on its part, but it was also reflective of the overwhelmingly positive—or tolerant or realistic—attitude that it seems to have adopted in relation to the literacy of its forces. Men who enlisted in the Company's army had ample opportunities for self-improvement, for its "establishments of European regiments included, in the 1820s, a school master, a reading master and writing master, later joined by two assistant school masters, a librarian and (for soldier's children) a school mistress."[29] Men such as William Pattison

---

[26] See, for example, L/MIL/5/391, Collections 134-8.

[27] Margaret Makepeace, *The East India Company's London Workers: Management of the Warehouse Labourers, 1800–1858* (Woodbridge: The Boydell Press, 2010), pp. 1, 73.

[28] Makepeace, *The East India Company's London Workers*, pp. 71–72.

[29] Stanley, *White Mutiny*, p. 44.

obviously delighted in the educational opportunities that opened up for them, as the following extract from a letter to his brother in July 1834 reveals: "I am now attending our regimental school, and hope I do not flatter myself in saying, 'that I improve in useful learning[.]' You must perceive I have in some measure improved; and it is a gratification to think we can communicate with each other, without the assistance of others."[30] We shall see in the next chapter that the Company's attitude to the literacy of its soldiers was in marked distinction to that of the Regular Army, which, we noted in the introduction, waited until the late 1830s before it began to establish libraries for its rank-and-file troops.

The second point that must be made about Colville's remarks is that they were significantly limited to "European Soldiers" and made no mention of the vast number of native troops upon which the power of the East India Company so hugely depended. Richard Holmes suggests, for instance, that there were some 232,000 Indians in John Company's army by the time of the Indian Rebellion in 1857, as opposed to a figure of some 45,000 European soldiers, a figure that was much the same in 1835.[31] Sir Charles's failure to mention native soldiers in relation to the libraries is replicated throughout the early records, and it becomes very clear that the institutions were initially intended only for European troops. It is not until much later in history of the libraries that we find evidence of native troops using (some of) the institutions. The report that was returned in relation to the library at Bangalore for 1855, for example, indicates that native troops were now being numbered among the readers there: "The returns of issues for 1854 were 3745 2/3 those of 1855 ... shewing [sic] an increase in the demand for reading—this is partly attributable to the increase in the number of Europeans now serving at the Station in Her Majesty's 43rd Regiment, and the Books being available to the Drummers of Native Corps, and the Staff Serjeants [sic] and others at Hoonsour."[32] The fact that there is no explicit mention of native troops using the libraries in the early records is obviously significant, but we cannot take it entirely for granted that the institutions were never used by such soldiers at this

[30] William Pattison to his brother, 20 July 1834, NAM 1967-02-66-2, 3.

[31] Richard Holmes, *Sahib: The British Soldier in India, 1750–1914* (London: HarperCollins, 2005), p. 81.

[32] "Extracts from the Annual Reports for 1855 upon the Soldiers' Lending Libraries of this Army," Fort Saint George, Military Cons. of August 1856, Nos. 131 & 132, L/Mil/3/1555. Henceforth, "Extracts from the Annual Reports for 1855 upon the Soldiers' Lending Libraries."

period. As we shall see in the next chapter, the day-to-day operation of the libraries evolved slowly, and there were differences between the ways in which they were operated by those responsible for them at a local level.

Colville's comments are significant for a further reason, however, and this is that they are reflective of the notion that the libraries could play a vital role in regulating the behavior and, potentially, the attitudes of the soldiers. As he put it, the establishment of the institutions was looked to as a means not only of contributing to the "Comforts and recreations" of the troops in India, but also of "lessen[ing] the inclination to vice, and induc[ing] … better principles and greater regularity of habits among the European soldiery." The link that Colville made here between reading and behavior clearly recalls the arguments of critics such as Gary Kelly, who emphasize, we noted previously, that reading at this period was perceived as a transformative activity that had to be carefully controlled.[33] As a professional army officer, and the son of the 8th Lord Colville, Sir Charles obviously assumed a proprietorial stance in relation to the libraries, and believed he had both a duty and a right to supervise the reading habits of the soldiers who were his inferior dependents.[34] By providing what he described as "well selected Books" to the libraries, and then by "regulating" and "superintending" the reading that was carried on within the institutions, Sir Charles—and the Company—clearly hoped to produce a "better" class of soldier in India and, presumably, to facilitate thereby the colonial and imperial process on the subcontinent.

The recognition that the East India Company may have envisioned using reading in this way raises a considerable number of questions for the modern scholar, and not the least of these relates to what criteria the company followed when choosing the books that it provided to its forces. Overwhelmingly, the evidence suggests, the company's choice of books was informed by class considerations, for a General Order of 1829 laid down that "European Non-Commissioned Officers and Privates [were]

[33] Gary Kelly, *Women, Writing, and Revolution, 1790–1827* (Oxford: Clarendon Press, 1993), p. 184.

[34] See Stephens, "Colville, Sir Charles (1770–1843)," *Oxford Dictionary of National Biography*, and Riddick, *Who Was Who in British India*, p. 81. The essential point I am making here holds true in relation to both Mountstuart Elphinstone and, indeed, John Adam, who acted as Governor-General of India for seven months following Hastings' departure. Elphinstone, for example, was the son of the 11th Baron Elphinstone and, while Adam did not come from such an exalted background, he was educated at Charterhouse and Edinburgh University. See Riddick, *Who Was Who in British India*, pp. 3 and 118.

to have the first choice of Books."[35] As the years went by, compilers of and contributors to lists and reports relating to the libraries thus became increasingly convinced that they were tasked with a very particular responsibility, which was to procure books that would appeal to and, ideally, improve this class of readers. It was plainly because of this that a minute from the 1820s observed that "societies at home" might be looked to as a source of books because "The publications they put forth are generally of a Religious nature, but they likewise comprise amusing Narratives, and other Compositions likely to attract the Common people." It is also why, some 14 years later, Brigadier-General Brown, the Commander of Artillery at Dum Dum, expressed the view that "The best standard works of fiction such as the Waverley Novels and the Books published for the information of Labouring Classes at home which are now coming out in various shapes and in periodical numbers would undoubtedly be received with interest."[36] The Company, it must be remarked, supplied "good" works of fiction such as the Waverley novels to the libraries from the very first, and correspondence from the 1830s reveals that it also took steps to provide both newspapers and "certain" periodical publications to the institutions. One letter from Madras in 1834, for example, observed that the expense of providing such works to the libraries had been limited to between one and half to two thousand rupees per year, and that the figure was to be defrayed by drawing upon regimental canteen funds; it also observed that the latter circumstance "afforded satisfaction to the Court."[37] In a similar fashion, letters and reports from the late 1830s and early 1840s suggest that works such as the *Penny Magazine* (1832–1845) and *Saturday Magazine* (1832–1844) were increasingly sought by—or for—the soldiers, and that the East India Company supplied them to the men. In a letter from 1840, indeed, Sir Hugh Gough, the Adjutant-General of the Army, expressed the opinion that such publications "should always form part of each [library], as being in great request, and calculated to be of much utility."[38]

[35] "General Order," Madras Presidency, Extract from Fort St. George Military Correspondence, F/4/1243/40911, p. 19.

[36] "Minute by the President," L/MIL/5/384, Collection 85A, p. 282, and "Report upon the Soldiers Libraries," p. 33.

[37] Military Letter from Madras, 5 August 1834, L/Mil/3/1162.

[38] "Copy of a Letter from the Adjutant-General of the Army, 17 March 1840," L/Mil/3/1331.

That said, the East India Company's libraries stocked authors whose appeal cut across class lines, such as Edgeworth and Scott, which is made clear by Sir William Henry Sleeman's account of his service in India. Recalling his one-time commanding officer, a Colonel Gregory, Sleeman observes—

> He was an old man when I first became acquainted with him. I put into his hands, when in camp, Miss Edgeworth's novels, in the hope of being able to induce him to read by degrees and I have frequently seen the tears stealing down over his furrowed cheeks as he sat pondering over her pages in the corner of his tent. ... It was impossible ever to persuade him that the characters and incidents of these novels were the mere creation of fancy; he felt them to be true, he wished them to be true, and he would have them to be true. We were not very anxious to undeceive him, as the illusion gave him pleasure and did him good.[39]

The first point that might be made about Sleeman's recollection of the weeping colonel, of course, is that it is illustrative of nothing so much as the persistence of the culture of sensibility well into the nineteenth century and, in particular, how this culture continued to forge contemporary notions of the military man of feeling. As Neil Ramsay observes, "In line with the broader development of sentimental culture during the late eighteenth century, Britain's cultural response to war was also heavily informed by concerns with feeling and sympathy," and at the "heart" of this culture "was a perception that feelings were foundational to the correct operation of morality and social behaviour."[40] In this context, Sleeman's description of the elderly officer was a highly charged one, for the colonel's tears were symbolic of both his own moral and cultural superiority and that of the nation which he served. They also demonstrated, though, that writers like Edgeworth—or, indeed, Scott—found readers among all classes, and Scott's popularity with soldiers in general was, indeed, something of which he was himself aware. As he put it in his journal entry for June 16, 1826, "I am sensible that if there be anything good about my poetry, or

---

[39] Francis Tuker, *The Yellow Scarf: the Story of the Life of Thuggee Sleeman or Major-General Sir William Henry Sleeman, K.C.B. 1788–1856 of the Bengal Army and the Indian Political Service* (London, Sydney, and Toronto: White Lion Publishers, 1961), pp. 26–27.

[40] Neil Ramsey, *The Military Memoir and Romantic Literary Culture, 1780–1835* (Farnham: Ashgate, 2011), p. 7.

prose either, it is a hurried frankness of composition which pleases soldiers, sailors, and young people of bold and active disposition."[41]

Class issues alone did not dictate the types of books that were supplied to the libraries, though, and a tension frequently existed between the works that authorities thought suitable and the demands of the soldiers themselves. The Company itself recognized this as the years went by, and made great efforts to supply readers with their preferred reading material. This, however, was no easy task, as the preferences of soldiers could vary greatly both within and between the different stations. Reports upon the library at Jaulnah in1855, for instance, pointed out that the books "least valued or read" at the station included "Scientific" works. This was in marked contrast to "some" of the readers at Mhow the same year, who were seeking "works of an educational tendency, especially in Arithmetic for them to study, & others, who look forward for employment as Overseers in the Department [of]Public works, [who] would like Books which would instruct them ... in Road making, Building, Surveying, &c. &c."[sic]. Other soldiers at Mhow were complicating matters further because they were requesting more "dramatic works for their perusal."[42] Amateur dramatics, it must be remarked, were hugely popular with soldiers, and it is tempting to suggest that the latter men were seeking such works to facilitate the kind of theatrical production that Emily Eden at one point encountered in Kurnaul: "They [that is, the privates at the station] did much better than the gentlemen amateurs at Meerut, and, except that the heroines were six feet high and their pink petticoats had not more than three breadths in them, the whole thing was well done: the scenery and decorations were excellent, and all got up by the privates."[43] Eden, it should be pointed out, traveled to India in 1835 with her brother, George, when he was appointed as Governor-General, and remained there with him until he was recalled in 1842.[44] We will meet with her again at the beginning of our next chapter, where we will consider her reflections on the kinds of isolated places where Europeans in India could find themselves.

[41] Walter Scott, *The Journal of Sir Walter Scott*, ed by W.E.K. Anderson (Oxford: Clarendon Press, 1972), p. 159.

[42] "Extracts from the Annual Reports for 1855 upon the Soldiers' Lending Libraries."

[43] Emily Eden, *Up the Country: Letters to her Sister from the Upper Provinces of India*, with an introduction and notes by Edward Thompson (1930; London and Dublin: Curzon Press, 1978), p. 104.

[44] Edward Thompson, introduction to *Up the Country*, p. ix.

Probably the earliest list of books in relation to the libraries, however, dates from the early 1820s[45]; it is entitled "List of Books sent to Bengal," and features 45 titles, including books of poems, texts relating to history and geography, and works of a religious or spiritual nature. That this list should feature works such as "A Family Bible," "Cowper's Poems," "History of England," "Goldsmith's Geography," or "An Account of the Battle of Waterloo" is hardly surprising; what is more interesting is the prominence that it gives to fiction. Maria Edgeworth's "Popular Tales" is the first such work mentioned, followed by "Arabian Nights' Entertainments, Robinson Crusoe, Peter Wilkins, Sherwood's Serjeant Dale, Leadbetter's Cottage Dialogues, Narrative of a Soldier of the 71st Regiment,[46] [and] Waverley and all the works of the same Author."[47] The prominence given to fiction on this early list is important, in the first place because it once again underlines the more positive—or realistic or tolerant—approach that the East India Company adopted in relation to the reading of its soldiers. However much they might have wished to limit readers to religious or instructional works, those responsible for the establishment of the libraries clearly realized that works of fiction could not be excluded. The works of fiction mentioned on the Bengal list are also important, though, because they are illustrative of the kinds of texts that the company went on to supply during the 1820s and early 1830s; that is to say, of works that were clearly chosen to appeal to, improve, and inspire their very particular projected readers: mainly lower-class men who were engaged in overseas military service. The *Arabian Nights Entertainments*, for example, is representative of the highly imaginative and extravagant oriental tales that went on to become a staple feature of the libraries; that is, of a type of fiction where the rules of probability are frequently suspended—or renegotiated—and where heroes and heroines

---

[45] I have suggested elsewhere that this list dates from 1819, but further reflection upon correspondence between the Court of Directors and India in the years between 1819 and circa 1823 convinces me this is too early. The Court refer in their letter to Bombay on 27 February 1822, for instance, to a letter they had sent to Bengal on 22 August 1821, wherein they noted that they had agreed to the suggestion to provide small libraries for soldiers in that presidency. The first books seem to have been sent to Bengal in 1822, so the list was probably generated at some point after August 1821. See "Military letter to Bombay [extract], 27 February 1822," L/MIL/5/384, Collection 85A, p. 275.

[46] The work meant here is probably *Journal of a Soldier of the 71st, or Glasgow Regiment, Highland Light Infantry, From 1806 to 1815*, which was published in Edinburgh in early 1819. My thanks to Catriona Kennedy, who first drew my attention to this text.

[47] "List of Books sent to Bengal," L/MIL/5/384, Collection 85A, p. 277.

encounter mischievous or malevolent genii and magicians as well as giants and monsters. The tales that appear in collections such as the *Arabian Nights* frequently have a moral, and provide a critical insight into the social conditions of the Persian, Indian, Arab, or Chinese cultures from which they emerged, but they are nonetheless marked primarily by their determination to contribute to the delight and entertainment of readers rather than their improvement. The story that frames the *Arabian Nights* collection facilitates this: Scheherazade tells stories to her husband, Schahriar, to stave off her always imminent execution, and readers, like Schahriar, find themselves enthralled by stories that promise to keep expanding.

Daniel Defoe's *Robinson Crusoe* (1719) and Robert Paltock's *The Life and Adventures of Peter Wilkins* (1751) are representative of a less extravagant type of fiction that goes to great formal lengths to stress the essential realism of both its central characters and their adventures. Each of these works begins with an account of the early life and family history of its protagonist, for instance, and provides exhaustive details that prove he had the wherewithal to survive in the strange new world he eventually discovers. By "employing a mass of circumstantial detail" in this way, Defoe and Paltock produce an "illusion of complete reality" in their stories; in other words, they persuade readers to accept the bigger lies in their narratives by first encouraging them to accept the many smaller ones with which they have been preceded.[48] In impressing these various "lies" upon their readers, moreover, Defoe and Paltock provide them with careful descriptions of the countries and peoples that their heroes visit, and explain why their ideas about the world and God are profoundly affected by these encounters. This means that the fiction exemplified by works such as *Robinson Crusoe* and *Peter Wilkins* has an explicitly didactic as well as an imaginative dimension, encouraging readers to reflect upon and learn from the experiences of the central character. That said, this type of fiction is also informed by an obvious colonial or imperial imperative: both Crusoe and Wilkins become increasingly convinced of the essential superiority of Britain and the British in the course of their adventures, and turn themselves into the "prince[s] or lord[s]" of the "new" worlds that they discover.[49]

[48] Walter Allen, *The English Novel: A Short Critical History* (Harmondsworth: Penguin, 1954), p. 38.

[49] Daniel Defoe, *The Life and Adventures of Robinson Crusoe* (London: Penguin, 1965), p. 157.

Walter Scott did not publicly acknowledge his authorship of the Waverley Novels until 1827, and these were typically grouped together or consigned to their own separate category on East India Company library lists. In these historical novels, Scott skillfully blends elements drawn from the romance, the National Tale, and the novel of manners, brilliantly evoking the atmosphere of past ages and breathing life into a vast cast of colorful characters. Although there are many remarkable women in Scott's novels, the works are primarily preoccupied with men, and their attempts to make sense of the complex political and social situations that they encounter. Frequently, this involves a display of physical as well as moral courage on their parts, with characters—such as Waverley, Ivanhoe, or Rob Roy, for instance—finding themselves compelled to bear arms and/or ponder the qualities and obligations of fighting men. In *Rob Roy*, for example, the narrator is hugely impressed by Captain Thornton, a British officer, whose courage and intelligence enables the men under his command to conduct themselves in battle with all "the firmness of English soldiers." Threatened with death at the hands of the rebels led by Rob Roy's wife, he remarks, "I am wise enough to know how to die ... without disgracing the service."[50] The prominence afforded to Scott's novels on this and later lists is not too surprising, given the truly sensational effect that the publication of these works had upon the early-nineteenth-century reading public. Readers of all classes read them, in America and Russia, as well as in Britain and continental Europe, and the works have been credited with "open[ing] up the novel to the male gender as both writing and reading, establishing novel writing as a literary activity, and legitimating novel reading as manly practice."[51] The Company's willingness to admit works like Scott's to its libraries so early in the nineteenth century is clearly worth noting because it is was in contrast to what was happening in many libraries and reading clubs in Britain at this period. That said, however, it is important not to overstate this point. Fiction was a staple of circulating libraries from the late eighteenth century, a circumstance that was lamented by contemporaries who feared the social effects of these institutions, and there is strong evidence to suggest that its status steadily

---

[50] Sir Walter Scott, *Rob Roy* (London: Penguin, 1995), pp. 368, 394.

[51] Andrew Hook, introduction to *Waverley*, by Sir Walter Scott (London: Penguin, 1972), p. 9; Ina Ferris, *The Achievement of Literary Authority: Gender, History, and the Waverley Novels* (Cornell University Press: Ithaca and London, 1991), p. 80.

improved during the 1820s.[52] One further point must be made about the presence of Scott's novels in the soldiers' libraries before we move on, and this is that it is reflective of the Company's willingness to purchase expensive books for the institutions. *Waverley* was priced at 21 shillings in 1814, for example, but a record-breaking 31.5 shillings became the standard price for all of Scott's three-volume novels following the publication of *Kenilworth* in 1821.[53]

An unexpected category on the Bengal list is represented by Mary Martha Sherwood's *Memoirs of Sergeant Dale, His Daughter and the Orphan Mary* (1815), a tale originally published for a juvenile audience. The selection of such works may have been predicated on an awareness of the poor reading skills of many of the soldiers who would use the libraries, or on recognition of the youth of some of the potential readers. Stanley observes, for instance, that one of the "most notable contributions" of the East India Company's military seminary at Addiscombe was "to preserve [some of the officer cadets] from arriving in India at an even more vulnerable age" than was necessary: "After passing an unexacting entrance examination, young men of between fourteen and sixteen spent two years pursuing a curriculum heavy with arcane mathematics and light on idiomatic Hindoostanee ... Cadets were appointed to the engineers, the artillery, and to the infantry in order of what passed for academic merit. Most infantry and all cavalry cadets, however, were appointed 'directly,' arriving in India without any preparation and little guidance."[54] It is in this context plainly significant that one of the contributors to the 1845 report on the Gun Carriage Manufactory library in Madras observes, "The books ... have been much read during [this year], nearly all the Artificers and Pupils

---

[52] See, for example, Peter Garside, "The English Novel in the Romantic Era: Consolidation and Dispersal," in *The English Novel 1770-1829: A Bibliographical Survey of Prose Fiction Published in the British Isles, Vol. II: 1800–1829*, ed. by Peter Garside, James Raven, and Rainer Schöwerling (Oxford: Oxford University Press, 2000), pp. 15–103. For details of holdings of fiction in circulating and subscription libraries between 1800 and 1829, see P.D. Garside, J.E. Belanger, and S.A. Ragaz, *British Fiction, 1800–1829: A Database of Production, Circulation & Reception*, designer A.A. Mandal http://www.british-fiction.cf.ac.uk (accessed 24 January 2007).

[53] See William St. Clair, *The Reading Nation in the Romantic Period* (Cambridge: Cambridge University Press, 2004), pp. 120 and 203. On how costs of newly published books rose in the Romantic period, see p. 120.

[54] Stanley, *White Mutiny*, p. 30. On the history of Addiscombe, see J.M. Bourne, "The East India Company's Military Seminary, Addiscombe, 1809–1858," *Journal of the Society for Army Historical Research*, Vol. LVII, No. 232 (Winter 1979), pp. 206–222.

read them, and I am very certain the Library continues to be a useful means of improving the minds and characters of the men and boys under my Command."[55] In any event, writers like Sherwood played a crucial role in constructing notions of both childhood and adulthood that were emerging in the late eighteenth and early nineteenth centuries, and manifestly addressed themselves to adult and child audiences alike. Those responsible for Company libraries may have hoped that, by reading works like these, soldiers would internalize "appropriate" attitudes to gender, class, or race, and thus become more tractable in their behavior. Another point that must be made about Sherwood's *Serjeant Dale*, of course, is that it may have been seen as particularly appropriate for East India Company soldiers because much of the book is set on a military station in India.

The leading category of fiction on the Bengal list is represented by Maria Edgeworth's *Popular Tales* (1804) and Mary Leadbetter's *Cottage Dialogues* (1811–1813), which were aimed at a lower-class readership. Edgeworth's text, for example, was explicitly aimed at readers "beyond circles which are sometimes exclusively considered as polite," while Leadbetter's work—as its title suggests—was intended for perusal by the inhabitants of Irish cottages. In her advertisement to the second part of the work in 1813, moreover, Leadbetter noted with satisfaction that an English edition of the first part had also been "the means of introducing the Dialogues to the notice of the *Society for bettering the condition of the Poor*, who were pleased to extract and publish some Dialogues for the use of English Cottagers." Despite their formal differences, both of these works had a similar didactic mission: namely, to educate and improve lower-class readers by emphasizing the importance of generosity, thrift, chastity, sobriety, and good temper.[56] Thus each of these books also reassured upper-class readers that popular education was not to be feared, as it would encourage the lower classes to respect the essential superiority of their "betters." This is evidenced in Leadbetter's text by the continuing positive emphasis that the enlightened lower-class protagonists place on the "Quality," and by the way in which the hero of Edgeworth's "Lame Jervas", for example, stresses that it was his upper-class master's benevolence that made possible his story of rags-to-riches.

[55] Adjutant-General's Letter of 4th June, 1847, No. 480, forwarding Extracts from the Annual Reports for 1845, L/Mil/3/1457.

[56] Richard Lovell Edgeworth, preface to *Popular Tales* by Maria Edgeworth, 3rd edition. (London: J. Johnston, 1807), vol. 1, p. v; and Mary Leadbetter, *Cottage Dialogues among the Irish Peasantry*, Part II (Dublin: John Cumming, 1813), pp. vii–viii.

Describing the works of Edgeworth and Leadbetter in this way is useful only to a certain point, which again underlines the two greater points that must be made about all of the fictions with which the East India Company anticipated supplying its men. Firstly, and as we noted earlier, all of the titles on the first and subsequent lists were evidently chosen because of the Company's conviction that they would peculiarly appeal to their projected readership—that is, men engaged in overseas military service. This is probably most immediately apparent in the cases of works like the *Arabian Nights Entertainments*, *Robinson Crusoe*, *Peter Wilkins*, or the Waverley Novels, which overtly celebrate (manly) attributes such as courage, curiosity, and acquisitive desire and, in the case of the first three texts, portray foreign lands as places of opportunity and fabulous riches. It is in the latter context, for instance, that the heroine of "The Story of Zobeide" makes a trading voyage to the Indies, and discovers a town where the inhabitants have all been petrified. When she visits the royal apartments, she is amazed by "a throne of massy Gold, raised several Steps above the Floor, and enriched with large inchased Emeralds, and a Bed upon the Throne of rich Stuff embroidered with Pearls." What surprises her most, though, is "a Diamond as big as the Egg of an Ostrich," which lights up the whole room.[57] Edgeworth's, Sherwood's, or Leadbetter's works also seek to promote positive images of masculinity, though, and, in the cases of *Popular Tales* and *Memoirs of Sergeant Dale*, trace the (colonial and imperial) adventures of heroes in places like India, the West Indies, America, and China. Moreover, one of the stories in *Popular Tales*, "Murad the Unlucky," is clearly indebted to the *Arabian Nights* in terms both of its characters and setting. Edgeworth's didactic aim in her tale is to prove that "prudence has more influence than chance in human affairs," and she accomplishes this by contrasting the behavior of Murad and Saladin, two characters at the court of the Grand Seignor of Constantinople.[58]

The more realistic fiction of *Robinson Crusoe* and *Peter Wilkins* is similarly indebted to the extravagant fiction of the *Arabian Nights*, most obviously to the stories of Sinbad the Sailor and his seven voyages. Like Crusoe and Wilkins, Sinbad is insatiably curious, and disregards the advice

[57] *Arabian Nights' Entertainments: Consisting of One Thousand and One Stories, Told by the Sultaness of the Indies, to divert the Sultan from the Execution of a bloody Vow he had made to marry a Lady every Day, and have her cut off next Morning, to avenge himself for the Disloyalty of his first Sultaness, &c.*, English translator not given, 4 vols., 10th edn (Dublin: W. Whitestone, 1776), vol. 1, pp. 180–81.

[58] Edgeworth, *Popular Tales*, vol. 2, p. 249.

of those who try to warn him that travel has its dangers as well as its rewards. In common with Defoe's and Paltock's heroes, Sinbad at first turns to prayer only when he is in dire straits, lamenting his foolish behavior and promising that he will henceforth submit his will—and life—to God. Typically, he forgets this promise once the immediate danger has passed, and it is this characteristic that makes his seven voyages possible. By the time Sinbad finally reaches true maturity—and stops travelling—he has amassed a fabulous fortune, which underlines another crucial similarity that exists between his and Crusoe's and Wilkins's adventures: all three are informed by an acute mercantile and colonial awareness. In Sinbad's case this is made particularly explicit: his "Passion for Traffick," he remarks, went hand-in-hand with his "Curiosity to see new Things," and he provides those who read his tale with scrupulous details about the riches of the lands that he visits.[59]

It is worth stressing the comparisons that exist between Sinbad, Crusoe, and Wilkins, because they illuminate the complex role that eastern literature—and its imitators—played in stimulating Western imperialism. The reading of works such as the *Arabian Nights Entertainments* affected Western readers in a variety of ways, Ros Ballaster points out, including inspiring many to "imagine the succession of a European Christian power to government in some eastern regions, particularly Britain in India."[60] The fact that the East India Company introduced texts such as "Persian Tales," "Turkish Tales," and "Tales of Genii" to its libraries during the 1820s and 1830s is therefore obviously important, for, in Edward Said's terms, these works also demonstrate the "complex ideological configuration[s] underlying the tendency to imperialism."[61] It must be remarked here that the Company added to the other types of fiction that featured in its libraries during these years, and so works such as "Castle Rackrent," "Cottagers of Glenburnie," "Don Quixote," "Gil Blas," "Devil on two sticks," "Baron Munchausen," and "Alfred and Galba" began to appear on lists of books exchanged between those responsible for the institutions.[62] Again,

[59] *Arabian Nights' Entertainments*, vol. 1, p. 221.

[60] Ros Ballaster, *Fabulous Orients: Fictions of the East in England, 1662–1784* (Oxford: Oxford University Press, 2005), p. 35.

[61] Edward Said, *Culture and Imperialism* (London: Chatto and Windus Ltd., 1993), p. 82.

[62] See, for example, "Larger List of Books for the four principal stations viz., Bombay, Poonab, Kauria, and Maloonga to be applied for the Court of Directors," L/MIL/5/384, Collection 85A, p. 284.

all of these works were evidently chosen as particularly appropriate for soldiers, either because they would contribute to their moral improvement or stimulate their desire for adventures in foreign lands. At one point in his adventures, for instance, Baron Munchausen encounters "a fleet of British East India men," and learns from their officers "of their affairs in India, and the ferocity of that dreadful warrior, Tippoo Sahib, on which I resolved to go to India and encounter the tyrant."[63]

It is important to exercise caution, however, when speculating that those responsible for the establishment or operation of the libraries may have perceived possible links between soldiers' reading and the imperial enterprise in which the company was engaged. As East India Company records demonstrate, some of these individuals entertained considerable reservations about the types of books that these libraries should stock, and even about the libraries themselves. Commenting on an early 1820s' list of books, for instance, Sir Charles Colville remarked, "The list, I think, will bear reconsideration generally and a greater number of Historical books should I think be introduced among other changes. I doubt for example if Scott's novels can be deemed a generally appropriate selection for such … establishment[s]."[64] In his comments on the library at Cawnpore in 1832, Brigadier-General Murray was for his part insistent "that more harm than advantage accrues from Institutions which congregate Soldiers of different Corps together, and that it is as well to confine the Readers to their Bible and Prayer Book."[65] These reservations are typical of the anxieties that frequently coalesced around the figure of the lower-class reader at this time and, as our chapters on the Regular Army will demonstrate, they persisted well into the Victorian period.

There is a further point that we must bear in mind when considering possible links between reading and empire, and this is that soldiers' responses to books in the Company's libraries may have been informed by their previous reading experiences. As Louis James has pointed out, early-nineteenth-century innovations in papermaking and mechanical printing produced "a wave of cheap publications … [that] helped to create the new working-class reading public."[66] The East India Company drew the majority of its

---

[63] Rudolf Erich Raspe, *The Travels and Surprising Adventures of Baron Munchausen* (1785; Sawtry, Cambridge: Dedalus, 1993), p. 256.

[64] L/MIL/5/384, Collection 85A, p. 283.

[65] "Report upon the Soldiers Libraries," p. 57.

[66] James, *Fiction for the Working Man*, pp. 10–11.

rank-and-file soldiers from this public, which invites speculation as to how men whose previous reading experience may have been limited to cheap periodicals such as *The Mirror of Literature, Amusement and Instruction* (1820–1837), or to a more sensational periodical such as *The Tell-Tale* (1823–1824), responded to the types of books that the Company supplied. The Company also drew a significant number of its troops from Scotland, particularly "during periods when Scotsmen exerted a powerful grip on the Directorship."[67] Scotland, of course, is pointed to by critics as the place where the "reading habit" was early and peculiarly "democratized ... thanks to the strong Calvinist tradition of Bible study and the consequent emphasis upon schooling for all."[68] The Scottish common reader drawn from this environment, one might assume, may have been more literate than his English, Welsh, or Irish counterparts, but that fact alone does not tell us whether he read the books in Company libraries, or how he read them.

There is a further reason why caution must be exercised when using the East India Company records to explore links between reading and Empire, and this relates to the role that the Society for Promoting Christian Knowledge played in the establishment of libraries for soldiers. The SPCK anticipated the Company by establishing libraries at some of the stations in the early 1820s, supplying books that were overwhelmingly grave or didactic in nature. The Company tried to rectify this situation when it took over these libraries from the society, which is in the first instance made clear by two lists that were generated in relation to libraries in the Bombay presidency. List A, titled, "Books which may be obtained from the Bombay District Committee of the Society for Promoting Christian Knowledge," is relatively short, and is primarily concerned with works of a spiritual or religious nature. Apart from "Robinson Crusoe" and "Gay's Fables," there is no real light reading on the list. List B, "Additional Books to be obtained from the Court of Directors," is much longer and more ambitious, and includes a section titled "Poetry, Tales, etc.," which makes some concessions to imaginative literature, featuring Shakespeare, *Paradise Lost*,

[67] Alan J. Guy, "People who will stick at nothing to make money?: Officers, Income, and Expectations in the Service of John Company, 1750–1840," in Alan J. Guy and Peter B. Boyden (eds), assisted by Marion Harding, *Soldiers of the Raj: The Indian Army, 1600–1947* (London: National Army Museum, 1997), p. 50.

[68] Richard D. Altick, *The English Common Reader: A Social History of the Mass Reading Public, 1800–1900* (1957; Columbus: Ohio State University Press, 1998), pp. 9–10. See also Rose, *Intellectual Life*, pp. 16–18, 59–61, and, St. Clair, *Reading Nation*, pp. 241–42, 251–52.

Arabian Nights, "Persian Tales," "Turkish Tales," "Edgeworth's Popular Tales," the Waverley novels, and *Peter Wilkins*.[69] However, book lists of what were originally SPCK libraries are far more austere. An 1829 list for a Bangalore library, for example, has spiritual and religious works aplenty, but Edgeworth or Scott is conspicuously absent. Indeed, works such as "Instructive Tales of Mrs. Trimmer" or "Country Parishioner Instructed" represent the lightest reading on this list.[70] Much the same can be said of the books held in 1829 at the libraries at St. Thomas's Court,[71] or Bellary,[72] although the latter did have a copy of *Robinson Crusoe*, as did Vizagpatam.[73]

In their reports for 1833 and 1834, most commanding officers and station chaplains were keen to stress the "beneficial results" of the libraries, but also to emphasize that the works supplied were largely "of too grave a nature to render their perusal an object of attention to the men."[74] They thus insisted that the libraries must in future offer a greater selection of books, fiction included. The commanding officer at Ghazeepore, for instance, asked for more "works conveying knowledge generally in a popular form. ... Sir Walter Scott's novels, books descriptive of military operations, and a volume of Elegant Extracts which is in the Library and Shakespeare's plays are very much called for by the men." He also emphasized that "a much too considerable proportion" of the books so far supplied "were purely moral and religious. ... There is no disinclination on the part of the men to read a moral tale but the moral and religious Treatises to which I allude lie on the shelves unopened."[75] A committee appointed to report on the Trichinopoly library in 1833 expressed similar sentiments: "Books of Voyages, travels, History, Biography, and such like are in great demand, [but] the very strictly religious Books are not read by the men." A memorandum produced in relation to Secunderabad in the

---

[69] L/MIL./5/384, Collection 85A, pp. 279–81.

[70] "List of Books in the Lending Library established by the S.P.C.K. at Bangalore on the 08th [sic] October 1829," F/4/1272/51087, pp. 23–28.

[71] "Proceedings of Station Committee assembled at St. Thomas Court on Tuesday the 8th September 1829 for the valuation of Books to be purchased...," F/4/1272/51087, pp. 38–41.

[72] "Proceedings of Committee assembled ... to value books ... at Bellary Lending Library ... 26th September 1829," F/4/1272/51087, p. 32.

[73] "... Proceedings of Committee assembled at Vizagapatam ... [18 November 1829]," F/4/1272/51087, pp. 45-48.

[74] "Report upon the Soldiers Libraries," pp. 23 and 18.

[75] "Report upon the Soldiers Libraries," pp. 46–47.

same year begins, "Few of the Books on Religious Subjects appear to have been read."[76] At Chunar, Lieutenant-Colonel Auriol observed, "the voyages, travels, Histories, and Sir Walter Scott's novels and poems have been most sought after and read by the soldiers, more particularly the novels." He therefore urged that "the remainder of Sir Walter Scott's novels and some other standard works of the same description" be added to the library, as well as "Biography, Dr. Johnson's Works, Publications of the Society for Promoting Useful Knowledge, some numbers of Blackwoods Magazine, and the Edinburgh Review and one of the cheaper Encyclopedias."[77] Major-General Sir S. Whittingham, commanding Meerut Division, wrote that while "Military and Historical Works should doubtless form the chief part of a soldier's library … all Walter Scott's Novels, some good Works of Travels, and the maps of Europe[,] Asia[,] Africa and America" should be included as well.[78] Lieutenant-Colonel Arnold, commanding the 16th Lancers at Cawnpore, was firmly convinced "that the best description of Books to be provided for the use of Soldiers would be 'Novels,' 'Romances' or 'Books of Travels.'"[79]

The desire of officers to secure a wider selection of books for their soldiers is hardly surprising; what is more remarkable, perhaps, is that this wish was also expressed by some of the station chaplains. The chaplain to the garrison at Fort William, for example, suggested that "General Literature—Copies of the Series of Works published under the titles of National Library—Family Library—Chalmers, ditto [et cetera et cetera] a complete set of the novels by Sir Walter Scott" should be supplied to the libraries, as well as voyages, works of Divinity, and texts published by the Society for the Diffusion of Useful Knowledge.[80] The chaplain at Dinapore recommended that any books of "general interest" be purchased, as well as "Histories, Travels, Campaigns, Books of Geography with some few volumes of Modern Poetry and popular science, [which] will be read by the soldiers with avidity." He also suggested that existing holdings of periodicals should be added to, and further remarked that

---

[76] "Report on Soldiers Libraries and Indent for Books," F/4/1428/56391, Madras Military, Collection No. 1, pp. 23 and 27. Hereafter "Report on Soldiers" Libraries and Indent for Books.

[77] "Report upon the Soldiers Libraries," pp. 48–49.

[78] "Report upon the Soldiers Libraries," pp. 79–80.

[79] "Report upon the Soldiers Libraries," p. 58.

[80] "Report upon the Soldiers Libraries," p. 30.

the publications of the Society for Promoting Christian Knowledge were "peculiarly adapted to institutions of this nature."[81]

One of the most enthusiastic advocates of the libraries was the Reverend Edward White, the chaplain at Cawnpore, whose detailed report into the Eastern and Western libraries at that station bring those institutions—and the men who used them—particularly to life. The Reverend White provided a glowing account of the soldiers' responses to the library at the western end of the cantonment, and supported his remarks with a detailed list he made of the library's holdings and usage between March 1 and November 6, 1832. This demonstrates that tales or fiction constituted the largest percentage of the library's holdings (approximately 33.3 % of 57 titles), and that these were the works most frequently borrowed by the men (32.3 % of 1,608 issues). The work taken most often from the library was the "Cottager's Magazine," which was issued 64 times (accounting for nearly 4 % of the total number of issues). The next most "popular" works were the "British Plutarch" (at 59 issues or 3.7 %), "Shipwrecks and Disasters" (at 57 issues or 3.5 %), "British Encyclopedia" (52 issues or 3.2 %), and "Cook's Voyages" (50 issues or 3.1 %). The most popular works of fiction in the library were "St. Ronan's Well" (at 37 issues or 2.3 %), and "Edgeworth's Tales" and "Esop's Fables" (both of which were issued 34 times or 2.1 %). The Reverend White reveals that he and his fellow chaplains supplemented the reading material available at the western library at Cawnpore by adding 12 further titles, mostly of a spiritual or religious nature. The most popular of these additional works was "Tracts in Small vols.," which was borrowed 200 times; this accounts for nearly 60 % of the total number of issues for the chaplains' books, or for nearly 10.3 % of the total issues at the western library when figures for both lists are added together. The Reverend White also notes that "Tracts in Small Vols." comprised 56 volumes, so it may be assumed that he added together the number of issues for several parts. Fifty-eight works were held in the Eastern library at Cawnpore, with tales and fiction accounting for 20 titles (or 34 % of the holdings).[82]

The Meerut station's report likewise includes a list of the books held in the station library on November 1, 1832, and the librarian there observed

[81] "Report upon the Soldiers Libraries," p. 42.

[82] See "Western Library, State[ment] shewing the number of works and volumes in that Library, as also the number of times each has been taken out for the purpose of being read since the 1st March 1832, [dated] Cawnpore 6th November 1832," in "Report upon the Soldiers Libraries," pp. 67–68.

"that from 30 to 40 vols. [were] read daily by the European Soldiers and many more would be read if more Books were in the Soldiers Library." The Meerut library list includes "Edgeworth Tales, Arabian Nights, Gay's Fables, Gullivers Travels, Don Quixote, … Cottagers of Glenburnie, … Robinson Crusoe, Old English Baron, Canterbury Tales, Tales of the Castles, Peter Wilkins, Gil Blas, [and] Tales of My Landlord" under the heading "Historical[,] Voyages[,] Travels," and consigns 15 works by Scott—as well as John Galt's *Ringan Gilhaize, or The Covenanters* (1823)—to "Novels or Romances." It must be remarked here that Galt's novel traces how several generations of the Gilhaize family are affected by the social, political, and religious upheavals of mid-sixteenth- to late-seventeenth-century Scotland, and so it is therefore possible that the compilers of the Meerut list mistook the novel for one of Scott's works.[83]

The consigning of Scott's works to a separate category illustrates perceptions of genre at this period, and also reveals that those in charge of the soldiers' libraries gradually came to realize that the Waverley novels were, after all, particularly "appropriate … for such … establishment[s]." Scott's popularity with the soldiers, it must be remarked, was evidenced in a variety of ways over the years. A list of books that were "worn out by long usage, and require to be replaced" at Ghazeepore on October 26, 1832, for instance, begins with titles for 18 of his novels (or novel series).[84] The 1849 report upon the library at Moulmein for its part revealed that the Waverley Novels were the most frequently borrowed works at the station, having been issued 150 times during the year. This is in comparison to the figures for the next most frequently borrowed works at the station, which were "The World in Miniature" (at 50 issues); "Recollection of an Artillery Officer (11 issues);" and "Chelsea Pensioners," "Southey's Life of Nelson," and "Twenty Five Years in the Rifle Brigade" (each of which was issued 10 times).[85] Issue figures were also given in relation to some individual titles by Scott, but these appear to have been counted separately from the figure given for the Waverley Novels. It must be remembered, of course, that the multi-volume nature of Scott's novels would have an upwards effect on borrowing figures for his works

The details relating to the actual usage of libraries like Meerut or Cawnpore are both revealing and important, but must be contextual-

---

[83] "Report upon the Soldiers Libraries," pp. 84–85.
[84] "Report upon the Soldiers Libraries," p. 48.
[85] L/Mil/3/1506/[1850].

ized in terms of other factors that affected the soldiers' reading habits
and preferences. As contributors to reports variously acknowledged over
the years, boredom coupled with the limited selection of books that was
available sometimes meant that a library's contents were read again and
again by the men. A major complaint of soldiers, for example, was that
frequently the same selection of books was sent out to libraries at the
different stations, and the chaplain at Dinapore at one point stressed the
annoyance of newly arrived troops when they discovered that the library
there held the same books as at Agra, their former posting. The chaplain also observed that about two hundred men used the library, and
remarked he had no doubt the figure would be higher but for the fact
that the same works were sent out to all of the stations.[86] The committee reporting on the library at Trichinopoly in 1833 for its part noted
that, because the 54th Regiment and the Company of Artillery had been
stationed at the garrison for upwards of eight months, "it is a fact that at
this very time when the books have been read once or twice by almost
every man, they are now, rather than not read at all, taking out again the
works they have already read."[87] The figures provided by the Cawnpore
or Meerut libraries plainly do not take account of this rereading of books
by frustrated and bored soldiers, nor, indeed, of the number of illiterate
men who had books read to them by their comrades—a practice, we shall
see in the next chapter, that became more common as rules relating to the
libraries were gradually relaxed.

That said, surviving records in relation to usage patterns in the soldiers'
libraries provide invaluable information for scholars, and reveal the different factors that affected readers' ability to use the institutions. An 1833
memorandum on the library at Masulipatam, for instance, observed that
the library had been open on the Tuesdays, Thursdays, and Saturdays of
the preceding year, and that an average of 45–50 volumes a week had
made their way into the hands of readers during this period. The memorandum also noted both that usage of the library had ebbed and flowed
in accordance with troop movements, and that different types of readers
and reading could be found in different companies and regiments. During
the time that the Madras European Regiment was at the station, it thus
remarked, works of history and "Tales" were most in request, but following the arrival of the 45th Regiment "the Works in the library of a religious

[86] "Report upon the Soldiers Libraries," p. 19.
[87] "Report on Soldiers' Libraries and Indent for Books," p. 24.

nature and more serious turn have been far more read." Significantly, the memorandum also observed that the Artillery at Masulipatam had not used the library at all, firstly, because they had a small library themselves and, secondly, because they would have to travel a great distance to fetch books ("nearly three miles").[88] An early 1833 memorandum on the library at Poonamalee noted that the "utility" of the institution appeared to be increasing, as "the different classes [were] evincing a great desire to read." The librarian at the station attended at the library every day from between 3 and 5 in the afternoon and, on average, issued between 19 to 25 books. This figure could be higher, according to the library committee, as the supply of "a greater variety" of works would be "likely to induce a still further number of applicants."[89]

The recognition that soldiers of *all* classes desired to read and that a better and wider supply of books would lead to more readers particularly affected men like Reverend White, who worked hard to impress the point on those in authority. The contents of the two libraries at Cawnpore, he thus declared, had been repeatedly exchanged with each other, and the chaplains had circulated their own reading material in an attempt to augment the men's supply. The concerned chaplains had also purchased cheap religious works from England, and sold them to soldiers at cost price in the library. The last supply of the latter, he observed, "was sold off immediately it arrived, and proved quite inadequate to the demand." The library "at the <u>Western</u> end of Cantonment," the Reverend White further insisted, had "not been regarded with indifference by the men of His Majesty's 44th Regiment, a Regiment in which the number of uneducated Catholics is particularly great. In that Corps the allurement the Library holds forth has excited a taste for reading in many men who never before exhibited it, and, if that allurement be sustained and increased by the supply of additional Books, I confidently believe a taste for reading will become universal."[90] The Reverend White's condescending remarks about Catholics is relevant to a point that was raised by Colonel Shelton, who was one of the officers at Cawnpore. Clergymen, the Colonel warned, must be mindful at all times of "the various denominations of Christians of which the army is composed," and "carefully avoid introducing into [libraries] any works that may in the slightest degree court controversy or

---

[88] "Report on Soldiers' Libraries and Indent for Books," p. 10.
[89] "Report on Soldiers' Libraries and Indent for Books," p. 31.
[90] "Report upon the Soldiers Libraries," p. 63.

Religious discussion."[91] White plainly could have been more sensitive in this regard, for, despite the large number of Catholic readers at Cawnpore, he included Grace Kennedy's proselytizing works on his list of suggested titles.[92] A Roman Catholic soldier who selected the writer's *Father Clement; A Roman Catholic Story* (1824) from a library's shelves, for instance, might have been surprised—and, perhaps, offended—to discover that the tale traces how the Roman Catholic Maria and Basil Clarenham are persuaded to embrace the Protestant faith by the Montagues, their relations. Even the eponymous hero appears to undergo a deathbed conversion at the end: he declares that he dies in "The Church of Christ," but refuses to specify that he means the Roman Catholic Church at the urging of Mr. Warrenne, his (scheming) Jesuit confessor.[93]

Later reports on the libraries sometimes provided a more detailed glimpse of the types of readers who were using them and the reading rooms at the different stations. An 1849 report in relation to Fort St. George, for example, revealed there were 780 applicants to use the facilities there in 1848, which represented an increase of 262 on the previous year:

Applicants, 1848	
Commissioned Officers	48
Rank Nos. 4th Regiment	124
Rank Nos. 25th Regiment	531
Veteran Company	18
Store Serjeants	6
Staff Serjeants	4
Sappers and Miners Serjeants	2
Conductors	13
Sub [?] Conductors	4
Garrison Band	4
Medical Pupils	30
Miscellaneous	4[a]

[a]"Return of Books in the Lending Library at Fort St George for 1849," L/Mil/3/1506 [1850]

---

[91] "Report upon the Soldiers Libraries," p. 60.

[92] "Report upon the Soldiers Libraries," p. 69.

[93] Grace Kennedy, *Father Clement; A Roman Catholic Story* (Edinburgh: William Oliphant, 1824), p. 355.

The report returned in relation to Cuddalore for 1855 for its part included the following observation: "The European Pensioners, as well as Effective Soldiers who have occasionally visited the station on sick leave or Furlough, have derived great benefit and amusement from its Books."[94]

Overall, then, East India Company material in relation to the soldiers' libraries provides fascinating insights into the history of the institutions and, in so doing, make three things particularly clear. Firstly, the records demonstrate that the majority of individuals who contributed to official reports were keen to stress that the libraries were having a beneficial effect on the soldiers and, alongside this, their appreciation of "the liberality of the Court of Directors in their establishment."[95] That this should be the case is hardly surprising, given that the majority of those who were involved in drawing up the reports were either Commanding Officers or Military Chaplains; in other words, individuals who would have been all too aware of the potential benefits of praising the Company's various efforts to ameliorate the condition of the men. For this reason, the recollections of individuals such as Staff-Sergeant Bancroft are particularly useful, for they give an insight into the views of the men themselves. Bancroft was himself the son of a soldier, and joined the Bengal Horse Artillery at the age of nine as a boy recruit; he eventually rose to the rank of Staff Sergeant and, as such, was ideally placed to observe the behavior and conditions of soldiers in India over many years.[96] In his memoir, Bancroft significantly observed not only that he "saw a wonderful change for the better in the habits of the men before he left the old Bengal Horse Artillery," but also stressed that this was a direct result of the efforts that were made to improve the recreational facilities of the troops: "[I] saw the habit of drunkenness, and even the habit itself, reduced almost to a minimum in other troops, and batteries, and [take] credit for having [myself] assisted in the good work in [my] own. This wasn't done by punishment! but by the introduction of a reading-room, a coffee shop, and malt liquor, but not much of the latter."[97] It must be remarked that Bancroft's memoir was first published in late-nineteenth-century Calcutta by the Army Temperance Association Press, and he dedicated it to "The Rev. J. Gelson

---

[94] "Extracts from the Annual Reports for 1855 upon the Soldiers' Lending Libraries."

[95] Adjutant-General's Letter of 4th June, 1847, No. 480, forwarding Extracts from the Annual Reports for 1845, L/Mil/3/1457.

[96] Major-General B.P. Hughes, introduction to *From Recruit to Staff-Sergeant* by N.W. Bancroft, p. 5.

[97] Bancroft, *From Recruit to Staff-Sergeant*, p. 38.

Gregson, The Apostle of Temperance in the British Army and the Soldier's Friend." Both of these circumstances obviously would have influenced the way in which he chose to depict soldiers in his memoir and, especially, his determination to stress that men were definitely "improved" by the provision of facilities such as reading rooms.

The second point that is made clear by East India Company records is that the soldiers' libraries had a protracted evolution, and whether they flourished depended hugely on, firstly, the attitudes of the Commanders-in-Chief of the different presidencies and, secondly, those of local commanding officers. As Lockyer points out, Madras was particularly fortunate in terms of its Commanders-in-Chief "in that it obviously had a succession of Commanders who showed great interest in the libraries."[98] The truth of this assertion is illustrated, firstly, by the wealth of material that survives in relation to the libraries of that presidency and, secondly, by evidence of the efforts that were made to prompt Bengal and Bombay to be more proactive in this regard. One 1837 letter to Bengal, for example, notes the receipt of annual reports from Madras in relation to the "advantages of each library," and observes the Company is "desirous of being furnished with a similar Report from your Presidency also."[99]

The third thing that the East India Company record reveals, though, relates to the way in which the day-to-day operation of the institutions clearly evolved at different rates at individual stations. Overwhelmingly, the records suggest that those on the ground in India quickly realized that they faced considerable challenges when trying to run libraries, problems that their counterparts in England never faced. The first part of our next chapter therefore will demonstrate how the responses of such individuals to these challenges profoundly affected the early reading experiences of soldiers who used the libraries; the second will illuminate more closely the "where," "how," and "why" of soldiers' reading on the subcontinent.

[98] Lockyer, "Provision of Books and Libraries," p. 150.
[99] "General Order Modifying System of Establishment and Regulations approved," Letter dated 30th Jan. 1837 (No. 10), E/4/753.

CHAPTER 3

The Reading Environment, and Readers, in India

"[I]t is easy for a man to loll in his easy chair, in dressing gown and slippers, and write long articles on drunkenness and immorality of the Army in general (and the army of India in particular), but place the same individual in the one of the stations on the plains of India, in the capacity of a private soldier, and see how eloquently he will defend temperance." So wrote Private Waterfield in his recollection of the years he spent in India between 1842 and 1857, wherein he recounted some of the miseries of the soldier's life on the subcontinent. One of the main reasons why the men drank so much, he declared, was because they were tormented by vermin, and the consumption of alcohol—particularly before sleeping—gave them some relief. Remembering one of the stations where he found himself stationed with the 32nd Regiment of Foot, he described it as "a miserable hole. The barracks was infested with all kinds of reptiles, scorpions, centipedes, triantilopes, snakes, etc. [sic], several of our men received some severe bites." The soldiers' general discomfort was added to by the fact that there were more men than there was space at the station, and "a great many ... had to make their beds on the rough brick floor."[1]

Soldiers' responses to India could vary greatly, and some of them, such as John Pindar, stressed that they found life there much more pleasant

[1] Robert Waterfield. *The Memoirs of Private Waterfield, Soldier in Her Majesty's 32nd Regiment of Foot, (Duke of Cornwall's Light Infantry) 1842–57*, edited by Arthur Swinson and Donald Scott (London: Cassell & Co., 1968), pp. 33–34, 47.

© The Editor(s) (if applicable) and The Author(s) 2016   63
S. Murphy, *The British Soldier and his Libraries, c. 1822–1901*,
DOI 10.1057/978-1-137-55083-5_3

than they had expected. Pindar arrived in India roughly three years after Waterfield left it, and expressed the view that "it was only those who revelled in the canteen, imbibed the killing drink of the country, or were too indolent to indulge in out-of-door exercise, that had cause to complain of the effects of an Indian climate." Further, "there were very few privates but who were able to keep their own-bat man, cook, barber, &c. [sic], as a few pice was all the expense for these."[2] The truth of the soldier's experience of India probably fell somewhere between these two extremes, but it is clear that the early nineteenth-century cantonments and stations were often primitive and isolated places. Emily Eden suggested as much, for example, in letters that she wrote to her sister from India, during the years that she spent on the subcontinent with their brother George. She dismissed Meerut, for instance, which was then the most important station in upper India, as "a large European station—a quantity of barracks and white bungalows spread over four miles of plain. There is nothing to see or to draw," and "Kurnaul" as "a great ugly scattered cantonment, all barracks, and dust, and guns, and soldiers." Eden also underlined her sense of the essential isolation and boredom of Europeans at the stations, intimating that many must have felt entirely cut off from the world: "How some of these young men must detest their lives! M.—was brought up entirely at Naples and Paris, came out in the world when he was quite a boy, and cares for nothing but society and Victor Hugo's novels, and that sort of thing. He is now stationed at B., and supposed to be very lucky in being appointed to such a cheerful station. The whole concern consists of five bungalows ...."[3]

Eden's concern was with upper-class men, but the East India Company's decision to establish libraries for soldiers was at least partly informed by its growing awareness of the conditions in which these mainly *lower*-class men served. Soldiers in India had vast amounts of time on their hands, the Company recognized, and precious little with which to fill it. "[T]he duty here is pretty easy" was how William Braithwaite put it: "[I]n the morning I read until breakfast time, from breakfast time until dinner time in writing and cyphering, in the afternoon reading again until

---

[2] John Pindar, *Autobiography of a Private Soldier* (Cupar-Fife: Printed in the "Fife News" Office, 1878), p. 24. A "pice" was a small copper coin that was worth less than a farthing. See Henry Yule and A.C. Burnell, *Hobson-Jobson: The Anglo-Indian Dictionary*, Wordsworth reference series (1886; Ware, Hertfordshire: Wordsworth, 1996), p. 703.

[3] Emily Eden, *Up the Country: Letters to her Sister from the Upper Provinces of India*, with an introduction and notes by Edward Thompson (1930; London and Dublin: Curzon Press, 1978), p. 7.

parade time[.] [I]n the evening either in walking or playing [?]."[4] By the late 1830s, most commanding officers and chaplains were complimenting the Company on the wisdom of the initiatives that had been introduced to improve the welfare of soldiers; they stressed, for example, that the men were hugely appreciative of the libraries that had been provided for them, and intimated that such facilities were definitely contributing to their moral improvement. Remarking upon the success of the library at Dinapore in 1832, for instance, an unnamed chaplain at the station observed that he would "say generally ... the minds of those soldiers who use the Library are better regulated and their conduct more becoming them as men and as Christians, then [sic] it would have been had they been left to their own Resources, and their very limited means of finding useful occupation for the many leisure hours which the European Soldier in India has at his own disposal."

Significantly, this chaplain advanced a further point, and suggested that the beneficial effects of the garrison library were hugely due to the fact that he had modified his attitude to the "where" of the reading of the soldiers. He was put in charge of the library in October 1829, he thus remarked, and "chiefly attribute[d]" the improved circulation and, implicitly, effect of the books since then "to [his] having permitted [them] to be taken by the soldiers into their Barracks."[5] The link that the chaplain drew here between the men's site of reading and their subsequent behavior was an important one, and illustrative of one of the prevailing opinions about reading at this period. Put simply, many believed that the site of reading was a problematic issue; that certain places—such as in bed, for example—were unsuitable for reading, and sites where such activity should be discouraged. This had the result that, over time, reading itself came to be "carefully presented as a privileged activity," which had "to be guarded by protectors and modulated by codes of conduct."[6] This meant that considerable anxiety frequently coalesced about not only what books readers were reading, but also where—and how—they read them. The chaplain's observations in relation to how library policy was modified at Dinapore were there-

[4] William Braithwaite, Letter to his mother, 05 November 1832, NAM 1976-05-75.

[5] "Report upon the Soldiers Libraries, and recommendation that they should be formed into Regimental, instead of Station, Libraries, and that the number of Books be increased," F/4/1486/58611, Collection No. 4, p. 43. Hereafter "Report upon the Soldiers Libraries."

[6] James Raven, "From promotion to proscription: arrangements for reading and eighteenth-century libraries," in James Raven, Helen Small, and Naomi Tadmor (eds), *The Practice and Representation of Reading in England* (Cambridge: Cambridge University Press, 1996), pp. 179–81.

fore important because they simultaneously acknowledged *and* inter-rogated one of the most important views of reading in the early nineteenth century: specifically, the notion that little good could comes of reading that was carried on in "inappropriate places."[7] Indeed, his account of the success of the library at Dinapore was informed by a very particular and contrary suggestion: that the behavior of the reading soldiers at the station improved once rules relating to the site of reading were relaxed.

This suggestion, this chapter shows, is to be traced in much of the material that exists in relation to the East India Company's libraries, which demonstrates that both chaplains and commanding officers manifested a marked determination to defend to the Company their decision to allow greater reading freedom to soldiers. In the very early days of the libraries, it is clear, the East India Company attempted to regulate scenes of reading at their stations in India by issuing a series of rules that stressed the privileged nature of the institutions. Although the Company does not appear to have directed explicitly that books could not be removed from the libraries, this seems to have been the initial conclusion—or conviction—of those who were responsible for their day-to-day operation, who dictated that men should only read in rooms that were under the supervision of persons such as chaplains, schoolmasters, or librarians. The impractical nature of this policy obviously became more evident as the years went by, and those responsible for the libraries appear to have become convinced that it did not take sufficient account of the peculiar nature of military service upon the subcontinent. This realization in due course caused chaplains and commanding officers to modify their attitude in relation to the removal of books to barracks, a decision they subsequently labored to explain to their superiors. One ambition of this chapter, then, will be to examine the reasons why the East India Company—and its agents—initially tried to regulate scenes of reading at military stations in India; another will be to consider how rules governing reading at the stations evolved to take account of the peculiarities of the Indian environment and military service. Informing both parts of the discussion will be a determination to illuminate scenes of military reading in early to mid-nineteenth cen-tury India and, thereby, illustrate some of the physical and geographical "determinants ... that helped to shape the ... reading life" of soldiers on

[7] Raven, "From promotion to proscription," p. 180.

the subcontinent.[8] In so doing, this chapter draws wherever possible upon the letters and memoirs of soldiers, as well as upon official records, and thereby allows the men to speak for themselves.

The first thing that must be said here is that the history of the East India Company's lending libraries for soldiers is a somewhat complicated one, for records make clear that their establishment took place at different times in the three presidencies.[9] What the records also show is that the Company's policy in relation to the physical nature of the libraries evolved slowly, and there was initial indecision as to whether books should, or could, be housed in already existing buildings, or whether it would be necessary to provide new spaces. Overwhelmingly, the evidence suggests, libraries were originally established in a somewhat ad hoc fashion, and where books were housed depended very much on circumstances at the different presidencies and/or stations. Thus, it was that early correspondence in relation to the libraries in Bombay simply suggested that books should be sent out to the different stations and kept in the charge of the chaplain and clerk upon their arrival; issues such as where the books should actually be read, it remarked, could be sorted out at a later stage.[10] By the late 1820s and early 1830s, attitudes were obviously shifting, and authorities were beginning to pay more attention to where the libraries were housed. It was in this context that the Military Board in Fort St. George was instructed in 1830 to ascertain whether existing "Public buildings ... could be wholly or in part appropriated" for this purpose and, if not, to obtain estimates for providing new space.[11] It is also why the 1834 report upon libraries in Bengal both commented upon the East India Company's former generosity in relation to the establishment of the institutions and suggested how they might be placed on a more secure physical footing: "Before the [?] practice of economy had been so rigidly enforced as it now is, Government had sanctioned the purchase of Buildings for the reception of Books at ... nine different stations ... These buildings ... might now be sold, and with the proceeds of the sale a room might be added to every Regimental

[8] Stephen Colclough, "Readers: Books and Biography," in Simon Eliot and Jonathan Rose (eds), *A Companion to the History of the Book* (Malden, Massachusetts; Oxford; and Carlton, Australia: Wiley-Blackwell, 2007), p. 59.

[9] For accounts of the establishment and early development of the Company's three presidencies, see Philip Lawson, *The East India Company: A History* (London and New York: Longman, 1993), pp. 46–48, and Linda Colley, *Captives* (New York: Pantheon Books, 2002), pp. 246–251.

[10] L/Mil/5/384, Collection 85A, p. 283.

[11] "Military Letter from Fort St. George [extract], 15 June 1830," F/4/1272/51087.

School House, large enough for a Library." This suggestion, it must be pointed out, was made in a very particular context: namely, in light of the recognition that regimental libraries had been established by this time in nearly all of the corps in India, and a subsequent debate about whether the Company's libraries should be used to form the basis for the further provision of such facilities to the troops.[12] The Commander of the Bengal forces, Major-General Watson, was firmly in favor of this proposal, largely because a number of commanding officers had advanced this opinion and he took their recommendations seriously. Several of these men, including a Colonel Faithfull at Cawnpore, emphasized that there were "many inconveniences attendant" upon the garrison library system as it was then being operated, including the fact it meant soldiers had to "[quit] their own Lines" to get books and, consequently, were vulnerable to "exposure."[13] What caused Watson and other like-minded individuals to hesitate was the recognition that the libraries they were considering breaking up belonged to the East India Company, and their establishment had represented a significant decision—and considerable financial outlay—on the part of the Honourable Court of Directors. By 1834, however, the Court gave its assent to the proposed change and,[14] in 1836, a General Order directed—

> that the books of the several station libraries shall be divided equally (with reference to the number of Troops or Companies belonging to each,) amongst the Eur. [sic] Corps quartered in the different Cantonments, to serve as a nucleus on which Regl. [sic] libraries may be formed. These libraries are to be kept up and supported from the portion of the Canteen Fund balances, directed [in an earlier General Order] to be specifically set apart for that purpose ...[15]

It must be pointed out that, notwithstanding either this General Order or the emphasis that 1840s' correspondence placed upon the success of the regimental "experiment," there is much to support the suggestion that many of the libraries continued to operate on the garrison system.[16]

---

[12] "Report upon the Soldiers Libraries," p. 25.

[13] "Report upon the Soldiers Libraries," 21.

[14] See "Extract from a Letter dated 29 August, 1834 (No. 71)," E/4/744.

[15] *Abstract of General Orders from 1817 to 1840 (Both Included)*, compiled by Captain David Thompson (Delhi: Gazette Press, 1840), p. 11.

[16] See, for example, "Military Letter from Bengal, 30 September 1841 [extract]," Bengal Military Collection No. 12, Reports Relating to Soldiers' Libraries, F4/1949/84727.

Although there are references to the libraries of individual corps—such as the "Troop of Horse Artillery" at Jaulnah in 1855, for instance[17]—most are still listed under the place names of garrisons, and some reports—such as that in relation to Fort Saint George for 1845—refer to "the Garrison Lending Library" explicitly.[18] The fact that some libraries appear to have continued to operate on the garrison system may have been partly due to cost. In 1841, for example, the Court responded to a letter it had received from Bengal, wherein authorities had pointed out the prohibitive expense of fully implementing the regimental system:

> It being found that to erect separate Buildings for Regimental Libraries within … Bengal alone would cost the sum of 50,000 Rs even tho' some Stations should still be unprovided for, it has been determined, after calling for the opinion of three experienced Commanding Officers of H.M.'s Regiments (a majority of whom were however in favor [sic] of separate Buildings) to limit the expense to that of fitting up a Room for the Library in the several Barracks for European troops.[19]

Correspondence between the Court and Bengal in 1856 further suggests that decisions about the type of library provision were sometimes dictated by issues relating to both reader usage and station size: "The construction of buildings for Regimental Libraries authorized only when made use of, and Station Libraries at small stations in Pegu where Madras Troops are quartered."[20]

In any event, the complicated nature of the early history of the libraries is worth noting, because all of the evidence suggests it had a significant impact on the reading experiences of soldiers. This was in the first place true because those responsible for the day-to-day operation of the libraries evidently worried greatly about the books that were in their care, and interpreted regulations laid down by the East India Company to mean that they should not allow soldiers to take them away and read them in their barracks. That this should have been the

---

[17] Fort Saint George, Military Con. of August 1856, Nos. 131 & 132, [comprised of] "Extracts from the Annual Reports of 1855 upon the Soldiers' Lending Libraries of this Army," L/Mil/3/1555.

[18] Letter of 4 June 1847 from the Adjutant General forwarding Extracts from the Annual Reports for 1845, L/Mil/3/1457.

[19] Reproduced in Court's Letter of 3 February 1841 to Bengal, E/4/765.

[20] Letter of 8 October 1856, Bengal Despatches, E/4/839, p. 413.

case is hardly surprising, for the net effect of the rules that were promulgated in relation to libraries was to emphasize the valuable nature
of the books that were being supplied to the stations in India; to stress
that they were fragile as well as expensive, and so *everyone* involved
should take careful steps to ensure that they were neither damaged nor
lost. To illustrate the several issues that are at stake here, it is useful in
the first instance to focus on rules that were promulgated in 1822 in
relation to the establishment of libraries at "seven principal military
stations" in Bombay, for these manifested an overwhelming preoccupation with issues relating to both the preservation of the books and
reader supervision. Thus it is that the first of these "Rules for Stationery
[sic] Libraries" directed that a station's library was "to be under the
immediate direction of the Chaplain at the Station, and under him
in charge of an [sic] European Soldier," and it emphasized that the
hours of the institution were to be "fixed by the Chaplain ... [who] may
make any Regulations for [its] management ... with the consent of the
Commanding Officers." Rule two ordered that a library "Register" had
to be kept, wherein should be recorded to "whom, and, on what day,
[a] volume was lent, and on what day returned," while the third rule
declared that any volume borrowed needed to be returned by the bor-
rower "within fourteen days, but may be reissued to him at the direction of the chaplain." Rules four and five declared that volumes were
not to "be transferred from one Person to another, nor shall any person
except under special circumstances have more than one Book at a time,"
and that "No Book shall be alienable under any circumstances whatever,
and every Book admitted into the Library shall contain these rules on
the inside."[21]

One ambition of these rules obviously was to impress upon readers
the special nature of the libraries, and this was made even more explicit
by regulations that were issued in August 1829 in relation to envisaged
libraries at 12 stations in the Madras presidency. Among other issues,
these decreed that the institutions were "to be under the care and superintendence of Committees composed of the Commandants of Stations,
Military Chaplains, and Principle Station and Staff Officers," and that
the books supplied were "to be deposited in Locked Book-Cases in the
Station School Rooms, and placed under the immediate charge of the
School Masters, who will each be allowed five Rupees per [mensem?], for

---

[21] Collection 85A, L/Mil/5/384, pp. 278 and 281.

dusting the Books, and keeping a correct Register of the volumes, and an Account of those lent." Books lent from the library were—

> on no account to be transferred, but every Book is to be brought back the week after it has been received, when it may be either returned the following day to the borrower for further perusal, or exchanged for another. … In the event of any Book being wantonly injured, the Person by whom it was borrowed, [is] to be subject to such penalty as the Committee at the Station may see fit to impose …[22]

Again, there is a marked emphasis here upon the need to ensure the physical preservation of books, and what the evidence suggests is that this resulted in the decision of authorities to ensure that soldiers could only read in the environment where the books were kept; in other words, only in rooms (or spaces) that were either specifically set aside for that purpose, or which were shared with schoolmasters or chaplains. In part, this policy was probably the result of a perception that such a (centralized) system of storage and access would facilitate the physical preservation of books, for, as Albert Hervey's account of the depredations of white ants in India makes clear, librarians on the East India Company stations experienced challenges in this regard that their counterparts in England never faced:

> The best way to keep them [that is, the ants] from attacking clothes, books or papers, or indeed anything, is to get *paetrolium* [sic] (it is procurable almost everywhere in India), or tar, should the former not be within reach; and rub the legs of chairs and tables or the bottoms of boxes and trunks, and the backs of pictures, &c. &c.[sic] as well as to keep a bright look out against their incursions, having the carpets and mats frequently taken up, the floors well swept and sprinkled with wood ashes; all the incipient passages destroyed, and a little *paetrolium* poured into every opening. Your whole property must undergo a constant watchfulness and examination, and there is a probability of your keeping them off; but if not, one night will be the ruin of you.[23]

The anxieties that the individuals responsible for the libraries experienced in relation to the books make themselves felt in different ways in material relating to their history at the stations, and it is clear that they devoted

---

[22] Extract from Fort St. George Military Correspondence, 18 August 1829, F/4/ 1243/40911, pp. 13–17.

[23] Captain Albert Hervey, *A Soldier of the Company: Life of an Indian Ensign*, edited by Charles Allen (London: Michael Joseph, 1988), p. 164.

great thought to how best to look after the works in their care. Referring to the rule directing that books should be placed in locked bookcases in schoolrooms, for instance, the Committee at Trichinopoly anxiously observed that there was no schoolroom at the station, and remarked that they had "requested the Reverend Joseph Wright would have the kindness to take charge of the Books until the pleasure of the Government is known."[24] Another report, for Cannanore in 1839, stressed that the library was "kept with great care," but pointed out that "the climate [was] unusually destructive to Books."[25] Soldiers themselves, incidentally, sometimes remarked upon the tremendous difficulties that they faced in trying to preserve *their* belongings in India; Sergeant Greening, for instance, observed: "White ants destroy everything not made of iron, and one has to keep books and clothes &c. [sic] in tin boxes to escape destruction.."[26]

A further factor plainly informed the decision to confine reading to the places where the books were stored, and this related to the nature of the readers themselves. The Company's libraries, as we have seen, were primarily intended for, and used by, lower-class soldiers, and those responsible for the institutions were from the very first convinced that such readers had to be subjected to both "good regulations and a watchful superintendence"; in other words, that their reading had to be carefully controlled.[27] It was clearly in this context that soldiers were at first refused permission to take books away with them to their barracks, and instead made to sit in rooms where their reading was subject to monitoring and supervision. As the years went by, though, authorities obviously began to realize that such a policy did not make sufficient allowance for the realities of military life in India; in the first place, that it failed to appreciate the very real problems that could result from providing spaces that encouraged soldiers from different regiments to congregate together.[28] As an 1834 report upon the libraries concluded:

[24] "Proceedings of the Committee assembled ... at Trichinopoly for the purpose of balancing the Books intended to be purchased for the use of the Station Library," F/4/1272/51087, p. 29.

[25] Copy of a Letter from the Adjutant General of the Army, 17 March 1840, L/Mil/3/1331, No. 262.

[26] Diary of W. Greening, 90th Regiment, Scottish Rifles, NAM 1983-07-121, p. 17.

[27] Military letter from Bombay [extract], 29 January 1823, L/MIL/5/384, Collection 85A, p. 274.

[28] We saw Brigadier-General Murray's opinion of this practice in our previous chapter. See page 51.

[W]hen out of sight of their own Non-Commissioned Officers, [soldiers] are apt to get into mischief, and it is difficult to believe that the Librarian, who is generally some quiet sort of person, selected by the Chaplain for his piety, would be able to restrain or over-awe a few half drunk soldiers. Besides, it may be deemed objectionable that the men should have so ready an excuse to quit their lines, as going a mile and a half to the Library for a Book.[29]

Factors relating to discipline, therefore, played a key role part in per-suading those responsible for the libraries to allow soldiers to take books back with them to their barracks, but so, too, did the realization that the implementation of this policy would contribute greatly to the comfort and physical safety of soldiers. John Mercier MacMullen, for instance, remembered his delight at being able to borrow books from the library to read in his barracks: "I was so fortunate as to ferret out ... an old edition of Scott's works ... I feel it is impossible to describe what pleasure it afforded me after returning from office, to stretch myself on my charpoy, raising my head as high as I could by doubling up my pillow, and thus to read 'Guy Mannering' until I fell into my custom-ary sleep at three o'clock."[30] Officers too, as we saw earlier, pointed out the dangers of men having to cover "immense" distances under a blazing sun to read a book in a library, and stressed that permitting the soldiers to take the books away with them would lessen both their daily physical exertion and their vulnerability to exposure. The fact that this latter issue remained of major concern to authorities is evidenced by the later testimony of commanding officers, who stressed that the libraries were proving particularly successful in this regard. The report returned in relation to the Cadet Establishment at Bellary in 1855, for example, declared that the library was "an inducement to some Cadets to remain in Quarters during the heat of the day when otherwise they would seek out-door amusement," while that in relation to the European Artillery Veteran Company at Cuddalore for the same year remarked the "Books [were] useful in keeping many of the men in-door when they would otherwise be out in the midday sun."[31]

---

[29] "Report upon the Soldiers Libraries," p. 24.

[30] "By a Late Staff Sergeant of the 13th Light Infantry" [John Mercier MacMullen or McMullen], *Camp and Barrack Room; or, The British Army as it is* (London: Chapman and Hal, 1846), p. 155. Hereafter "MacMullen, *Camp and Barrack Room*."A charpoy was "the common Indian bedstead, sometimes of very rude materials, but in other cases handsomely wrought and painted." See Yule and Burnell, *Hobson-Jobson*, p. 185.

[31] Fort Saint George, Military Cons. of August 1856, Nos. 131 & 132, L/Mil/3/1555.

The granting of permission to soldiers to read in barracks had a further benefit: it meant they had to spend less time in what was sometimes the very poor accommodation in which libraries were housed. Commenting upon the "generally ... unserviceable and dilapidated state" of the books in the library at Agra in 1832, for example, Colonel R.H. Sale pointed out that "beneficial results [have been] derived from the Establishment even in its present cramped state. It affords amusement and occupation for men who of necessity have much idle time on their hands and that too in a climate where sedentary habits must prevail." He continues, "[S]ince the destruction by fire of the Building appropriated for the Station Library, no eligible place appears to have been allotted for that purpose. The hovel now occupied, (a mud Gadown[32] containing two appartments [sic] 12 ft square outward walls 7 ft high) being quite inadequate and uninhabitable."[33] Concern about the physical state of the libraries grew in the 1830s, and this helped inform the discussion about whether to reestablish them on a regimental basis. Notwithstanding this, it is clear that libraries—and readers—continued to find themselves in places that were sometimes far from ideal, and which often served more than one purpose. One officer, for example, a Lieutenant-Colonel Bell, reported that the "Library Room [at his station was] merely a part of the Verandah of the Barracks partitioned off, and [it was] not sufficiently commodious." Another reported that a similar practice was being followed at Cawnpore, where "part of the Verandah of the Barracks [had] been fitted up for that purpose." At Dinapore, there was no room "fitted up exclusively for the library" of the 21st Fusiliers, and it was instead "placed in the room occupied as a Tailor's Shop."[34] In some garrisons, such as Bangalore, the library also doubled as a reading room, and "a great number of Soldiers report[ed] daily for the convenience of selecting the Book and perusing it on the spot."[35] Later in the century, when the libraries along with all other aspects of military life in India were under the control of the Regular Army, Lieutenant-Colonel W.B. Laurie drew attention to the superior nature of the reading arrangements that existed on the subcontinent. "Among intelligent European soldiers serving in India," he

[32] A "Godown" was "A Warehouse for goods and stores; an outbuilding used for stores; a store-room." See Yule and Burnell, *Hobson-Jobson*, p. 381.

[33] "Report upon the Soldiers Libraries," pp. 86–87.

[34] Bengal Military Collection No. 12, "Reports Relating to Soldiers' Libraries"[1841], F4/1949/84727.

[35] Copy of a Letter from the Adjutant General of the Army, 17 March 1840, L/Mil/3/1331, No. 262.

remarked, "reading must ever form a chief source of delight. … [Reading and recreation rooms] are very attractive in India, and may either be found in the same room as the library, or separate, which is by far the best, and is the most general plan."[36] That said, glimpses of some of the libraries and the reading rooms at this time suggest that men like Laurie may have been overly enthusiastic in their remarks, and that some readers were still reading in conditions that were far from ideal. The library of the 1st Battalion, 4th Foot at Poona in 1865, for instance, contained—

> 1,300 works of various kinds, and 20 newspapers and periodicals are taken in. A club and reading room is established in one of the unoccupied barrack rooms. The room is divided into two by a temporary canvas wall; one-half is comfortably fitted up with coir matting,[37] arm chairs, &c. [sic] as a reading room, in which there is a table set apart for soldiers to write their letters, &c., paper, envelopes, pens and ink being furnished to subscribers.
>
> In the other division of the room there are four bagatelle boards, draught, backgammon, and chess boards, dominoes &c.; and in this portion of the club is the coffee-shop, at which tea, coffee, lemonade, soda water, fruit, bread, meat, tobacco, and other refreshments can be obtained.[38]

This description of the library and reading room at Poona is important because it invites us to think more closely about the soldiers who read in conditions like these; to consider both what motivated them to read in the first place, and the quality of their reading life. What becomes clear from letters and memoirs of soldiers is that the men who used the libraries in India—or who purchased their own reading material—did so for a variety of reasons, and complex motivations frequently informed both their literary tastes and reading practices. Some soldiers, like John Pindar, for example, plainly used the libraries because they recognized that the facilities afforded them something they might not otherwise have enjoyed: the opportunity to convert idle time into self-improvement. Pindar began,

---

[36] W.B. Laurie to the Secretary of the Council of Military Education, 8 May 1868, Appendix II—No. 13 to *Fifth Report by the Council of Military Education on Army Schools, Libraries, and Recreation Rooms* (London: HMSO, 1869), p. 69.

[37] "Coir" is the "fibre of the coco-nut husk, from which rope is made." See Yule and Burnell, *Hobson-Jobson*, p. 233.

[38] "A. Libraries and Lectures" in Appendix III—No. 7 to *Third Report by the Council of Military Education on Army Schools, Libraries, and Recreation Rooms* (London: HMSO, 1866), p. 42.

he observed, "to use [his] spare moments replenishing [his] mind with information from books or surroundings, for every British regiment in India is possessed of a good Library—a blessing which cannot be too highly appreciated by the private soldier. The books are carefully selected and well calculated to inform and improve the mind." Too many "young soldiers," he insisted, failed to appreciate the marvelous opportunity represented by the libraries, and unfortunately allowed "the brightest time of their life to escape from their grasp, thinking little of the present and far less of the great hereafter." In this "great age of books," he continued, "there is no soldier that has not the opportunity to improve and enrich his mind, and make himself acquainted with the world's history. Shame it is for any young man in this highly cultivated age to pass through the world and become none the wiser of all the beauties and wonders surrounding him on every side. No man has no more time for this purpose than the British soldier." As for himself, he declared, "I have felt more pleasure in my barrack room poring over the almost inspired pages of a Milton, a Cowper, or a Thomson, than I would amidst the attractions of all the gin palaces in the world."[39]

Thomas Quinney obviously was just as intent to improve himself as Pindar, and so took the advice of a fellow Scotsman who befriended him shortly after his arrival on the subcontinent. This "kindly" individual conducted Quinney around his new barracks, and "directed my special attention to the library and school-room, stating that, if I wished to improve myself, I never could have a better chance, as I would receive books, in abundance out of the former, and everything requisite in the latter, without costing me a single *pice* (halfpenny)." The men at the station, Quinney observed, could "sit and read in the library, or carry books home to the barrack-room as they [thought] proper." The soldier in India, he concluded, lived "like a gentleman compared with the British labourer. When he mounts guard the whole of his bedding is carried after him by the cooks, and spread in a cot in the guard-room, so that he can stretch himself out on it and take a nap, or read his book when he is not wanted for sentry; and as he is four hours off sentry for every two hours on, he has plenty of time to read or rest."[40]

[39] John Pindar, *Autobiography of a Private Soldier* (Cupar-Fife: Printed in the "Fife News" Office, 1878), pp. 22–23.

[40] Thomas Quinney, *Sketches of a Soldier's Life in India by Staff Sergeant Thomas Quinney, Honorable East India Company's Service* (Glasgow: David Robertson and Edinburgh: Oliver & Boyd, 1853), pp. 30–31, 34–35.

One of the things that becomes clear from accounts such as these is that soldiers who read became singularly adept at adapting themselves to their peculiar circumstances; most obviously, they became accustomed to the fact that their reading would be constantly interrupted. In some cases, such as the one that Quinney describes, this was because of the very nature of the soldiers' daily existence; of the fact that they were trying to snatch precious moments for reading in between a range of other activities, such as sentry duty, for example, or sleep, or drill. In other cases, however, the interrupted nature of soldiers' reading had to do with the manner in which books and newspapers reached them in India, which was, to say the least, a laborious process. Remarking in one letter that he was "now—by the kindness of a friend reading ... 'Smiles and Tears,'" Richard Hardcastle also noted that he was "rather bothered having to wait from the interval of the arrival of one mail until another arrives for the reading of another of the paper."[41] In another letter, he again pondered what was actually involved in getting letters or newspapers to him, thereby underlining why these articles were so treasured by soldiers on the subcontinent: "Your letter and papers have been 59 days on their journey of 19,000 miles, that is from Undercliffe to Allahabad having in that time been in nearly all sorts of conveyances, on the rail, on the sea, on the back of camels and lastly on the shoulders of a blackman who to forward our letters has to run at the speed of a racehorse through jungles and forest midst the roar of wild beats [sic] and the scream of jacksls [sic]."[42] The tale whose next install-ment Hardcastle was so anxious to read, by the way, was John Frederick Smith's "very long-running" serial *Smiles and Tears: A Tale of our Times*, which first began to appear in *Cassell's Illustrated Family Paper* in 1857.[43] "The chief plot" of the tale, according to Hardcastle, was "the incident of the Sepoy Revolt on which the Author draws very large."[44]

What the recollections of men like Hardcastle and Quinney also reveal, though, is that soldiers became adept at reading wherever they found themselves; more than this, that they became experts at seeking out places where they could read relatively undisturbed. Remembering how he and his comrades were warned against climbing the rigging of the ship that

[41] Richard Hardcastle, Letter of 21 November 1858, Photo Eur C332, p. 107.

[42] Hardcastle, Letter of 3 January 1858, Photo Eur C332, p. 31A.

[43] Catherine Delafield, *Serialization and the Novel in Mid-Victorian Magazines* (Farnham: Ashgate, 2015), p. 89.

[44] Hardcastle, Letter of 21 December 1858, Photo Eur C332, p. 107.

carried them out to India, for instance, Quinney also recollected that he ignored this injunction once he realized that doing so would afford him the opportunity of reading in blissful seclusion. "Notwithstanding" the fact that being caught would have meant him either losing his "grog" or being fastened to the rigging for a couple of hours as a punishment, he observed: "the foretop was a favourite retreat of mine, where I often sat or lay reading a book for hours together."[45] Quinney's emphasis here upon the fact that the foretop functioned as a place of "retreat" for him during his passage to India has a further significance, of course, for it reminds us that many soldiers plainly turned to reading in an attempt either temporarily to escape the difficult conditions in which they found themselves and/or find the degree of solitude or privacy that they dearly craved. William Stephen Raikes Hodson of the celebrated Hodson's Horse, for example, described how reading could help soldiers living under canvas survive the coming of the "hot winds" in India, and suggested those who had never been there could not understand what this time was like on the subcontinent:

> This sounds a very mild word, but you should only just try it! … It feels as if an invisible, colourless flame was playing over your face and limbs, scorching without burning you, and making your skin and hair crackle and stiffen until you are covered with "crackling" like a hot roast pig. This goes on day after day, from about eight or nine o'clock in the morning till sunset … The only resource is to get behind a tattee (or wet grass mat) hung up at one of the doors of the tent, and to lie on the ground with as little motion as possible, and endeavour to sleep or read it out.[46]

---

[45] Quinney, *Sketches of a Soldier's Life*, p. 17.

[46] William Stephen Raikes Hodson, *Twelve Years of a Soldier's Life in India: Being Extracts from the Letters of the Late Major W.S.R. Hodson, B.A. Trinity College, Cambridge; First Bengal European Fusiliers, Commandant of Hodson's Horse, Including a Personal Narrative of the Siege of Delhi and Capture of the King and Princes, Edited by his Brother, the Rev. George H. Hodson, M.A.* 2nd ed (London: John W. Parker & Son, 1859), pp. 23–24. "Hodson's Horse" was raised by Hodson as an irregular cavalry unit at the time of the Indian Rebellion, and was celebrated for its actions at both the siege of Delhi and later at Lucknow (where Hodson died of wounds). The unit went through various changes in the course of the nineteenth and early twentieth centuries and, in 1921, became—following amalgamation with the 10th DCO Lancers, Hodson's Horse—Hodson's Horse, 4th DCO Lancers. It subsequently became a regiment of the new Indian Army in 1947. See John F. Riddick, *Who Was Who in British India* (Westport, Connecticut and London: Greenwood Press, 1998), p. 175, and R.G. Harris and Chris Warner, *Bengal Cavalry Regiments, 1857–1914*, Men-at-Arms series (1979; Botley, Oxford: Osprey, 2000), pp. 17–21.

William Douglas agreed with Hodson about the dreadful effects of the heat in India, but also suggested that books were not equal to what the soldiers faced. "We certainly had books," he wrote, "but how could they be read with a hot stifling wind passing through the room, scorching all that it touched."[47]

Yorkshire man Richard Hardcastle's attitude to India vacillated during the time that he spent there, and the letters that he sent home to various family members suggest he tried to "read out" the conflicting emotions that he experienced during his service on the subcontinent. On the one hand, he—

> found in India what I zealously sought after in England prior to and since I became a soldier—the power, the ability to confirm my mind strenuously and firmly on a subject until I have mastered it. I sought this at home but never found it. I know that quiet solitude was all that I required. ... I have now a study five times as big as your [that is, his parents'] little back parlour well stocked with books and I can already apprise the results of my persever-ance [sic] and I make constant and daily use of it ...

On the other hand, however, Hardcastle's letters also demonstrate that the "solitude" he found in India was sometimes tinged by an almost over-whelming sense of loneliness and homesickness, and that reading was a vital means through which he tried to remain connected to his former life. Advising his younger brothers on their reading, for example, he cautioned them against the "low trash that comes out in penny numbers. Read Jane Eyre first. This must be your minimum and nothing lower."[48] It is only when we read a later letter, though, that we discover that Hardcastle's love of Charlotte Brontë's work was not entirely predicated upon his apprecia-tion of its literary merits; specifically, that it was also to do with the fact that anything by or about the Yorkshire novelist had the ability temporar-ily to transport him to familiar scenes and places. "Bye the bye," he wrote his parents, "this last few days, would you believe it, I have spent all my spare time at Haworth near Bradford. There in mind though, [sic] cooped up in an Indian bungalow. Yes I have been reading the life of my dear friend Charlotte Brontë. She was a friend, for has she not beguiled many a solitary hour of mine away." Urging his parents to read both the life of

[47] William Douglas, Private, 10th Royal Hussars, *Soldiering in Sunshine and Storm* (Edinburgh: Adam and Charles Black, 1865), p. 2.
[48] Hardcastle, Letter of 14 May 1860, Photo Eur C332, pp. 156–58.

Brontë and *Jane Eyre* (1847), he admitted: "Perhaps they won't have such a charm over you as they have over me. I like them because they describe old localities that I sometimes think I shall never reach again."[49]

Hardcastle repeatedly pleaded with family members to send him newspapers, which, he revealed, were one of the most powerful means of connecting men like him with far-distant and much-loved places:

> News from home! What a power of meaning these three words contain. Reading of well known and familiar haunts[,] I feel for the time transported to the dear place—and, as it were, an eye witness of what is going on miles from where I sit. ... I no sooner get your papers than I am besieged by all the Yorkshire men in the Troop who all at once ask "After you Bombadier with a look at the paper[.]" "Any news?" "Tell me," a fellow ... cries. I could not, if I were inclined deny them—for I know they are as anxious as myself to hear from dear old Yorkshire.[50]

Hardcastle eventually was appointed as a librarian at one of the libraries at Meerut, and one of the first things he did was order "out from England a whole host of papers and they have already begun to arrive. This mail I read the Weekly Despatch, Bell's Weekly Messenger, Punch, Illustrated London News, Home News, London Journal, Reynolds' Miscellany, Family Herald, Chamber's Journal, All the Year Round, Cassell's Family Paper, Lesson Hour and some others."[51] This list not only suggests that Hardcastle delighted in his new-found ability to satisfy his own reading tastes as a librarian, but also gives some indication of the time that soldiers like him had on their hands.

Reading, then, could temporarily transport soldiers to the places that they had left behind them, but it also helped to connect them to loved ones who were far distant. Writing to his "dear Friend John" in 1858, for example, Sergeant John Ramsbottom remarked: "you say that you often think of them happy hours which we have spent together over a pipe

---

[49] Hardcastle, Letter of 24 August 1860, Photo Eur C332, p. 175.

[50] Hardcastle, Letter of 21 November 1860, Photo Eur C332, p. 96. Amanda Laugesen has made a similar discovery in relation to Australian soldiers' preference for newspapers during the First World War, observing: "Newspapers were a staple of soldiers' reading, and soldiers especially desired newspapers from home." See Amanda Laugesen, "*Boredom is the Enemy*": *The Intellectual and Imaginative Lives of Australian Soldiers in the Great War and Beyond* (Farnham: Ashgate, 2012), p. 31. We will return to the issue of soldiers and newspapers in Chap. 4.

[51] Hardcastle, Letter of 23 May, 1860, Photo Eur C332, p. 161.

and the papers[,] I often think of them too." Significantly, Ramsbottom responded to his friend's query as to whether he was "as fond of reading as [he] was before" with an observation that conjures up an evocative image of the night-reading that was carried on by soldiers in India: "I am still very fond of reading and sometimes read for hours together[.] We have got a fine library here and their [sic] is some splendid works in it[.] Sometimes I sit reading the whole of the night."[52] John Mercier MacMullen also read at night in his barracks, and described the measures he took to make himself more snug: "I ... trimmed my lamp, and hung it close by the head of my charpoy, so that I could read by its light while reclining at my full length; and for the next five hours, that is till eleven o'clock, books were almost invariably my sole amusement."[53] The nocturnal reading habits of some of the soldiers who used the libraries obviously posed challenges for the individuals who supervised them, and not the least of these was ensuring that some form of lighting was available. It was in this context, clearly, that the library committee at Trichinopoly at one point begged leave to voice a major concern: namely, "that there [was] no allowance of oil for the use of the Library. ... [T]he Quarter Master of the Regiment cannot spare any for the use of the Library and the Committee recommends a small quantity being allowed for this purpose, sufficient for one light all night."[54] Reading at night-time obviously appealed to soldiers in India not only because it helped to while away the long hours, but also because the heat then and, presumably, the noise would have been less intense.

Some soldiers obviously read for a further purpose, of course, and this was to find spiritual comfort and/or the fortitude to face the particular temptations or dangers with which they were faced. William Pattison, for instance, informed his mother in one of his letters that a "Temperance Society" had been established at Dum Dum, and he had joined it on the first night: "There is an excellent Library attached to it, supported by the Officers ... [which] contains every description of Books, both moral and religious. I have derived great information from them all; but especially the life of Col. Gardiner, God grant that I may imitate the example of that good man."[55] Richard Hardcastle for his part criticized the soldiers who

[52] Sergeant John Ramsbottom, Letter of 23 May 1858, Ms. Add 59876.

[53] MacMullen, *Camp and Barrack Room*, p. 161.

[54] "Report on Soldiers Libraries and Indent for Books," F/4/1428/56391, Madras Military, Collection No. 1, p. 25.

[55] William Pattison to his mother in letter to his brother, 13 October 1837, NAM 1967-02-66-2, 3.

read their Bibles in India in 1857 only when "danger" was clearly immi-
nent: "Cowards!—Cowards!—all! They would not read their Bibles when
there was no danger but now they are face to face with it they feel their
deficiency."[56] One private, who enlisted in the 92nd Regiment of Foot in
the late eighteenth century, clearly worried about the way in which life in
the army affected his reading and, in particular, his devotion to the Bible.
During a voyage home to Portsmouth from Gibraltar, he thus declared:
"I read something more in my Bible, but much more still in any other
book I could find; sometimes it was a novel, sometimes a history or play:
sometimes it was a book of religious cast; but this was rare: I read anything
I could get, to the neglect of the Bible."[57]

William Taylor, whom we shall meet again in our next chapter, went
with the 4th Light Dragoons to India in 1823, and remembered reading
aloud from a Catholic prayer book to comfort a dying Irish comrade:
"Taking the volume, I read several of the beautifully worded and impres-
sive passages with which the Roman Catholic ritual abounds, and I was
rejoiced to perceive a soothing effect on his mind. He at first shed tears,
but gradually became calmer, and it was evident he was more at peace
with himself." Leaving this individual to sleep, Taylor later "returned to
his bed side, [and] the poor fellow was dead."[58] Taylor's recollection of
this scene is obviously a poignant one, but it also demonstrates that the
realities of life—and death—in the military were such that soldiers were
frequently inclined to respect—or at least tolerate—convictions and opinions that were different to their own. It was obviously in this context, for
example, that the above-mentioned private from the 92nd Regiment of
Foot recalled an incident from his service in late 1790s' Ireland, where he
described his willingness to carry a book for a comrade whose religious
persuasion was different to himself: "I carried Gray's Sermons in my knapsack, to oblige a comrade who was a Methodist, but who had not room for
it in his."[59] It must be remarked here that this was an act of considerable
generosity, especially given the amount of equipment that soldiers often

[56] Hardcastle, Letter of 6 December 1857, Photo Eur C332, p. 19.
[57] Not given, *Narrative of a Private Soldier in His Majesty's 92nd Regiment of Foot. Written
by Himself. Detailing many Circumstances Relative to the Insurrection in Ireland in 1798; the
Expedition to Holland in 1799; and the Expedition to Egypt in 1801; and Giving a Particular
Account of his Religious History and Experience. With a Preface by the Rev. Ralph Wardlaw*,
D.D., 2nd ed (Glasgow: University Press, 1820), p. 7.
[58] William Taylor, *Life in the Ranks*, 2nd ed (London: T.C. Newby; Parry, Blenkarn & Co.,
1847), pp. 146–47.
[59] Not given, *Narrative of a Private Soldier*, p. 33.

found themselves carrying. Philip O'Flaherty, for instance, sent a letter from Scutari camp during the Crimean campaign, wherein he observed that the soldiers' "burden [was] heavy, for beside our ordinary kit, each man has to carry a camp kettle, a tin pot and bill-hook."[60] A soldier's life in the Crimea was obviously a somewhat different affair to a soldier's life in late-eighteenth-century Ireland, even if that latter soldier was in Ireland primarily because of the 1798 rebellion. That said, the basic point remains the same: soldiers had to carry most of what they needed for themselves, and so carrying a book for a comrade was a generous gesture.

Some soldiers were keen to stress that their devotion to the Bible survived even in the army; others again emphasized that they tried to share the fruits of this reading—and sometimes physical Bibles as well—with the non-Christian peoples whom they encountered. Sergeant Gowing, for example, recalled an episode from his time in India, describing what happened one day when "some eight or ten native boys" approached him as he sat reading outside of his tent. Remembering a box in which he knew that he had "several small bibles [sic]," he gave orders for this to be opened: "When the top layer of books was taken off, and the poor boys got a look into the box, they exclaimed in rapture, while their little black eyes glistened again, 'Those are the books, Sir, those are the books.'"[61] Gowing's recollection of this scene is very clearly a product of its nineteenth-century moment, and there is much here to make modern readers feel uncomfortable. It also can be argued that Gowing probably shaped his description of this scene very carefully in order to meet the expectations—and cultural assumptions—of his projected audience, and to reinforce their perception of the superiority of the civilization that both he and they represented. All of that said, though, Gowing's account of this encounter between a British soldier and some native children in nineteenth-century India underlines the fact that soldiers like him were not always the subjects of the missionary impulse—that they were, in fact, sometimes its agents. This is also demonstrated by Philip O'Flaherty's description of the manner in which he passed his "leisure hours" in Turkey during the Crimean campaign, which, he declared "were divided into three parts: first, translating several passages of my Bible into Turkish; then telling them over and over again to the people; and, lastly acquiring other useful knowledge."

[60] Philip O'Flaherty, *Philip O'Flaherty: The Young Soldier* (Edinburgh and Dublin: John Shepherd and Shepherd & Aitchison, [1855?]), p. 12.
[61] Timothy Gowing, *A Soldier's Experience; or, Things not Generally known, Showing the Price of War in Blood and Treasure* (Colchester: Benham & Co., 1883), pp. 194–95.

O'Flaherty, it must be remarked, recorded his experiences in letters that he sent to the Reverend Michael Brannigan, and these were eventually published to raise subscriptions for the mission school in Mayo where this gentleman was minister. Brannigan was responsible for O'Flaherty's conversion to Presbyterianism when he was a young boy, and so the soldier's determination to convert Turks to Christianity was clearly predicated upon a determination to replicate a process from which he felt he had benefitted himself. It was obviously in this context that he professed a desire in one of his letters to go to Turkey or Russia if he were able eventually to purchase his own discharge, and "do good to the followers of the false prophet." It was also, no doubt, why he attached a particular significance to the Bible that was sent out to him "for the purchase of which the money was collected at the Corn Exchange. ... I shall carry it with me in my bosom wherever I go. *Where I fall, it shall fall.*" Many soldiers guarded their Bibles jealously, but this one was sent to O'Flaherty by individuals who *ipso facto* approved of his conversion; as such, it probably was a peculiarly powerful and personal symbol of his spiritual development.[62]

As the years went by, authorities on military stations in India increasingly realized that soldiers read in various ways and places, and recognized that there were benefits to allowing men to take books out of the places where the libraries were stored and back with them to their barracks. One of the greatest of these benefits related to the reach of the books, for it became clear that the adoption of this practice had the potential to introduce the works to a wider audience. In the first place, and as officers such as Lieutenant-Colonel Piper observed, the decision to allow men to take books to their barracks facilitated "the participation which those men who cannot read have in the advantage of the Library, by getting their Comrades to read aloud to them which could not be permitted in a reading room."[63] Colonel Shelton elaborated upon this point, remarking that books read in this way afforded "Amusement to each as can read and through them to their Comrades who cannot, it is but fair therefore to infer that the hours spent thus, both by readers and by listeners, have been advantageously stolen from the time that might possibly have been spent

---

[62] O'Flaherty, *Philip O'Flaherty. The Young Soldier*, pp. 22, 3–4, 27, and 10. O'Flaherty was actually in Turkey when he made his remark about going either there or to Russia for the purposes of facilitating the conversion of non-Christians, so presumably he meant he would return once he secured his discharge.

[63] "Report upon the Soldiers Libraries," p. 47.

in riot and drunkenness."[64] Before we move on here, it must be remarked that the recollections of some soldiers suggest that libraries and reading rooms were often noisy spaces, notwithstanding rules to the contrary, and there clearly were occasions on which it was permitted to read aloud. William Douglas, for example, vividly described the scene in his regimental library whenever a paper arrived with news of what was happening in the campaign in the Crimea: "Always on the day when a mail was due, our regimental library would be crowded, awaiting the arrival of the *Poonah Observer's Extra*, and the noise and hubbub made on its coming contrasted favourably with the silence and attention paid when one would get on the table and 'Horse Guards' or read it aloud to all assembled.."[65]

The manner in which John Fraser was introduced to the pleasures of poetry demonstrates a further benefit of allowing soldiers to take books to their barracks: it afforded men a greater opportunity of influencing each other's reading tastes. Fraser owed his introduction "to the slopes of Parnassus" to two brothers called Bob and Harry Norton, whom he first met at Chatham before the trio embarked for India. The friendship of the three young men continued at Agra, and the brothers, who were keen scholars, encouraged Fraser "by their example." Both of these brothers loved poetry, but this seems to have been particularly true of Bob who "could string rhymes with a skill far beyond the rest of us." When he came to write his memoir many years later, Fraser therefore conjured up a particularly poignant scene, and one that was no doubt replicated in different ways in many barracks: "I see him best sitting on the steps of the veranda, with the cool white arches of the barrack-room behind him and the five smooth steps of the plinth below. A poetry book lay open on his knee and he would take the pipe out of his mouth for a minute to tap the page with it as he turned to me: 'John, get this into your memory and there'll be less room for ordinary stuff.'" Fraser noted in his memoir that he would "always be tremendously grateful" to the Norton brothers "for awakening [his] latent and, till then, almost unsuspected love of poetry": "[M]any times in my life, even to-day, looking out on Tower Green with the well-thumbed and yellow-leaved copy of Keats in my hand, I have thought of those two very good friends."[66]

[64] "Report upon the Soldiers Libraries," p. 61.
[65] Douglas, *Soldiering in Sunshine and Storm*, p. 13.
[66] John Fraser, *Sixty Years in Uniform* (London: Stanley Paul, 1939), pp. 86–88. Fraser refers to "Tower Green" as he ended his years in uniform as one of the Yeoman Warders of

Significantly, individuals such as the Reverend White worked hard to defend their decision to extend the "privilege" of reading at the stations in India; he insisted that at Cawnpore, for instance, it had gone in hand-in-hand with the introduction of regulations that were designed to ensure both the preservation of books *and* their introduction to a wider audience. From 1829, he thus observed, soldiers were allowed to take books back with them to their quarters, and chaplains imposed extra duties upon the librarians; these required the men to recover the costs of missing books from whomever had mislaid them, and also to bring "weekly supplies of suitable Works to the sick in Hospital, and to the Prisoners in Solitary Confinement." Reverend White also stressed that he attached particular significance to the latter duty, but observed that "unhappily the limited number of the Books in the Library[,] particularly of a religious character[,] ... prevented the Librarian from fulfilling it to the extent desired."[67] Initiatives like these plainly were not confined to Cawnpore, and efforts were made at other places to provide books for hospitalized or otherwise invalided soldiers. In 1840, for example, the Court expressed its approval of "the Establishment of a Library at Landour for the use of the Invalid Soldiers" and, in 1858, authorized a monthly allowance to facilitate the provision and preservation of books for the hospital in Fort William.[68] John Mercier MacMullen's account of visiting a sick friend in hospital, it must be remarked, suggests that the provision of books to soldiers in such places led to some very curious scenes: "In the corner of his tent a group of some three or four had assembled around a clay lamp, one of them reading aloud from 'Charles O'Malley' an account of some of Mickey Free's exploits, which caused peals of laughter; while a few feet apart from them, a poor wretch was writhing in the bitter pangs of dissolution."[69]

What the comments of men like the Reverend White finally reveal, though, is that authorities took the decision to facilitate further reading at stations like Cawnpore in the hopes of reaching—and morally improving—more soldiers; in other words, they sanctioned a modification of their origi-

the Tower of London.

[67] "Report upon the Soldiers' Libraries," pp. 62–63.

[68] Court's Letters to Bengal on 23 December 1840 and 21 April 1858, Bengal Despatches, E/4/764, pp. 843 and 444.

[69] MacMullen, *Camp and Barrack Room*, p. 201. The work being read here was Charles Lever's *Charles O'Malley, the Irish Dragoon* (1841), which recounts the adventures of the eponymous hero - and his manservant, Mickey Free - during the Peninsular wars.

nal attitude to scenes of reading at the military stations in the hopes of producing more—and better—actively reading soldiers on the subcontinent. Significantly, the chaplain was for his part keen to stress that this was precisely what happened at Cawnpore, which, he emphasized, everyday proved the wisdom of the initial decision to provide libraries for the men:

> With respect to the moral benefits that have accrued from *this* Institution, I am of opinion that if in some of the Readers the strength of immoral habits unhappily has prevailed against the influence of newly acquired knowledge, still if inquiry be instituted, it will be found that a very large proportion of the Readers have made a moral advancement, which in its progress towards perfection has already put the sound policy and true philanthropy of Government in the Establishment of Military Libraries beyond all controversy and doubt.[70]

Men such as White had a vested interest in the success of the libraries, of course, and their praise of the effects of the institutions sits uneasily alongside newspaper commentary from the period which continued to comment upon "the extent of the moral degradation" that prevailed among the soldiers.[71] Nonetheless, White's testimony about the Cawnpore libraries is obviously valuable, and not least because it provides a vital insight into how the usage of such spaces evolved upon the subcontinent. The reverend tried hard to impress upon authorities the fact that other classes of individuals could benefit from the Honourable Company's wisdom in establishing the libraries and reading rooms; he emphasized that women, for example, might be improved if they were admitted to spaces originally intended purely for soldiers. This had already been tried in the reading room of the Western library at Cawnpore, he pointed out, and his implication plainly was that this experiment could be usefully replicated across the subcontinent:

> [It] has afforded to the Chaplains an unobjectionable place for assembling one Evening in every week, the Women of His Majesty's 44th Regiment, for the purpose of reading or lecturing on some interesting article of Female Biography,—The minds of many have thus been awakened to the importance of those Family and Religious Duties so generally and so fearfully violated by Females of this class in India.[72]

---

[70] "Report upon the Soldiers Libraries," p. 64.
[71] *The Delhi Gazette*, 14 June 1837.
[72] "Report upon the Soldiers Libraries," p. 65.

This seems to be the earliest reference to women using the station libraries or reading rooms, but it is impossible to be entirely certain that they were unable to use them before this. The 1829 rule that declared that "European Non-Commissioned Officers and Privates [were] to have the first choice of 'Books'" in the libraries of Madras, for example, also decreed that "Committees [had] the power of lending Books, not required by European Soldiers, to such other persons as may engage to observe the rules of the Institution," and the fact that individual libraries exercised their autonomy on this point makes itself felt at different places in the records.[73] For example, the 1849 report in respect of the library at Moulmein observed that it appeared "to be of much utility to many of the Residents in Cantonment, as well as to the European Soldiery."[74]Mary Martha Sherwood's *Memoirs of Sergeant Dale, His Daughter, and the Orphan Mary*, incidentally, treats of precisely the kind of women of whom White was clearly thinking, thereby suggesting another reason why the tale might have been felt to be suitable material for the libraries that the Company was establishing. Mrs. Simpson and Jenny, the reader discovers, are two of the worst wives in the barracks in India where part of the tale is set, largely due to their fondness for alcoholic spirits. The drunken pair at one point quarrel so violently that their soldier husbands have to separate them, and they eventually die due to their over-consumption of alcohol—and disgraceful behavior—on an excessively hot day. The narrative underlines the point that is being made by remarking: "it would have been well for [them], if they had loved their Bible more, and what they called pleasure less."[75]

There is another point to be made about the Reverend White's decision to use one of the reading rooms at Cawnpore to facilitate evening lectures for women, however, and this is that it is illustrative of the crucial significance these spaces plainly came to assume at many of the stations. In his recollection of his time in India, for example, Thomas Quinney remembered that "ministers [used to] visit the barracks once or twice during the week, and hold prayer meetings in the library for all

---

[73]Extract from Fort St. George Military Correspondence, 18th August 1829, F/4/1243/40911, p. 17.

[74]From Lieutenant Colonel R.I.H. Vivian, Adjutant-General of the Army to Lieutenant Colonel C.A. Browne, Secretary to Government, Military Department, No. 98, L/Mil/3/1506 [1850].

[75]Sherwood, Mary Martha. *Memoirs of Sergeant Dale, His Daughter, and the Orphan Mary*, 3rd ed (London: F. Houlston and Son, 1816), p. 96.

who wish[ed] to attend"; he also recalled how he and his comrades were on one occasion "all assembled in the library" by their captain in order to inquire into some arrack that had gone missing from the barracks.[76] On the one hand, we can point to the shortage of accommodation at many barracks and stations as the reason why libraries and reading rooms sometimes fulfilled purposes other than those for which they were originally intended. On the other hand, though, the recollections of men like Quinney—and White—also suggest that the libraries and reading rooms took on a greater significance for the men who supervised and/or used them; that is to say, they came to be seen as spaces that represented learning and/or authority.

There is a further point to be made about the significance that the soldiers' libraries came to assume over the years, though, and this is that it on one occasion at least led to a dispute between the individuals who were responsible for operating them on a local level. The trouble, ironically, arose at Cawnpore, where it appears that one of the chaplains became too proprietorial about the books that were in his charge. In a letter dated July 2, 1839, the Court thus observed they were "concerned to perceive the want of cordiality that has long subsisted between the Military Authorities and Chaplains" at Cawnpore, noting they were "glad that the Bishop [had] noticed the impropriety of Mr. Jenning's conduct, tho' less explicitly than we could have wished." This gentleman, it appears, had refused to obey an order of the commanding officer at the station, which was intended to facilitate the breaking up of the books in the libraries and, thereby, presumably facilitate the implementation of the regimental "experiment"; specifically, the Reverend Jennings had failed either to attend a committee or furnish a catalogue of the books at Cawnpore "on the grounds that he was not amenable to the Military Authorities" there. Regrettably, the finer details of what happened at Cawnpore in the late 1830s may be destined to remain elusive, for the Court regretfully observes that "[s]everal papers connected with this case, including the correspondence of Mr. Jennings," were not forwarded from Bengal.[77] It requires no great leap of the imagination, however, to speculate that the Reverend Jennings believed that the latest innovation in relation to the operation of the libraries was misguided, and not in the best interests of the soldiers.

---

[76] Quinney, *Sketches of a Soldiers' Life*, pp. 35–36, 85.
[77] India Ecclesiastical, 2 July 1839, Bengal Despatches, E/4/759, pp. 966–970.

In his consideration of the history of books and of reading, Robert Darnton points out that it is vital to recover as many clues as possible about "where" books were read; this is "more important" than we might think, he suggests, "because placing the reader in his setting can provide hints about the nature of his experience."[78] One of the things that this chapter has tried to do is illustrate the fact that soldiers in nineteenth-century India read in a wide variety of places: in buildings that had been either built or hired for the purpose, for example, or in the spaces that resulted from curtaining off part of a barrack room or veranda; they also read in what were sometimes makeshift beds, or in the nooks and crannies that they foraged out for themselves. The soldiers, we have seen, also read at all sorts of times: they snatched random moments between sentry duty and sleep, for instance; they read during the hottest part of the day when it was virtually impossible to move, or at night, when it was cooler and more quiet on the stations. The soldiers, moreover, read for a variety of reasons: because they were bored and in search of momentary amusement or distraction; because they were determined to improve themselves in educational terms; because they were fearful, or felt themselves peculiarly in need of the comfort that they could find only by turning to God. Soldiers also resorted to reading when they were lonely and/or homesick, and when the picking up of a newspaper or a book could connect them emotionally to far-distant, and much loved, people or places.

The fact that the soldiers appreciated the libraries that the East India Company provided for them was emphasized again and by the individuals who oversaw their day-to-day operation; authorities at Fort St. George in 1836, for example, declared that some of the men there had supposedly "taught themselves to read on purpose" so that they could "profit" from this wonderful innovation that had appeared in their midst.[79] Soldiers' appreciation of the libraries, furthermore, was demonstrated by their memoirs and letters, which intimated that those men who could read—however imperfectly—often turned to them as another way of coping with the challenges that they faced on the subcontinent. According to authorities, and to some of the soldiers themselves, the libraries that were provided had one very particular effect upon the men who used them:

[78] Robert Darnton, *The Kiss of Lamourette: Reflections in Cultural History* (London and Boston: Faber and Faber, 1990), p. 167.

[79] Collection No. 20—Books for Soldiers' Libraries, E/4/1701/68730, p. 9.

namely, they improved the morale *and* morals of soldiers, and lessened their tendency to indulge either in drink or other disreputable behavior. Thomas Quinney, who greatly appreciated the institutions, was firmly of this opinion, and urged authorities to persist in their efforts to ameliorate the condition of troops. It was essential, he wrote, to—

> provide means for the profitable employment of the soldier's leisure hours. Much good has been done in this way by libraries and coffee-rooms. Care should be taken that the books consist of such as blend information and instruction with amusement, and newspapers from editors of genuine principle, so that the leisure of the soldier may be judiciously spent, which will have the effect of engendering steady habits, and teach him to entertain a due respect for himself, as well as his superiors.[80]

Joachim Hayward Stocqueler (1800–1885) was an Anglo-Indian journalist, who edited several periodicals in Calcutta and also published on Anglo-Indian Affairs.[81] He commented four years after Quinney on the efforts that were being made to improve soldiers in India, and offered a more measured view of the effect that the provision of facilities such as libraries was having on the troops. He began, for instance, by noting that "crime [was] more rife [in India] than elsewhere" because "the heat of the climate and the monotony of a soldier's existence induce a more frequent resort to the bottle and the dram, and drunkenness is the source of the greater portion of a soldier's offences." That said, he also suggested that much had been accomplished on the subcontinent, and that "drinking to excess [was] by no means as common … as it was in former years": "More attention is paid to the moral culture of the men, and to arrangements for their healthful amusement. Attending libraries during the heat of the day, and cultivating their gardens in the morning and evening, at stations where gardens are possible, occupy a great deal of the time of the men pleasantly and profitably."[82] The scene that Stocqueler painted was an idyllic one, and conjures up images of soldiers pottering about on army stations, dividing their time between improving their gardens and themselves. Ironically, of

---

[80] Quinney, *Sketches of a Soldier's Life*, p. 174.

[81] Peter Stanley, *White Mutiny: British Military Culture in India, 1825–1875* (London: Hurst & Company, 1998), p. 5.

[82] Joachim Hayward Stocqueler, *The British Soldier: An Anecdotal History of the British Army, from its Earliest Formation to the Present Time* (London: Wm. S. Orr & Co., 1857), p. 157.

course, Stocqueler published his book in the very year that was to shatter the East India Company's relationship with India, and alter forever the nature of Britain's relationship to the subcontinent. The effects of the Indian Rebellion of 1857 reached into every aspect of British life in India and, of course, had profound consequences for the Indians themselves. One of the most immediately significant outcomes of the rebellion in terms of what we have been discussing, however, is the fact that the East India Company's "three native armies, with their twelve European regiments, came under the control of the crown. The European infantry were added to the Line, as the 101st to 109th Foot, and the three regiments of cavalry became the 19th, 20th and 21st Hussars."[83] Henceforth, in other words, the soldier in India was part of an army that had for a long time resisted providing facilities such as libraries to its rank-and-file forces, and our next chapter will begin by considering why this should have been the case.

[83] Douglas G. Browne, *Private Thomas Atkins. A History of the British Soldier from 1840 to 1940* (London & Melbourne: Hutchinson & Co., 1940), p. 198.

CHAPTER 4

The Regular Army's Libraries

William Taylor began his military career in 1823, when the commencement of hostilities with the Burmese Empire "rendered large drafts from our home forces necessary." He had risen to the rank of sergeant in the fourth Light Dragoons by the early 1830s and had become increasingly aware that he needed something other than the canteen "for the occupation of [his] leisure hours." Upon discovering that several of his fellow sergeants were of the same opinion, he decided to form a library for the use of non-commissioned officers, "and accordingly made an application to the Colonel for leave to write to London for books." This "old martinet," however, reacted with horror and incomprehension to the suggestion and dismissed it out of hand: "A library, and what the devil do you want with a library? No, no, you want to make the men all lawyers, and we have too many of them already. If things go on like this, you'll soon take command of the regiment out of my hands. The only two books fit for a soldier, are the articles of war and the bible [sic]." Taylor pleaded with his commanding officer, urging him to at least give the men permission "to subscribe for a few newspapers." The colonel also refused this request, on the following grounds: "To teach you sedition, and make you more rebellious than you are. ... Once for all I tell you that I am not one of your 'march of intelligence' men. I never knew a good soldier yet who was fond of

© The Editor(s) (if applicable) and The Author(s) 2016
S. Murphy, *The British Soldier and his Libraries, c. 1822–1901*,
DOI 10.1057/978-1-137-55083-5_4

your trashy books, or seditious newspapers, and I shall not be the first to introduce such a bad precedent into the service."[1]

Taylor's commanding officer would not have been the first to introduce such a precedent into the army, for we have already seen that some regiments began to establish libraries for soldiers beginning in the late 1700s. His reaction to Taylor's suggestion, though, is a useful place for us to begin our consideration of the history of garrison libraries in the Regular Army, as it illustrates several of the reasons why the army for so long resisted officially establishing such facilities for its rank-and-file forces. "As late as 1823," it was reported, for instance, "the Chaplain General ... was instructed in the matter of providing a reading library for the troops at Portsmouth, that 'His Royal Highness [the Duke of York] will on no account sanction so unnecessary and so objectionable an institution.'"[2] The "suspicion" with which the King's and then the Queen's army viewed literacy was the result of many factors, including the perception that "books tended 'to make soldiers question the wisdom of their officers, and fit them for being ringleaders in any discontent.'"[3] In part, this was a class-conditioned response to the men who made up the rank-and-file within the army, for many contemporaries believed that the worst sort of men typically enlisted. "The French system of conscription," as the Duke of Wellington put it, "brings together a fair sample of

---

[1] William Taylor, *Life in the Ranks*, 2nd edn (London: T.C. Newby; Parry, Blenkarn & Co., 1847), pp. 3, 285–87. Taylor's recollection of this scene reveals the Colonel was particularly alarmed by the fact that the men wished to subscribe to the *Weekly Despatch*, "which about this time contained a series of excellent articles on corporal punishment" (p. 286).

[2] T.A. Bowyer-Bower, "The Development of Educational Ideas and Curricula in the Army during the Eighteenth and Nineteenth Centuries," Thesis submitted to the University of Nottingham for the Degree of Master of Education, May, 1954, pp. 65–66. Frederick Augustus, the second son of George III, was first appointed as Commander-in-Chief of the army in 1798, but was forced to retire from the post in 1809 as a result of a scandal involving his mistress and her efforts to extract money from officers in return for recommending their promotions. He was reappointed to the post again in 1811, and held it until his death in 1827. See H.M. Stephens, "Frederick, Prince, Duke of York and Albany (1763–1827)," rev. John Van der Kiste. *Oxford Dictionary of National Biography*, Oxford University Press, 2004; online edn, Oct 2007 [http://www.oxforddnb.com.remote.library.dcu.ie/view/article/10139, accessed 10 July 2015].

[3] This was the view of Henry Marshall (1775–1851), military surgeon, author, statistician and reformer. Quoted in Peter Stanley, *White Mutiny: British Military Culture in India, 1825–1875* (London: Hurst & Company, 1998), p. 43.

all classes; ours is composed of the scum of the earth—the mere scum of the earth."[4]

This negative view of the British soldier persisted well into the nineteenth century, despite the fact that the benefits of greater literacy among soldiers were increasingly recognized from the early 1700s. General Wolfe, for example, issued a series of orders in 1749 that "clearly indicate" he expected the non-commissioned officers under his command to be able to produce written reports, and the various military publications that were produced in the last 25 years of the century reveal "that the Soldier, and particularly the Non-Commissioned Officer, was expected to be able to read, write[,] and undertake a little figuring."[5] In part, the growing recognition of the need for literate soldiers was the result of the "gradual change that was taking place in military tactics," firstly, during the wars with France in North America and, secondly, during the wars with Napoleon. The shift away from the "rigid lines" of men that had been favored by Frederick the Great resulted in greater movement among soldiers on the battlefield and, consequently, called for men who were more able to think and act for themselves.[6]

It was in this context that more emphasis was placed on education in the army from the early nineteenth century on, although it has to be stressed, firstly, that efforts in this regard were often the result of the initiatives of a few enlightened individuals rather than general policy and, secondly, that these efforts were frequently met with great hostility. Many officers, for example, held the same view as Taylor's colonel and believed that Bibles and drill books were the only reading material that soldiers needed. This was one reason army chaplains remained the only official source of reading matter for soldiers until the libraries were established, facilitating the distribution of materials provided by societies such as the Society for Promoting Christian Knowledge and the Naval and Military Bible Society.[7] Societies like these were hugely keen to reach the reading

---

[4] Quoted in Peter Burroughs, "Crime and Punishment in the British Army, 1815–1870," *English Historical Review* 100: 396 (July, 1985), p. 548.

[5] Bowyer-Bower, "Development of Educational Ideas," pp. 8–9. Wolfe was still a major in 1749.

[6] Bowyer-Bower, "Development of Educational Ideas," p. 10.

[7] See Bowyer-Bower, "Development of Educational Ideas," p. 65, and K.A. Manley, "Engines of Literature: Libraries in an Era of Expansion and Transition," in Giles Mandelbrote and K.A. Manley (eds), *The Cambridge History of Libraries in Britain and Ireland, Vol. II, 1640–1850* (Cambridge: Cambridge University Press, 2006), pp. 520–21.

soldier, as we noted in our second chapter, and so the Naval and Military
Bible Society, for example, proudly reported in early 1840 that it had since
its foundation distributed over 356,000 bibles to soldiers and seamen.[8]

The further factor that hampered educational initiatives in the army,
though, was a particularly interesting one, for it had to do with the resis-
tant attitude of many of the men themselves. As Victor Neuburg points
out, some soldiers plainly viewed efforts to "improve" them with a mix-
ture of suspicion and resentment, which was made particularly clear when
the Bedford Militia tried in 1809 to compel non-commissioned officers to
attend school. One of the men who protested, a Sergeant Richard Warden,
was so vociferous in his objections that he found himself imprisoned and
the subject of a court martial (although all of the charges against him were
subsequently dismissed). Warden, however, was so incensed by what had
happened that he went on successfully to take a case for damages on the
grounds of false imprisonment; and this, Neuburg remarks, profoundly
affected "the development of education in the army, for the judge gave a
ruling which was to bedevil it for some years to come: 'It is no part of the
military duty to attend a school, and learn to read and write. If writing is
necessary to corporals and sergeants, the superior officers must select men
who can read and write.'" The final appeal in the case—which was known
as Warden versus Bailey—was heard in 1811, and the Adjutant-General of
the army issued an order a few months later ordering the establishment
of "a regimental school in each battalion or corps 'for the instruction of
young soldiers, and the children of soldiers.'" The judgment that been
handed down in relation to the case made it impossible for the army to go
any further; whether soldiers chose to attend the schools that were being
set up for them remained, until the introduction of compulsory attendance later in the century, up to them.[9]

The attitudes of men like Warden reinforced the negative image that
many had of soldiers, which persisted well into the Victorian period. John
Edward Acland-Troyte, for instance, was compelled by personal circumstances to enlist in the ranks in 1873, and remembered in his memoir
that this at first seemed to him "like breaking cast, and doing an injury
to myself and belongings." Acland-Troyte clearly entertained a very

[8] *Bengal Hurkaru*, 4 July 1840.
[9] Victor Neuburg, *Gone for a Soldier: A History of Life in the British Ranks from 1642* (London: Castell Publishers, 1989), p. 72. Neuburg notes that "from 1879 it was a statutory offence for a soldier not to attend school if he had been ordered to do so."

low opinion of the men with whom he now found himself serving, and consequently recalled the "surprise and delight" that he experienced upon seeing "a man using a tooth-brush" when he first went to use the ablution room: "It put me at my ease at once, but I soon found that numbers of men did the same, and that, in *that* as in many other things, I had inwardly maligned the British Soldier."[10] Horace Wyndham, incidentally, also commented upon the fact that it was "no uncommon thing to see a soldier using a tooth-brush," remarking, "but in this article of toilet he is economical, and does not object to procure it at second hand when possible."[11] Negative stereotyping of soldiers, however, had many consequences, including the fact that it prompted many of the men to live up—or down—to the view of them held by their officers and superiors. As John Mercier MacMullen put it in 1846—

> [T]he British soldier is a neglected man. He is looked on in every country as a being of inferior species: as the paria [sic] of the body politic; and thought to be almost incapable of moral or social improvement. His own officers despise him, and the public at large despise him. Surely then, when he finds himself treated with universal contempt, it cannot be a matter of surprise that he loses all self-respect, and becomes the reckless and degraded being that he is. He has no one to represent him in parliament; no one to advocate his cause, as that of the peasant or mechanic is advocated; no wonder then, while these are progressing in the grand march of improvement, that he is still a being of the last century.[12]

The army's decision to begin to establish libraries for non-commissioned officers and soldiers in the late 1830s represented a major shift in attitude on the part of authorities and was a consequence of several factors: In the first place, the army had before it the example of those regiments that had already begun to set up libraries for themselves overseas, although many of these—at least at first—were intended for the exclusive use of officers.[13] Secondly, concerned individuals and societies had also made increasing

---

[10] Anon. [John Edward Acland-Troyte], *Through the Ranks to a Commission* (London: Macmillan & Co., 1881), pp. 3, 39–40. Henceforth "Acland-Troyte, *Through the Ranks.*"

[11] Horace Wyndham, *The Queen's Service: Being the Experiences of a Private Soldier in the British Infantry at Home and Abroad* (London: William Heinemann, 1899), p. 44.

[12] "A Late Staff Sergeant of the 13th Light Infantry" [John Mercier MacMullen or McMullen], *Camp and Barrack Room; or, The British Army as it is* (London: Chapman and Hall, 1846), pp. 141–42.

[13] Bowyer-Bower, "Development of Educational Ideas," p. 66.

efforts from the early 1800s to provide reading materials for those who found themselves on the ships of either His Majesty or the merchant navy, and suggested that this was something that should not be neglected. The influence of the Quaker Elizabeth Fry and her Ladies' Committee of Prison Reformers was also important, for these, too, tried to persuade the government to take "a more active role in libraries for prisoners, as well as sailors and soldiers."[14] And, of course, the East India Company's libraries had by this time been up and running in India since the early 1820s, and Regular Army soldiers were clearly appreciative of their presence on the subcontinent.

According to Colonel John Henry Lefroy, however, who was appointed as the Inspector-General of Army Schools in 1857, the army's shift in attitude toward the provision of libraries for soldiers was primarily "an indirect result of the remarks of the Inspectors of Prisons in Great Britain … on the imprisonment of military offenders."[15] In their 1837 report, the Inspectors had observed that the "dark cells" to which military offenders were typically consigned had "the effect of hardening and brutalizing those … confined in them … It may be also proper to remark, that in a light cell the salutary effect of reading and instruction may be expected." Crucially, the Inspectors also revealed that their preoccupation with the possible reading and instruction of military offenders arose directly from their conviction that too much emphasis was being placed by the army on punishing "*bad soldiers*"; much more should be done, they stressed, to "reward" and "encourage" the "*good soldier*," who was often overlooked among the troops:

> Nothing would have a greater influence in encouraging good habits, and in supplanting bad ones; in raising the tone of discipline, and the general character of the soldiery, than the consulting [of] the comforts and interests of the good soldier, and the conferring upon him those marks of distinction upon which the men greatly pride themselves, and which, however intrinsically slight, are, in the soldier's esteem, of the very highest value, and a source of the very greatest gratification.[16]

---

[14] Manley, "Engines of Literature," in Mandelbrote and Manley (eds), *The Cambridge History of Libraries in Britain and Ireland*, *Vol. II*, pp. 520–521.

[15] J.H. Lefroy, Brevet Colonel, Royal Artillery, *Report on the Regimental and Garrison Schools of the Army, and on Military Libraries and Reading Rooms* (London: HMSO, 1859), p. 51. Henceforth, Lefroy, *Report*.

[16] *Inspectors of Prisons, Great Britain: Second Report* (London: HMSO, 1837), pp. 56, 65.

Encoded here, we might think, is an excellent example of Michel Foucault's argument that, in discipline, "punishment is only one element of a double system." It was the army's growing awareness of the importance of the other element, that is, "gratification," that helped influence its decision to introduce Good Conduct Badges and pay for deserving soldiers and, crucially for our purposes, to begin officially to provide books and libraries to rank-and-file forces.[17] Her Majesty's Treasury thus started the process toward the foundation of garrison libraries in August 1838, granting funds for the establishment of such institutions at 50 large and 100 smaller military stations[18]; and John MacDonald, the Adjutant-General, issued the order in 1840 that noted Her Majesty's pleasure in commanding that "a library and reading room shall be established for the use of the Non-Commissioned Officers and Soldiers at each of the principal barracks throughout the United Kingdom and the Colonies." Significantly, the order also noted that General Lord Hill, the Commander-in-Chief, was "gratified in being authorised to announce to the Army the adoption of a measure from which the most beneficial results are expected. The object of these institutions … is to encourage the soldiery to employ their leisure hours in a manner that shall combine amusement with the attainment of useful knowledge, and teach them the value of sober, regular, and moral habits."[19] By 1844, according to the *Queen's Regulations* of that year, libraries and reading rooms had been established as per the earlier order, and the army's initiative was truly up and running.[20]

The emphasis that the 1840 order placed on the fact that the libraries were intended to edify as well amuse the soldiers during their "leisure hours" is clearly important, because it reminds us that the men under discussion were largely drawn from the working classes. This was the case because the army "was unable to broaden its appeal or its social composition" during the nineteenth century, and remained "principally dependent

---

[17] Michel Foucault, *Discipline and Punish: The Birth of the Prison*, trs. from the French by Alan Sheridan (1975; London: Allen Lane, 1977), p. 180. On the introduction of Good Conduct Badges, et cetera, into the army, see Byron Farwell, *The Encyclopedia of Nineteenth-Century Land Warfare: An Illustrated World View* (New York and London: Norton & Co., 2001), p. 359.

[18] See Lefroy, *Report*, p. 51.

[19] Reproduced in Bowyer-Bower, "Development of Educational Ideas," p. 71.

[20] *The Queen's Regulations and Orders for the Army,….First of July 1844*, 3rd edn (London: HMSO, 1854), p. 253.

on the unskilled, casual labourer" for much of the 1800s.[21] As Richard Holmes put it, "The British army was—with a few notable exceptions— a body of poor men officered by rather richer ones."[22] There is a further significance to this point, however, for it also invites us to recognize that the establishment of libraries for soldiers had motivations other than purely military ones, and must be contextualized in terms of the wider concern with working class leisure at this period. As we have already noted in our introduction, concern about "public leisure" grew in Britain post-industrialization, and contemporaries increasingly became convinced that the provision of facilities such as libraries would ameliorate the conditions of working-class life and, arguably, facilitate greater social control.[23] The army's decision to establish libraries for its non-commissioned officers and soldiers in the late 1830s clearly must be situated against this backdrop, and it is thus significant that two of the rules promulgated in relation to the institutions envisaged a disciplinary relationship between literate soldiers and those in authority, anticipating that the libraries would enable the public rewarding of "good" soldiers and the punishment of "bad" troops. "Books are not to be lent from a Library except to men of exemplary character," rule 7 stated, "and the indulgence of being thus entrusted with Books belonging to the Library by special Order of their Commanding Officer is to be regarded by their Comrades as an additional and distinguished mark of their trustworthiness." Rule 4 held, however—

> Whenever a Soldier may have subjected himself to Punishment, he shall, while under such punishment, be deprived of his right of admission to the Reading Room; and further Lord Hill approves of a discretion being vested in the Commanding Officer to deprive a Soldier of the privilege of admission to the Reading Room, for a limited period not exceeding three weeks, upon his being satisfied that the privilege had in any manner been abused.[24]

One the one hand, the army's promulgation of these rules reminds us once again that authorities looked to the provision of libraries at least in

---

[21] Peter Burroughs, "An Unreformed Army? 1815–1868" in David Chandler (General ed) and Ian Beckett (Associate ed), *The Oxford History of the British Army*, (Oxford and New York: Oxford University Press, 1996), p. 169.

[22] Richard Holmes, *Sahib: The British Soldier in India, 1750–1914* (London: HarperCollins, 2005), p. 221.

[23] See page 13 above.

[24] Reproduced in Bowyer-Bower, "Development of Educational Ideas," pp. 72–73.

part as a disciplinary measure, and that soldiers were encouraged to view access to reading as both a reward *and* marker of good behavior. On the other hand, though, we must recognize that the men in question were largely drawn from the working classes, and that this is a clear example of reading being used or envisaged as a tool that would facilitate social control. The context, obviously, was a military one, but the wider significance of what was being attempted cannot go unremarked.

Pointedly, later orders and memoranda in relation to the libraries manifested a continuing anxiety both to emphasize the beneficial effects of the libraries and reading rooms and to remind everyone involved that they were in the first instance established for rank-and-file troops. A "Circular Memorandum issued to the Army at Home and Abroad" in December 1852, for instance, noted the decision of the Secretary-at-War and the General Commander-in-Chief "to allow the Officers of the Army to participate in the advantages afforded to the Troops" by the libraries, but also stressed that such men must "bear in mind, that these ... have been formed at the public expense, for the express benefit of the Soldiers of the Army." Although it was now proposed to allow books to circulate among the officers, this "concession [had] been made with the clear understanding that it shall in no case be allowed to interfere with the free use of the Books by the Non-Commissioned Officers and Men."[25] Newspaper commentary from the period suggests that orders like these may have been prompted by a very particular circumstance, and this was the growing recognition that the libraries were being utilized by readers for whom they were never originally intended. *The Bucks Herald* for 24 May, 1845, for example, reported that "The Secretary at War having heard that in some instances officers of the army" were being allowed to use the libraries, "has the direction of the commander-in-chief [sic] to express his opinion that these institutions should be reserved solely for the use of the soldiers, and to desire commanding officers of regiments and others to forward the due carrying out of the original intentions of the government."[26]

Evidence relating to the garrison libraries from the late 1830s to the early 1850s suggests their evolution was a protracted affair, partly because the enthusiasm of authorities in relation to army reform in general was not consistent during these years. It was obviously in this context that an editorial on

---

[25] See *Addenda to the Queen's Regulations and Orders for the Army, From the First of July, 1844, to the Thirty First of March, 1854* (London: HMSO, 1854), p. 213.

[26] *The Bucks Herald*, 24 May, 1845.

the soldiery in the *Daily News* of 4 June, 1846 both criticized the fact that efforts at army reform were "in a great measure confined to externals," and singled out the provision of libraries for soldiers for particular praise:

> The experience of those *corps* in which regimental libraries[27] have been established, is most encouraging. There cannot be a finer sight than that of the handsome manly fellows (non-commissioned officers and the pick of the privates) who are generally deputed to select occasional additions to the library, turning over a bookseller's stores, making their remarks on each volume, and choosing with deliberate discrimination.[28]

Commenting on the court martial of a private soldier in the 7th Hussars later that same year, though, the newspaper made an explicit link between this individual's use of "threatening and disgustingly abusive language" and the fact that the army was not devoting sufficient attention to the welfare of its recruits: "No books are provided for his entertainment or instruction during the intervals of duty. ... Regimental, barrack, and garrison libraries, as well as schools, should be established, and the canteen discouraged."[29]

The attitude of individual commanding officers, it is clear, was a major factor in determining whether libraries were established, or thrived, at the different stations. *The Cork Examiner* for 3 June, 1846, for example, reported the comments of a Royal Marine stationed upon Spike Island, who lamented the lack of facilities available to the troops: "[It] is a 'prison-house' scarcely a mile in circumference ... destitute of any and every resource but the Canteen; the soldiers' only recreation is in turning over the stones on the beach at ebb-tide, knee-deep in mud, and searching for cockles." The situation at Camden and Carlisle Forts was similarly grim, he observed, and—

> the men's only amusement is in playing "pitch and toss" for the few spare pence which they possess, and which they cannot otherwise spend. Hawlbowline is another islet of no better repute, on which the men are prisoners ... and garrison libraries there are none anywhere where we are. In vain have we appealed to our Commanding Officer, ... who, having a wife and large young family,

---

[27] The sense of the editorial overall suggests that garrison rather than regimental libraries are probably meant here.

[28] *Daily News*, 4 June 1846.

[29] *DailyNews*, 7 October, 1846.

desires to live "unknowing and unknown," for economy's sake; but is it fair, is it just, that 650 men should be sacrificed. [30]

Troops at a particularly remote station in Canada fared considerably better, according to a piece reproduced in the *Dundee Courier* later that year, largely due to the efforts of their enlightened officer. Commenting on the considerable lengths to which this individual went to provide recreational outlets for his men, the piece observed: "in short, he knew how to manage them, and to keep their minds engaged; for they worked and played, read and reasoned; and so whiskey, which is as cheap as dirt there, was not a temptation which they could not resist." Pointedly, the writer of the piece continued—

> ... I feel persuaded, that now Government has provided such handsome garrison libraries of choice and well-selected books for the soldiers, if a ball-alley, or racket court, and a cricket ground, were attached to every large barrack, there would not only be less drinking in the army, but that vice would ultimately be scorned, as it has been within the last twenty years by the officers.[31]

The sentiments that the writer expresses here are significant, as they remind us that the provision of libraries was but one of several measures advocated in the nineteenth century in the interests of improving what an 1862 report was to describe as "the social condition of the soldier"[32]; others included the establishing of schools and savings banks and, in 1863, the removal of canteens from private control.[33] The writer's comments are also important, though, because they underline the fact that a major impulse behind the provision of facilities like these was the hope that they would

---

[30] *The Cork Examiner*, 3 June, 1846.

[31] *The Dundee Courier*, 1 December, 1846.

[32] See *Report of a Committee appointed by the Secretary of State for War to inquire into and report on the present state and on the improvement of Libraries, Reading Rooms, and Day Rooms* (London: HMSO, 1862), p. 7. Hereafter *Report of a Committee*.

[33] On the protracted history of schools in the army, see Bowyer-Bower, "Development of Educational Ideas," pp. 10–15; John M. Brereton, *The British Soldier: A Social History from 1661 to the Present Day* (London: Bodley Head, 1986), pp. 51–53, 69–71; and Neuburg, *Gone for a Soldier*, pp. 69–72. On reform efforts, see Correlli Barnett, *Britain and her Army, 1509–1970: Military, Political, and Social Survey* (Harmondsworth: Penguin, 1970), pp. 272–324; Burroughs, "Crime and Punishment in the British Army," *passim*; Edward M. Spiers, *The Army and Society, 1815–1914* (London and New York: Longman, 1980), especially pp. 145–76, for the post-Crimean period, and pp. 177–205, for the Cardwell Reforms.

lessen the soldiers' propensity for drunkenness and "vice," which, we will see below, remained of huge concern well into the Victorian period.

Efforts in relation to army reform proceeded slowly, however, primarily because the attitude of authorities and the general public alike waxed and waned during these years. In part, this was because the majority of the population was largely indifferent to the plight of military, and thought of soldiers only when their own lives or interests were threatened. This was something that clearly occupied the thoughts of Sergeant Jowett in 1854, when he "celebrated" a miserable Christmas in the Crimea: "Little does a man think, when seated by his fire-side at home, what hardships his own countrymen are enduring for his sake. I often wonder if a soldier will be treated the same in England as he used to be."[34] A turning point did come about as a result of the Crimean War (1853–56), as extensive newspaper and journal coverage alerted the public to the true extent of British losses in the campaign and the reality of the day-to-day life of the British soldier. Coverage of the war impressed upon readers the essential humanity of the British soldiers that were involved in the campaign; it reminded them that the men were human beings who were being called upon to fight and, perhaps, die, for a government and public that seemed largely indifferent to what they were suffering. As William Howard Russell declared in one of his famous dispatches to *The Times*—

> It is now pouring rain, the skies are black as ink, the wind is howling over the staggering tents, the trenches are turned into dykes, in the tents the water is sometimes a foot deep, our men have not either warm or waterproof clothing, they are out for twelve hours a time in the trenches, they are plunged into the inevitable miseries of a winter campaign, and not a soul seems to care for their comfort or even their lives.[35]

Growing public concern about the welfare of British forces in the Crimea played into the hands of individuals who insisted it was time to institute real reform in the army, including, of course, Florence Nightingale, who insisted it was entirely possible to improve British soldiers: "Give them opportunity promptly & securely to send money home—& they will use it. Give them a School & a Lecture & they will come to it. Give them a

---

[34] William Jowett, *Memoir and Diary of Sergeant W. Jowett, Seventh Royal Fusiliers* (London and Beeston, Nottinghamshire: W. Kent & Co. and B. Porter, 1856), p. 46.

[35] Published on 25 November 1854, quoted in David Murphy, *Ireland and the Crimean War* (Dublin: Four Courts, 2002), p. 173.

Book & a Game & a Magic Lanthorn [sic] [that is, a slide projector] & they will leave off drinking."[36] Nightingale had long been an advocate of the importance of reading for those recovering from illness or injury, as Michael D. Calabria points out, and was careful to ensure that books and newspapers were provided to soldiers in her care at hospitals in the Crimea; she also "became active in evaluating and improving army libraries, reading rooms, and soldiers' institutes, or establishing such institutes wherever needed." Crucially, moreover, "In the years following her return from the Crimea, she gathered advice on all of these subjects from a variety of experienced military men with whom she had worked during the war; she coordinated their efforts, pressed politicians to appoint parliamentary committees and procured resources and funds from the War Office or provided them herself." In this context, Calabria suggests, it is "tempting to attribute at least some of the change" in the late-Victorian military to the efforts of Nightingale (as well as to the associates with whom she worked).[37]

Dr. John Sutherland and Captain Douglas Galton were two of the men who worked closely with Nightingale, and both were appointed to one of the more important commissions to come out of the war: the 1857 Royal Sanitary Commission that was set up to enquire into the conditions of army barracks, the organization of hospitals, and the treatment of sick and wounded soldiers. This Commission produced its report a year after it was established, and among its findings was the shocking revelation that the mortality of some parts of the home-based army was "more than double" that of the civilian population.[38] Significantly, among the several causes that the Commission identified for the distressingly high rate of mortality among soldiers was the fact that the army provided so few recreational facilities to its forces. This was of particular concern, the commissioners pointed out, because of the peculiar nature of military life: "Perhaps no living individual suffers more than [the soldier] from ennui. He has no

[36] Quoted in Michael D. Calabria, "Florence Nightingale and the Libraries of the British Army," *Libraries and Culture* 29: 4 (Fall, 1994), pp. 368–69.

[37] Calabria, "Florence Nightingale," pp. 369–70 and 385.

[38] *Report of the Commissioners appointed to inquire into the Regulations affecting the Sanitary Conditions of the Army, the Organization of Military Hospitals, and the treatment of the Sick and Wounded, with Evidence and Appendix* (London: HMSO, 1857), p. xiii. The commissioners provided a table entitled, "Deaths per 1000 per Annum at Ages between 20 and 40," which demonstrated that the mortality of the Horse Guards, for example, stood at 20.4 as opposed to the figure of 10.314 for miners and 6.055 for agricultural laborers, respectively (p. xi). Hereafter *Report of the Commissioners*.

employment, save his drill and his duties; these are of a most monotonous and uninteresting description, so much so that you cannot increase their amount without wearying and disgusting him."[39]

The commissioners were here in point of fact drawing upon the evidence of Colonel the Honourable James Lindsay, who had stressed in his testimony to the commission both that soldiers had a "considerable amount of leisure [time]" to fill, and that the government and military authorities consequently had a "duty" to provide "means of recreation" for its forces. The "great object" of all involved, he argued, should be to render a soldier's barracks more like his "home," and provide him with "pursuits" so that he would not be tempted to go "outside" in search of amusement. The provision of such facilities would have a fourfold effect, according to the colonel, for it would improve the mental as well as the physical well-being of soldiers and lessen the tendency to "dissipation" and "crime" among the troops: "I can speak from experience that where you have opportunities of employing the men, you decrease the dissipation; if you give them amusement, they take an interest in it."[40] There are several points to be made about the colonel's observations, and the first of these is that they clearly echo the kinds of arguments that were put forward by soldiers themselves. In one early-nineteenth-century memoir, for example, a private soldier observed that he might have "turned out a habitual drunkard" while serving with the 92nd Regiment of Foot in Gibraltar, largely because of the peculiar combination of circumstances that drove many of the men out of their barracks each evening. Some of these were to do with Gibraltar itself, he remarked: "The wine is cheap; the place is warm; and in time of war with Spain, there is [sic] very little fresh provisions, and what is fresh, is very indifferent. There is a great deal of hard labour for the soldiers, for part of which they get extra pay: by the evening, many of them are fatigued, and actually need a refreshment beyond their ordinary provisions." Others again, though, had to do with the day-to-day reality of barrack life itself, which greatly destroyed what he described as the "social comfort" of the soldier:

> Many of the barrack-rooms are uncomfortable on account of their size, containing sixty or more men. ... [O]ne or two individuals can molest all the rest; so that select retired conversation cannot be enjoyed. Any thing of that

[39] *Report of the Commissioners*, p. xiv.
[40] Colonel the Honorable James Lindsay's evidence to the Commission on 22 June, 1857, in *Report of the Commissioners*, pp. 194–95.

kind is always ready to be interrupted by the vicious and ignorant, who do not fail to scoff and gibe at what they do not understand or relish themselves. Among so many men too, there will always be found some who take malicious pleasure in making their neighbours unhappy. ... This, along with other things, induces those who have a little money, to spend the evening in the wine-house with their more select companions.[41]

William Taylor, to whom we referred at the beginning of the chapter, for his part stressed the beneficial effects of the "excellent library" that he eventually succeeded in founding for both the non-commissioned officers and men as a result of the "patronage and assistance" of a new and more enlightened commanding officer:

> I do not know anything more calculated to reform dissipated habits, or prevent the young soldier from degenerating into them than resources of this kind. There are many men in the army who have really no taste for the drunken and noisy atmosphere of the pot-house, who are driven to it by the absence of mental occupation. Once there the effects of drink, or the force of example, betrays them into other excesses, and degradation and punishment follow as a matter of course.[42]

The second—linked—point that must be made about the arguments that Lindsay advanced to the 1857 Royal Sanitary Commission, however, is that they were clearly reflective of the types of arguments that were put forward from at least the late 1820s in relation to the need to ameliorate the conditions of working-class life; in particular, they made explicit the perceived link between the lack of leisure facilities for the general population and their subsequent misbehavior. In advancing his arguments, though, the colonel imbued them with a particular military significance, emphasizing that the poor living conditions and boredom of soldiers hugely contributed to the high rates of drunkenness, venereal disease, and crime that plagued Her Majesty's forces throughout the Victorian period. In relation to venereal disease, for example, nearly one-third of serving soldiers were being treated each year by the 1860s, a circumstance that

[41] Not given, *Narrative of a Private Soldier in His Majesty's 92nd Regiment of Foot. Written by Himself. Detailing many Circumstances relative to the Insurrection in Ireland in 1798, the Expedition to Holland in 1799, and the Expedition to Egypt in 1801, and Giving a particular Account of his Religious History and Experience*, 2nd edn, *greatly enlarged* (Glasgow: University Press, 1820), pp. 5–6.

[42] Taylor, *Life in the Ranks*, pp. 288–89.

was directly responsible for the passing of the *Contagious Diseases Acts* in 1864, 1866, and 1869 respectively. These acts of parliament allowed for the inspection and, if necessary, treatment of women whom police identified as prostitutes in certain garrison and naval towns. The acts were controversial for a number of reasons: many women, for instance, objected to them on the grounds that they promoted a double standard in relation to sexual behavior (female prostitutes were inspected, while their male clients were not).[43] Significantly, the authors of an 1862 report on the military libraries, reading rooms, and day rooms were unable to conclude "without alluding to the monster vice of large garrison towns and military stations; namely, prostitution, and prostitution unmitigated by any precautionary remedial or sanitary arrangements whatsoever." Although acknowledging that it did "not enter into the scope of their instructions to consider how this evil may be kept in check," they begged "to call the attention of the Secretary of State to the subject, in the earnest hope that by the better supervision of licensed houses of entertainment, or by arming the military police with larger powers, the evil may be mitigated."[44]

Colonel Lindsay's remarks had a further importance: they revealed how "the sweeping Evangelical Revival of 1859" influenced attitudes to army reform. As Kenneth Hendrickson has pointed out, "civilian missionaries increasingly interested themselves in the reform of the military from this period, call[ing] on the men to change from within, relying on an ethic derived explicitly from evangelical Protestant Christianity." Rather than appealing to "efficiency, or even to the manly," they seized upon "cultural norms of femininity they believed the men would understand, and to which even soldiers might be expected to be open: mother, home, domesticity, and female purity." Women missionaries were particularly active and, significantly in terms of Lindsay's arguments, made "'the home,' and the female space it encompassed," central to their efforts.[45] By setting up soldiers' homes in Aldershot (1863) and Cork (1877) respectively, individuals such as Louisa Daniell and Elise Sandes helped develop a model of socialization that Alan Ramsay Skelley describes as "the dominant form of social

---

[43] See John Belchem and Richard Price (eds), *The Penguin Dictionary of Nineteenth-Century History*, Advisory, ed. Richard J. Evans (London: Penguin, 1994), p. 146.

[44] *Report of a Committee*, p. 13.

[45] Kenneth Hendrickson, "Winning the Troops for Vital Religion: Female Evangelical Missionaries to the British Army, 1857–1880," *Armed Forces and Society* 23, No. 4 (1997), pp. 617 and 625.

facility" for all ranks in the army up until the First World War.[46] We shall see in our next chapter, however, that the army's efforts to counter this model of socialization tried to use garrison and regimental libraries and reading rooms—as well as recreation rooms and Soldiers' Institutes—to keep soldiers within their barracks and, hence, improve men's attitudes and behavior. Lindsay's remarks are therefore finally significant because they reveal that a combination of influences affected the army's evolving attitude to reform: in particular, its growing awareness that it would have to be more proactive if it was sincere in its determination to tempt soldiers away from the "places of evil influence and example" that they tended to frequent in their leisure hours.[47]

The role that garrison libraries and reading rooms might play in this process struck authorities more forcibly from 1859, when Lefroy produced the report that provided them with their first real insight into the positive effects of promoting recreational reading among the forces. Lefroy, we noted earlier, was appointed as Inspector-General of Army Schools in Britain in 1857, two years before he produced his *Report on the Regimental and Garrison Schools of the Army, and on Military Libraries and Reading Rooms*.[48] This 80-page report, as its name suggests, was primarily concerned with the state of education in the army, but its analysis of military libraries and reading rooms revealed both the types of books that were supplied to soldiers at an official level, and the way in which the reading of these works was viewed by those responsible for providing them to the men. The overwhelming emphasis of the report was that the libraries and reading rooms were beneficial for soldiers; at the very least, Lefroy pointed out, they offered a further means of persuading "the young soldier" away from "the temptations of the town."[49] That said, though, Lefroy's report also reveals that he entertained a very particular anxiety in relation to the libraries and reading rooms: namely, that they were inculcating a desire for inappropriate reading among the men.

---

[46] See Alan Ramsay Skelley, *The Victorian Army at Home: The Recruitment and Terms and Conditions of the British Regular, 1859–1899* (London: Croom Helm, 1977), p. 164. Hendrickson puts it this way: "Prior to 1914, the Homes remained central to army post social life in Britain and the empire" ("Winning the Troops," p. 624).

[47] *Report of a Committee*, p. 4.

[48] On Lefroy's long and distinguished military career, see R.H. Vetch, "Lefroy, Sir John Henry (1817–1890)," rev. Roger T. Stearn, *Oxford Dictionary of National Biography*, Oxford University Press, 2004; online edition, Oct 2005 http://www.oxforddnb.com/view/article/16343 [accessed 24 April 2007].

[49] Lefroy, *Report*, p. 59.

Lefroy's report is hugely significant in terms of what it reveals about prevailing attitudes about literacy and, especially, about fiction, in the late 1850s, and so we shall consider it in some detail here.

One of the first things to observe about Lefroy's report is that it is marked by the singular pride he clearly felt when recounting what the army had accomplished by the time of its production. There were, he noted, "158 military libraries in 140 garrisons, exclusive of India," and stations where these had been established abroad included Quebec, Cape Town, Auckland, and Corfu.[50] Twenty "Regimental libraries" had also been established for the Royal Artillery and Royal Engineers at home stations, and ten more for those serving abroad (the latter included places such as Bermuda, the Cape of Good Hope, and St. Helena).[51] All of these institutions were under the general control of the commanding officers on the spot, he remarked, but they were managed on a daily basis by committees of subscribers; this was because experience had shown that the "most effectual way" of ensuring the success of the libraries or reading rooms was "to allow [soldiers] a voice in their management."[52] Lefroy further observed that admission to the libraries was by subscription, and that the rate was four pence a month for a private and usually somewhat more for a non-commissioned officer.[53] Subscription to the libraries, he pointed out, was hugely improved by allowing men to become subscribers at any time: "the number of subscribers at Shorncliffe rose in consequence from 13 % to 23 % of the troops [and] a similar result has occurred in many other garrisons."[54] A report that was produced three years later suggests either that Lefroy was being hugely optimistic here, or that Shorncliffe was not typical of other stations:

Returns received from 136 commanding officers and barrack masters ... showing the number of subscribers in their corps and the average daily attendance at the libraries and reading rooms, give the following result:

Strength	69,336
Daily attendance	6,073

[50] Lefroy, *Report*, pp. 52–54.

[51] Lefroy, *Report*, pp. 55–56. The decision to set up libraries for the Artillery and Engineers was approved in 1840.

[52] Lefroy, *Report*, pp. 56 and 61.

[53] Lefroy, *Report*, p. 56.

[54] Lefroy, *Report*, p. 58.

From this it appears that the daily attendance is no more than 8.76 % of the force, a result which not only falls far short of what is desirable, but of itself points out the necessity for improvement.[55]

Lefroy's report on the military libraries and reading rooms was manifestly informed by many different sentiments—the determination of an army officer to write a good report, for instance, or by his sense of military as well as patriotic pride—but it is marked primarily by his anxiety that the wrong types of books were being read by the men by whom the institutions were frequented. This was in the first place made clear to him by the reclassification of the works held in the libraries, for this revealed that "Works of entertainment and fiction" constituted the biggest class of reading being made available to the men:

	No. in the Catalogue
Books of reference	37
Biography	243
Works of naval and military history or narrative	290
Voyages and Travels	463
Works of entertainment and fiction	581
Poetry	104
General literature	409
Works of zoology, botany, and natural history	85
Works on serious and sacred subjects	208
Tracts	38
Total	2,759[a]

[a]Lefroy, *Report*, p. 57

The call for returns from "34 of the principal libraries" also underlined the popularity of "Works of entertainment and fiction": the titles were classed under four headings—"Books in constant demand, Books in frequent demand, Books occasionally, but not often called for, Books seldom or never read"—and the result "consigned the biggest part of all these libraries to the third and fourth classes." This circumstance

> proved that novels, tales, and light periodicals are almost the only books which soldiers at present appreciate. The writings of Miss Jane Austin [sic], Mrs. Bray, Bulwer Lytton, Cooper, Dickens, Miss Edgeworth, Miss Ferrier,

[55] *Report of a Committee*, pp. 6–7.

Fielding, James, Lever, Lover, Marryat, Miss Jane Porter, Scott, Smollett, invariably appear with figures indicating the highest degree of popularity, to which may be added those of Peter Parley and other superior children's books, Chambers' Journal, and the Penny Magazine; books of travels, military works (except the historical records of regiments), and works of general literature, with comparatively few exceptions, repose undisturbed on the shelves.[56]

Lefroy's anxiety in relation to the preferred reading of soldiers was reinforced by his analysis of "a list of 264 works which have been demanded since January 1, 1858, to replace copies certified to be worn out by fair use," which confirmed the "conclusion" that works of fiction were particularly valued by soldiers. "We find among them," he points out,

Class A, Books of reference	0
Class B, Biography	8
Class C, Naval and military works	17
Class D, Voyages and Travels	16
Class E, Books of entertainment and fiction	205
Class F, Poetry	10
Class G, General literature	7
Class H, Natural history	1
Class I, Religious works	0
Total:	264[a]

[a]Lefroy, *Report*, p. 57.

Lefroy helpfully attached an appendix to his report, which listed under several headings the titles of the books that had been worn out and replaced at the various libraries. This appendix is extensive and so we will not consider it in great detail here. What is worth noting, though, is that the list provides an invaluable insight into the *types* of books that were being supplied at an official level to military readers at this period and, even more significantly, perhaps, of which of these were actually preferred by the men. So, for example, we find lives of military and naval figures such as Napoleon, Nelson, and Wellington listed under the heading of Class B (Biography), and titles such as "Advice to the British Soldier," "Soldiers and Sailors," and "Military Sketch Book" under Class C (Naval and Military Works). Voyages and Travels listed include "Anson's Voyages,"

---

[56] Lefroy, *Report*, p. 57.

"Cook's Voyages," "Irish Tourist," and "Hall's Voyages in Siberia," while Class F (Poetry) includes the *Canterbury Tales* as well as the works of Cowper, Burns, and Byron.

No fewer than 205 titles are listed under the heading of "Books of entertainment and fiction" and, as we might expect, these include a wide selection of novels by popular male authors. There are, for instance, 19 titles by Sir Walter Scott mentioned, including *Waverley* (1814), *The Antiquary* (1816), *The Black Dwarf* (1816), *Rob Roy* (1818), *Ivanhoe* (1820), *The Bride of Lammermoor* (1819), and *Anne of Geierstein* (1829). Seventeen titles each are listed for James Fenimore Cooper and G.P.R. James, with the latter's works including *Richelieu* (1829), *King's Highway* (1840), and *Agincourt* (1844), and the former's *The Pioneers* (1823), *The Last of the Mohicans* (1826), and *The Deerslayer* (1841), as well as *Lionel Lincoln* (1825) and *Red Rover* (1827). Thirteen of Captain Marryat's works appear on the list, including *Frank Mildmay, or the Naval Officer* (1829), *Peter Simple* (1834), and *Mr. Midshipman Easy* (1836), while *Pelham* (1828), *Eugene Aram* (1832), *The Last Days of Pompeii* (1834), and *Zanoni* (1842) are among the nine works by Bulwer Lytton that are mentioned. Seven of Charles Dickens' works appear on the list, and these include *Sketches by Boz* (1835), *Nicholas Nickleby* (1839), *Martin Chuzzelwit* (1844), *The Old Curiosity Shop* (1840), and *A Christmas Carol* (1843). An entry for "Fielding's Works (Complete)" also appears.

While it is hardly a surprise to discover that the works of such highly popular male writers featured in the military libraries and reading rooms at this period, it is, perhaps, slightly more interesting to learn that works by late-eighteenth- and early-nineteenth-century female authors were also represented on the shelves of these institutions. Titles mentioned include Elizabeth Inchbald's *A Simple Story* (1791); Charlotte Smith's *The Old Manor House* (1793); Ann Radcliffe's *The Italian* (1796); Maria Edgeworth's *Castle Rackrent* (1800) and *Tales of Fashionable Life* (1809, 1812); Jane Porter's *Thaddeus of Warsaw* (1803), *The Scottish Chiefs: A Romance* (1810), and *The Pastor's Fireside* (1817)[57]; Amelia Opie's *Adeline Mowbray* (1804); Mary Brunton's *Discipline* (1814); and Susan Ferrier's *Inheritance* (1824), as well as *Pride and Prejudice* (1811), *Mansfield Park*

---

[57] Anna Maria Porter's *The Hungarian Brothers* (1807) is also mistakenly attributed to Jane Porter.

(1814), *Emma* (1816), and *Northanger Abbey* (1818) by Jane Austen.[58] We might be tempted in the first instance to account for the presence of such titles in the soldiers' libraries on pecuniary grounds; they were, after all, older and, therefore, cheaper than works by contemporary male authors, and for this reason alone were featured on many Victorian library shelves. That said, though, the same point clearly can be made about many of the works in the garrison libraries and, as we shall see below, later reports make clear that the men continued to read and, sometimes, explicitly request works by female authors. Recognition of this fact is important because it reminds us once again of the need to be cautious when advancing arguments about the type of reading a particular reader might prefer. This, indeed was a point that John Fraser raised in his account of his life in the army, where he both stressed his preference for poetry and remarked that anybody seeing him "absorbed in *Prometheus Unbound* might well regard it as a strangely incongruous scene." He continued—

> Yet it is not so, really, for the swashbuckling stories and poems of action and adventure do not appeal to the adventurers and men of action so much as the unthinking would imagine. After all most people read in order to get away from the realities of their normal lives, and so it is the clerk or shopman who delights in tales of adventure, and the more spiritual matter that appeals to the man who, LIVING adventures, doesn't need to read about them.[59]

Adventure tales, however, did feature on Lefroy's list, which included old favorites such as the *Arabian Nights, Gil Blas, Robinson Crusoe,* and *Gulliver's Travels* (1726). Works with an explicitly military or naval theme were also represented, and included Philip Meadows Taylor's *Confessions of a Thug* (1839), Peter Parley's *Tales of the Sea* (c. 1830), and various publications by the Reverend George Robert Gleig, including *The Hussar* (1837) and *Chelsea Hospital* (1838). Cheap publications which were explicitly aimed at and "helped to create the new working class reading public" also appeared, and included

---

[58] "Return showing the Number of Books which have been reported as worn out by fair wear and tear in Military Libraries, from 1st January to 31st December 1858," Appendix IX to Lefroy, *Report*, pp. 219–222.

[59] John Fraser, *Sixty Years in Uniform* (London: Stanley Paul, 1939), p. 86.

the *Penny Magazine*, the *Saturday Magazine*, *Chambers Journal*, and *Chambers Miscellany*.[60]

While we might be impressed to discover that the mid-nineteenth-century soldier was reading such a wide range of works, including fiction, Lefroy for his part was very concerned that these were the types of reading matter that were flying off the garrison libraries' shelves. To account for what he plainly perceived as an unpalatable circumstance, he raised the issue of the poor level of education of the average soldier, intimating that he was typically incapable of comprehending the "good" books on offer within these institutions:

> The bulk of subscribers to military libraries are quite incapable of appreciating books written for educated readers; the knowledge predisposed is far beyond their acquirements. Much even of the language is unknown to them. I have been repeatedly struck with the limited vocabulary of their own language possessed by uneducated soldiers, and the number of words there are in common use of whose meaning they have no idea or a false one.

Lefroy also suggested that the peculiar conditions of military life were such that soldiers were unable to apply themselves to a course of serious study: "a soldier's opportunities of reading are too desultory to incline him to begin large works, and it is curious to observe how entirely thrown away for the most part are such classics as Napier's History of the Peninsular War, the Wellington Despatches, and others of the solid and standard character." This latter point, he continued, accounted for what was

> a common complaint among the troops, that there is too little variety in the libraries, they find the same books everywhere, and have "*read them all.*" The *all* here means that limited number of books which they will read. There is reason to hope that the classification of the catalogue will tend to encourage a wider range of choice, and it cannot be doubted that light reading will by degrees infuse a desire for knowledge and lead the way to reading of a more improving character, as it has been found to do in the free libraries established of late years in Liverpool and other commercial towns.[61]

---

[60] Louis James, *Fiction for the Working Man, 1830–1850: A Study of the Literature Produced for the Working Classes in Early Victorian Urban England* (London, New York, and Toronto: Oxford University Press, 1963), pp. 10–11.

[61] Lefroy, *Report*, p. 58.

There are, of course, a number of points to be made here, and the first of these relates to literacy rates within the army at this period. As Lefroy recognized, many of the men who enlisted were barely literate, and growing recognition of this fact was one of the factors that prompted authorities to pay more attention to army schools. The different reports that the army produced between the late 1850s and late 1880s made significant claims in relation to its educational efforts, as we noted in the introduction, and suggested that the provision of schools, libraries, and reading rooms was having a tremendous effect on the reading and writing abilities of the men. By the late 1880s, though, the army became more realistic in measuring its educational outcomes, and the gap between its claims and the observations of men such as John Pindar began to lessen. Commenting on the state of the army in the 1870s, for instance, Pindar began by observing that "an educated recruit is as great a rarity now as I have ever seen during my close on twenty years' service," which was in sharp contrast to what authorities were claiming at this period.[62]

Lefroy's remarks about the potential of the garrison libraries are also significant, however, because they are reflective of an aspiration that many entertained in relation to free public libraries: that they could be used gradually to "improve" the reading tastes of the lower classes. It was because of this that fiction was recognized as something that could be used to entice lower-class readers, and why it was

> common practice to provide novels in both lending and reference departments. At Manchester, the aggregate issue of the reference department between 1852 and 1857 included over 160,000 books from the Literature and Polygraphy class, approximately one-third of these issues being novels ... A similar emphasis on fiction and recreational literature is evident in other early public libraries: Sheffield's lending department issue for 1856–57, for example, included 51.5 % miscellaneous and fiction titles, rising to 56.6 % in 1858–59. In Birmingham, the central library's total issue for 1868 included 73.5 % of books from the Literature and Polygraphy class, which incorporated novels ...[63]

Ironically, Liverpool, the one commercial center that Lefroy actually names, was "well-known for its high issues of fiction; in 1868, its reference department alone issued 189, 841 novels and romance, a fact that

---

[62] John Pindar, *Autobiography of a Private Soldier* (Cupar-Fife: Printed in the "Fife News" Office, 1878), Pindar, p. 165.

[63] Robert Snape, *Leisure and the Rise of the Public Library* (London: Library Association Publishing, 1995), pp. 22–23.

prompted [Edward] Edwards to comment that, for every novel reader in Manchester, Liverpool could boast ten."[64]

The hope that "light reading" would eventually lead soldiers to more improving works is to be traced again and again in the later reports on the garrison libraries, which once more reminds us of the comparisons that can be drawn between these institutions and the free public libraries at this period. A major concern of an enquiry that was undertaken two years later in relation to the soldiers' libraries, for example, was the nature of the reading material that was being supplied to readers and, overwhelmingly, the responses the committee received to its questions in this regard indicated that insufficient attention was being paid to the literary preferences of the men. "The whole body of the evidence shows that, of the books in each library, works of fiction have by far the largest amount of circulation, and next to these, biography, travels, adventure, and discovery." However, "Many complaints are made that this species of literature is scanty. There is an ample supply of books, many of them highly valuable, but the lists of works most in request ... show that in future it may be well to consult more than has yet been done the tastes and capacities of the general body of readers."[65] This committee attached an extensive appendix to their report, which detailed the books most in request in the libraries and, thereby, provided a fascinating insight into the types of reading that were being carried on at the different stations.[66] Some libraries, such as the Sappers' library at Chatham, simply provided a long "List of Books &c. most in request" during a given period,[67] while others, such as the Garrison library at the Royal Barracks in Dublin, listed popular books according to their different classes.[68] Other libraries, such as the one at Winchester, provided lists that identified the books most requested both from available stock and from titles that were unavailable

[64] Snape, *Leisure and the Rise of the Public Library*, pp. 22–23.

[65] *Report of a Committee*, p. 6.

[66] See "List of Books and Periodicals most in request at Home and Foreign Stations, selected from the replies to Question 11," Appendix No. 2 to *Report of a Committee*, pp. 16–33.

[67] "List of Books &c. most in request at the Sappers' Library, Royal Engineers [Chatham], for the Quarter ending 31st December, 1860," in Appendix No. 2 to *Report of a Committee*, pp. 17–18.

[68] The works are listed under "Class C," "Class D," and so on, in accordance with the classes assigned to different categories of works by the committee in their survey. See "Dublin, Garrison Library, Royal Barracks, Books Mostly Read" in Appendix No. 2 to *Report of a Committee*, p. 24.

118 S. MURPHY

but listed in the catalogue. The list in relation to the former at Winchester, for instance, reveals that 112 books were most frequently requested in the library, and that works of fiction—by authors such as Sir Walter Scott, Jane Porter, Charles Dickens, G.P.R. James, and James Fenimore Cooper—were among those that were most popular with the soldiers.[69]

Significantly in terms of our discussion above, the list of popular works at Winchester included Susan Ferrier's *Inheritance* and Jane Austen's *Mansfield Park*, and the list of the 280 books that were sought for but unavailable at the library further revealed that a wide range of works by female authors was being sought for by the men. These included Jane Austen's *Sense and Sensibility, Pride and Prejudice*, and *Northanger Abbey*; ten works by Anna Eliza Bray, including *De Foix, or Sketches of the Manners and Customs of the Fourteenth Century* (1826), *The White Hoods* (1828), and *Warleigh, or, The Fatal Oak: A Legend of Devon* (1834); a selection of works by the Scandinavian writer and feminist Fredrika Bremer, including *The Neighbours, A Story of Everyday Life* (1842) and *The Home, or, Family Cares and Family Joys* (1843)[70]; twelve works by Anne Marsh-Caldwell ("Mrs Marsh"), including *Tales of Woods and Fields* (1836), *Emilia Wyndham* (1846), *Mordaunt Hall, or, A September Night* (1849), and *Lettice Arnold* (1850); and a selection of titles by Mrs. S.C. Hall, including *Sketches of Irish Character* (1829) and *Lights and Shadows of Irish Life* (1838) and, under "Anna Maria Hall," *Buccanneer* (1831) and *Outlaw* (1835). Four works attributed to "Currer Bell" were also being sought for: *Jane Eyre, Shirley, Villette* (1853), and "The Tenant of Wildfire Hall" [sic]. Compilers of the list, or those whose requests it reflected, were obviously unaware that *The Tenant of Wildfell Hall* (1848) was the work of an entirely different "Bell."

Other libraries again, such as the First Garrison library at Limerick New Barracks, provided the committee with details of the number of times different classes of books were issued to the troops. The Limerick list entitled "Number of Books issued to the Troops from 1st January to 31st December 1860," incidentally, supports the committee's contention that fiction was most popular with the men:

[69] See "List of Books most in Request" and "List of Books often asked for, which are in the Catalogue, but not in the Library" at Winchester in Appendix No. 2 to *Report of a Committee*, pp. 19 and 20–21.
[70] Bremer's works were introduced into England through the translations of Mary Howitt. See Carol A. Martin, "Mary Howitt" in Janet Todd (ed), *Dictionary of British Women Writers* (1989; London: Routledge, 1991), p. 336.

Works of Reference	121
Biography	284
Military and Naval	710
Voyages and Travels	734
Entertainment and Fiction	8,544
Poets and Poetry	266
General Literature	499
Natural History	160
Sacred and Serious Subjects	233
Total Number Issued	11,551[a]

[a] In "List of Books and Periodicals most in request at Home and Foreign Stations, selected from the replies to Question 11," Appendix No. 2 to *Report of a Committee*, p. 26

In advancing their suggestions in relation to possible improvements to the libraries and reading rooms, the committee was keen to stress that more care should be taken in future to ensure they contained "a sufficient supply of books of the character shown in the evidence to be best suited to the tastes and opportunities of the soldier." Commanding officers would have to play a crucial role in this regard, they observed, exercising "supervision" to ensure nothing "of an improper character gains admission." A further point members of the committee were keen to make concerned the supply of newspapers and periodicals to soldiers: "All, or nearly all, Reading Rooms or Libraries are provided with a certain number of [these] ... We look upon this kind of literature as a very important element in the success of Reading Rooms, and are of opinion that the number of newspapers and periodicals ought to be more accurately proportioned to the numbers likely to require them."[71] The committee here was clearly responding to the observations of commanding officers such as Captain Kirk, of the 96th Regiment, Devonport, who had remarked: "With regard to literature I have come to the conclusion that libraries should be subordinate to news rooms; I feel certain that if the soldiers were consulted their wishes for newspapers and periodicals versus books would be 10–1. One very important point to be remedied is that the supply should keep pace with the demand."[72]

Evidence gathered by the Royal Sanitary Commission of 1857 had also stressed the importance of providing newspapers and periodicals to soldiers. In his testimony before the commission, for example, Major-General Lawrence stressed that, as the men were already being "flooded with all sorts of newspapers of the lowest and worst description," it was "most desir-

[71] *Report of a Committee*, p. 7.
[72] In "Summary of Special Reports," in Appendix No. 3 to *Report of a Committee*, p. 47.

able that they should be supplied with newspapers and periodicals of a good moral tendency in order to counteract the evil effects of the publications which they not only meet with at the public-houses, but which are sent to them in such numbers by their friends."[73] Lefroy, too, remarked upon the importance of newspapers in his 1859 report, noting that the failure to provide them at that time was detracting from the appeal of the institutions:

> Newspapers, properly speaking … are not at present furnished to any read-ing- rooms, and consequently a powerful attraction is wanting. Applications for them are very numerous, nor can we ever hope to combat successfully the temptations of the canteen and public-house while they are withheld. As the present library regulations … sanction their introduction under private arrangements, leaving it to the commanding officer to see that nothing of an improper tendency gains admission, there is no objection of principle to their being furnished, and the question resolves itself into one of principle alone.[74]

The army's shifting attitude to the provision of newspapers in the late 1850s and early 1860s is significant for a number of reasons, including the fact it was obviously to some degree predicated on a growing awareness of the tremendous importance that soldiers attached to this type of reading material. Writing to his family from Constantinople in 1854, for example, Joseph Reid observed, "George asks me if a Banffshire journal would be of any use to me, here a paper of any description is nearly worth its weight in gold."[75] John Pine for his part pleaded with his family to send newspapers to him in South Africa, declaring, "A letter or a newspaper coming to me will only cost you a penny each."[76] The army's changing attitude to newspapers and periodicals, however, can also be related to the development of mass circulation at this time, and an appreciation of the fact that it would prove increasingly difficult to prevent soldiers from accessing such material. Prior to this, the flood of cheap publications that resulted from early nineteenth-century innovations in papermaking and mechanical printing had alarmed authorities, prompting them to pass a series of acts intended to regulate this potentially seditious material. The lifting in 1855 of the last of the duties that had been imposed on newspapers, however, cleared the way for them to develop properly and

---

[73] Evidence of Major-General Lawrence C.B. to the Commission on 12 June 1857 in *Report of the Commissioners*, p. 128.

[74] Lefroy, *Report*, pp. 60–61.

[75] Letter of Joseph Reid, 14 May 1854, NAM 1999-03-130, no. 15.

[76] John Pine, Letter of 20 April 1852 from Fort Beaufort, NAM 1996-05-4, 3.

reach a mass readership. The army's decision to put the provision of news-papers to soldiers on a sounder footing at this time thus can be seen as pragmatic; the men were already reading such material, they recognized, and it was better to provide them with "appropriate" works.[77] It was in this con-text, then, that a number of different measures were put in place as the years went by to facilitate men's access to newspapers and periodicals, many of these at a local level. From May of 1896, for example, soldiers at the Curragh were able to purchase "the last editions of the Dublin evening newspapers ... [from the] library at 9.30 p.m. each evening."[78]

The committee that produced the 1862 report stressed a further point about encouraging soldiers to read "appropriately," and emphasized that a good librarian could make a huge contribution in this regard. If a librarian is "fond of his occupation, [and] knows the contents of the books in his charge, and the taste of the subscribers," they observed, "he can generally lead them by degrees to a higher order of reading." It was in light of this rec-ognition that the committee suggested that "inducements superior to those now held out" should be offered to attract suitably qualified candidates to fill librarian posts: "The present rate of pay is considered to be quite inad-equate"; it is also why they intimated that, when arranging accommodation for a library, proper allowance should be made for the librarian's quarters.[79]

All aspects of army education were placed under the supervision of the Council of Military Education from 1860, and this manifested an ongo-ing determination to improve the army's libraries and reading rooms and, consequently, the soldier. The council thus issued a report in 1862 that stressed that its views were "entirely in accordance" with those recently published by the earlier committee, and remarked that the "important step" of supplying "daily and weekly newspapers" to the libraries and reading rooms was already in hand.[80] Its report three years later included

---

[77] On the restrictive measures imposed on the early-nineteenth-century British newspaper and periodical industries, see James, *Fiction for the Working Man*, especially pp. 12–22; William St. Clair, *The Reading Nation in the Romantic Period* (Cambridge: Cambridge University Press, 2004), pp. 309–12; and the *Concise History of the British Newspaper in the Nineteenth Century*, available on the British Library's website at [www.bl.uk/.../findhelpre-stype/news/conscisehistbritnews/britnews19th].

[78] Con Costello, *A Most Delightful Station: The British Army on the Curragh of Kildare, Ireland, 1855–1922* (Cork: The Collins Press, 1996), p. 126.

[79] *Report of a Committee*, pp. 6–7.

[80] *First Report by the Council of Military Education on Army Schools* (London: HMSO, 1862), p. xvi.

a "Reprint of the Regulations for Garrison Libraries and Regimental Recreation Rooms" and, crucially, several of these revealed an on-going concern to regulate—or control—the reading habits of the soldiers. Regulation number 26, for instance, reminded commanding officers that, "when sanctioning the purchase of new books, ... a reasonable proportion of works of an instructive as well as interesting character, such as histories, travels, and general literature, should be obtained," while number 27 observed, "No works of an immoral tendency, or of a political or religious controversial character, can in any case be sanctioned." Should such "unfit" books find their way into the libraries, they were upon discovery—

> to be condemned, and forwarded to the Stationery Office as unserviceable; and the corps, out of whose funds they have been provided, is to be required to supply another work of equal value. Any such works are to be ordered by the commanding officer of the garrison to be condemned, and withdrawn from circulation without delay; and any works of an objectionable character are also liable to be condemned by the Field Marshal Commanding-in-Chief, on the report of the Council of Military Education.

Regulation 31 looked to the supply of newspapers and periodicals to the libraries and reading rooms, and intimated that the provision of such works should also be carefully controlled. Commanding officers therefore were required to "sanction" such reading materials before they could be introduced to the libraries or reading rooms, and to state in their "quarterly report what newspapers and periodicals [they had] allowed to be admitted."[81]

Regulations like these were clearly reflective of the fact that those who operated the libraries repeatedly encountered the same difficulty in terms of reader preference, and consequently lamented the fact that subscribers continued to be attracted "to one class of books, the very lightest that can be found." This, they declared, was largely because the soldiers did "not generally go to the garrison library and select for themselves. Certain works become popular in a regiment, and these go through the ranks with little change or variety."[82] Different strategies were suggested to try to counteract this tendency on the part of the soldiers, at both a local and

---

[81] See Appendix XV—No. 1 to *Second Report by the Council of Military Education on Army Schools, Libraries, and Recreation Rooms* (London: HMSO, 1865), pp. 216–221. The three rules cited are on page 219.

[82] *Third Report by the Council of Military Education on Army Schools, Libraries, and Recreation Rooms* (London: HMSO, 1866), p. xxxi.

an official level. The Reverend T.R. Maynard, for example, noted in 1864 that works of entertainment and fiction were "mostly read" by subscribers to the library at Canterbury, and that in an effort to remedy this, "*Special classified catalogues*" were printed up and sold to soldiers at two pence a copy: "The greater number of the subscribers to the library," he observed, "ask for those books which they have seen their comrades reading, but it is hoped that by the introduction of the catalogues ... they will be led to extend their choice, and select books for themselves."[83] The chaplain's circulation figures for 1865 in relation to the 2,478 books in the library suggests that this scheme had only limited success, and invites speculation that the true effect of the special catalogues may have been to alert readers to the full range of the books available in their preferred class:

Subject	No. of Vols.	No. of issues during 1865
Books of Reference[a]	51	–
Biography	227	5
Military and Naval	231	178
Voyages and Travels	312	166
Entertainment and Fiction	500	4,694
Poets and Poetry	84	105
General Literature	526	368
Science and Natural History	149	57
Sacred and Serious Subjects	155	10
Magazines and Periodicals	202	358
Books to assist in the preparation of lectures and not available for general circulation	41	–
Total	2,478	5,951[b]

[a]The chaplain notes that subscribers were not allowed to take books of reference from the library.
[b]"Notes on the Working of the Garrison Library and Recreation Rooms at Canterbury for the Year ending 31stDecember 1865," Appendix XVIII—No. 2 to *Fifth Report by the Council of Military Education on Army Schools, Libraries, and Recreation Rooms* (London: HMSO, 1868), p. 135

"Of class E (Entertainment and Fiction)," the chaplain remarked, "the tales and novels of Sir Walter Scott,[84] Bulwer [Lytton], Dickens, Marryat,

[83] In Appendix XV—No. 4 to *Second Report by the Council of Military Education*, pp. 235–36.

[84] The chaplain reports that the library had two complete sets of Scott's works, "of whose novels the 'Fair Maid of Perth,' (41 [issues]), 'The Pirate,' (32 [issues]), and 'The Heart of

Cooper, James, Lever, Ainsworth, Miss Austen, and Grant were the most read." "The book in this class most sought after," however, "was Edgar Poe's [sic] '*Tales of Mystery and Imagination*' [1852]. There were two copies in the library, and, together, they were taken out 45 times in the course of a year." The Reverend Maynard concluded his remarks on this class of works in the Canterbury library by observing, "Novels with a sensational title ... were constantly asked for." Annette Marie Maillard's *Matrimonial Shipwrecks* (1818); Susan Ferrier's *Marriage* and *Destiny* (1824); Marguerite Gardiner's *The Lottery of Life* (1842); and John Lang's *Too Clever by Half* (1853) were among the works the chaplain cited in this regard.[85]

The limited success of schemes like the one at Canterbury eventually persuaded the army to pay closer attention to the recommendations of men such as Lieutenant-Colonel Gleig, the Assistant-Inspector of Army Schools for South Britain, who suggested that books of a garrison library could be divided up between the recreation rooms of the different regiments at a station. This measure, the Council of Military Education observed in 1866, "would bring the men face to face with works of utility and interest, and induce many a man to take a higher class of book than he would otherwise think of doing."[86] Arguments like this helped shape the evolution of the library, reading, and recreation room system that developed during the last four decades of the nineteenth century, but, so, too, did the dawning realization that facilities like these probably were always going to appeal most to "good" soldiers, and least to the men about whom the army was most concerned.[87] As John Edward Acland-Troyte put it in his recollection of his brief stint in the ranks, "[I]n an army like ours, there are and always will be some bad characters who will not be satisfied with the quiet employment of the library and recreation room. But after all, what soldiers really like, and I think quite naturally, is, after the restraint of the day's duty and discipline, to smarten themselves up, and looking their best, to get outside the barracks."[88] It was recognition of this fact that prompted the army to pay more attention to the physical accommodation of the libraries and reading rooms from the early 1860s,

Mid-Lothian,' (31 [issues]), were the favourites."

[85] "Notes on the Working of the Garrison Library ... at Canterbury," pp. 135–36.

[86] *Third Report by the Council of Military Education*, p. xxxi.

[87] Brereton also makes this point, and draws upon the memoir below in support. See *The British Soldier*, p. 71.

[88] Acland-Troyte, *Through the Ranks*, p. 63.

particularly as authorities became more aware at this period of the lengths to which the owners of public houses, music halls, and brothels were going in their determination to entice soldiers into their premises. Consideration of the measures that the army pursued in this regard sheds crucial light on both the reading experiences of soldiers and the way in which attitudes to the reading environment evolved in the last four decades of the nineteenth century, and so it is to these issues that we will turn in our next chapter.

CHAPTER 5

The Reading Environment, and Readers, in the Regular Army

In 1861, Sir Sidney Herbert, the Secretary of State for War, instructed a committee to enquire into every aspect of Her Majesty's libraries, reading, and day rooms, and to put forward recommendations in relation to possible improvements. The report that this committee produced revealed, firstly, there were by now three types of libraries in existence in the British army: garrison libraries, which issued books to officers, non-commissioned officers, and men upon payment of subscriptions; regimental libraries, which operated on the same lines but belonged to the different regiments; and the Victoria libraries at Aldershot and Dublin, which issued books to regiments without payment.[1] The latter libraries had been established by the queen, as their name suggests, utilizing books that had originally been sent out to troops in the Crimea; the estimation in which soldiers there held these volumes was reportedly demonstrated by the fact that "not more than two were missing" when they arrived back in England again.[2]

Although the existence of these several libraries obviously was a positive development, the evidence suggests that they offered soldiers who used them "few inducements to quiet reading" at this period. This was the case

---

[1] *Report of a Committee Appointed by the Secretary of State for War to inquire into and report on the present state and on the improvement of Libraries, Reading Rooms, and Day Rooms* (London: HMSO, 1862), p. 5. Hereafter *Report of a Committee.*

[2] Thomas Carter, *Curiosities of War and Military Studies: Anecdotal, Descriptive, and Statistical*, 2nd edn, illustrated (London: Groombridge and Sons, 1871), p. 224.

© The Editor(s) (if applicable) and The Author(s) 2016
S. Murphy, *The British Soldier and his Libraries, c. 1822–1901*,
DOI 10.1057/978-1-137-55083-5_5

because "the majority" were accommodated "in a barrack room, or in some place not originally used as a barrack room," and it was very "rare indeed" to find one housed in an apartment that was both separate from other buildings and which had been purpose-built. "Generally," indeed, "one room" actually fulfilled "the two-fold purpose of library and reading room and, in some cases [was also] used as a librarian's quarters, notwithstanding regulations to the contrary. ...These rooms being usually of the ordinary barrack size are very deficient in space, and can only accommodate a very limited number of readers. ...Not unfrequently the rooms are deficient in window space, and consequently not so light and cheerful, and not so well adapted for their object as they ought to be." Many of the libraries also served as games rooms, as there was no other space available for this purpose. This meant that those men "who really desire[d] to improve themselves by reading [were] disturbed by the noise of the players, by talking, and continual references to the non-commissioned officer in cases of dispute; a result which shows that one room is insufficient for the requirements of even the smallest barrack."[3]

The fact that so many libraries found themselves in such poor accommodation is hardly surprising, especially given the poor state of army barracks in general at this period. Some improvements had been made in the years immediately following the Crimean War, but the "sheer magnitude of the task, which involved over 250 barracks accommodating 97,832 men in 1860," meant that progress was both slow and limited. The cost implications alone meant that the army tended to put the issue on the back burner once the public's attention had shifted elsewhere, and so a sustained program of building and renovation was not undertaken until the late 1800s and early 1900s.[4] The inadequate nature of the library and reading room accommodation, moreover, was the result of a very particular circumstance, and this was that authorities appear to have been largely indifferent to the issue when the institutions were first being established. The 1844 *Queen's Regulations and Orders for the Army*, for instance, simply noted that "suitable apartments" had been "appropriated" in the various stations where the facilities had been set up, and also instructed that these were to be "fitted up with shelves and bookcases, and ... during the winter months, to be supplied with fuel and light." The greater concern of

[3] *Report of a Committee*, pp. 5–6.
[4] Edward M. Spiers, *The Late Victorian Army, 1868–1902* (Manchester: Manchester University Press, 1992), p. 140.

the orders, though, was with the physical preservation of the books, and their primary ambition obviously was to convince those responsible for the day-to-day operation of the libraries to do everything possible both to protect the works in their care and defray losses arising from reader usage. Thus it was directed that—

> The Library and its contents are to be placed under the charge of the Barrack-Master, who assisted by an Officer of the Troops, not under the rank of Captain, and accompanied by the Quarter-Masters of the different Corps in Garrison, is to make a minute Monthly Inspection of the Books, for the purpose of ascertaining the losses sustained, and damage done, either designedly, or through neglect, during the month immediately preceding, and of assessing the charges for the same; and a similar Inspection is to take place at every movement or interchange of Troops.

Officers unable to agree among themselves as to the "amount to be charged to the Troops" were ordered to refer the question to the Commanding Officer for a final decision. No charges were to be made "for damage arising from fair wear and tear," and those who carried out the inspections were to exercise "their discretion" when considering the amount of a charge to be laid against an individual soldier; specifically, whether "the loss of, or damage done to a Book" was "the result of accident and not of design." If the latter proved to be the case, the inspectors were to recover the "full amount of damage ... from the soldier committing it."

The 1844 orders also placed great emphasis on the librarian's role in the preservation of the works that were provided, intimating that this was something for which he was particularly responsible. "With proper care and attention of the Librarian and his Assistants," the orders therefore observed, "a general charge against the Subscribers, or against those of any particular Corps, ought rarely to be necessary." Pointedly, the librarian was initially to be "assisted by a Non-Commissioned Officer from each of the Corps in the Garrison, until he [became] well acquainted with the persons and character of all the Subscribers."[5] Even the order that directed the distribution of "*Bibles, Testaments, Books of Common Prayer*, and such Religious Tracts as may be approved for the use of the sick in hospitals" was more concerned with the physical preservation of the books than with the condition of the men who read them, and there is no sense that any

[5] *The Queen's Regulations and Orders for the Army*, 3rd edn (1844; London: HMSO, 1854), pp. 253–55.

thought was given to "where" these sick or invalided soldiers might find themselves. Commanding officers thus were to facilitate the provision of these types of reading material to the men, and ensure "that whatever Books [were] transmitted … [were] distributed in the most appropriate manner;—and that the greatest attention be given to their preservation, which may be consistent with the free circulation and use of them."[6] Private Clarke, who was hospitalized during maneuvers at Aldershot in the mid-1890s, left an account of his experience that suggests it must have been difficult either to preserve—or read—books in the conditions that he describes: "[W]e lay in large marquees in nice beds and I was't [sic] allowed to get up so I had 8 days good rest. … We have had rain every day and nearly every day rain came in[.] [We are] wet through with no where to dry our cloths [sic] and wet blankets to sleep."[7]

There is another point to be made about the orders that were promulgated in relation to the provision of reading material to hospitalized soldiers, however, and this is that they were clearly reflective of the fact that the army and its chaplains viewed such men as peculiarly suitable subjects for "improvement." "H," for example, visited the reading room at the Herbert Hospital in Woolwich in 1868, and was "somewhat astonished" to discover that the "majority" of books that the chaplain had selected for the sick soldiers "consisted of such works as Scott's 'Church History,' Nelson's 'Fasts and Feasts,' &c. &.c" [sic]. "I venture to say," he declared, "that such books are hardly fitted for soldiers under any circumstances, and I am quite certain that they are not proper books for a military hospital. A soldier in hospital is more or less depressed from the effects of sickness, and should be supplied with books of an interesting character."[8] We shall see below that other types reading material could and sometimes did reach hospitalized men, but one of John Butterworth's letters from late-nineteenth-century India suggests that this "improving" impulse did not diminish. "In the hospitals here," he wrote, "we don't get anything to read except Drill Books and our Bible."[9]

The army's initial failure to pay proper attention to the soldiers' reading environment was clearly the result of a number of factors, including what

---

[6] *Queen's Regulations and Orders*, p. 217. These orders were concerned with "Divine Service" rather than Barrack Libraries.

[7] Private P.P. Clarke to his mother, 14 September 1896, NAM 1992-08-445.

[8] *Pall Mall Gazette*, 8 August 1868.

[9] John Butterworth, letter to Polly, 25 September 1896, Mss Eur D900.

Gwyn Harries-Jenkins has described as the "divisiveness" of the "British Armed forces" during the Victorian period:

> The largest group—the Army—comprised the line regiments and cavalry formations which were administered by the War Office and the Horse Guards. The second major group was the Scientific Corps, that is the Royal Artillery and the Royal Engineers who were controlled by the Board of Ordnance. The third part was the civilian commissariat which, under Treasury control, was responsible for the provision of arms and supplies to forces in the field …[10]

In this context, it is hardly surprising that it was sometimes difficult to get *anything* organized within the British military, for its several parts were both hugely territorial and frequently in competition with each other. The other factor that affected the early development of the libraries and reading rooms, though, was a very particular one, and related to the sheer scale of what was actually being attempted. The army's initial efforts, for example, were devoted to the setting up of libraries and reading rooms at 31 locations, and the designated barracks were in places as far apart as Manchester and Malta, Dublin, the Cape of Good Hope, Novia Scotia, and Ceyon.[11] By the time of Lefroy's report in 1859, as we have seen, the initiative was well and truly established, and there were, now, "158 military libraries in 140 garrisons, exclusive of India." Again, the reality of what the army had accomplished is best illustrated by considering the range of places where the libraries now found themselves: they were by this time in places as far apart as Aberdeen and Auckland, Scarborough and Sydney, Manchester and Montreal.[12] The provision of libraries to such a wide range of locations obviously was going to present authorities with considerable challenges,

---

[10] Gwyn Harries-Jenkins, *The Army in Victorian Society* (Hull: University of Hull Press, 1993), p. 2. Harries-Jenkins also points out that the other part of the British military was, of course, the East India Company army, which became the Indian Army (after the Indian Rebellion of 1857).

[11] See T.A. Bowyer-Bower, "The Development of Educational Ideas and Curricula in the Army during the Eighteenth and Nineteenth Centuries," Thesis submitted to the University of Nottingham for the Degree of Master of Education, May, 1954, p. 72. Thirty locations are named, but a library and reading room was to be set up at both the Royal Barracks and Richmond Barracks in Dublin.

[12] J.H. Lefroy, Brevet Colonel, Royal Artillery, *Report on the Regimental and Garrison Schools of the Army, and on Military Libraries and Reading Rooms* (London: HMSO, 1859), pp. 52–53. As we saw in Chap. 4, Lefroy also gave details of "[r]egimental" libraries that had

including how best to preserve and circulate books in such a diverse range of conditions and climates. Major J.G. Boothby, for example, who was the Assistant Local Inspector of Army Schools in Malta, recommended in 1861 that "a stove be supplied to the library [in Ricasoli] ... as the room is so damp in the winter and rainy season that the books become mildewed. The room has no fireplace."[13] Henry Clayton's account of his time in Quebec, though, revealed that the provision of heating there was a matter of survival for the *men*: "It is very hot here in summer but extremely cold in winter[.][W]e dare not venture far without being well covered[.]. [W]e have fur caps[,] Boots that come over our knees and flannel Drawers and Guernseys[.][W]e have also fires night and day in our stoves so that our rooms are very warm[.][W]e burn wood[.]I have had several Narrow escapes from frost bite in my ears."[14]

It was no doubt an awareness of the different challenges that were involved in setting up the libraries that prompted authorities largely to avoid the finer points of the accommodation issue, and to concentrate instead upon getting the books to the soldiers. The fact that they adopted this approach, however, had two very predictable outcomes: it contributed to the sometimes chaotic nature of the early libraries, and caused tremendous frustration to some of the individuals who were charged with implementing the system on the ground. Captain L. Smyth O'Connor, for instance, reported in 1843 on the state of affairs in the Windward and Leeward Islands, observing that soldiers at St. Ann's could not access the books and other materials that had been provided for them because no suitable accommodation was available: "In enumerating the various buildings absolutely necessary at St. Ann's[,] I must not omit one for the library, for the non-commissioned officers and men. Books, periodicals, and maps have been received, and are ready for distribution, but as yet as yet it has not been possible to procure even a shed for a reading-room." Pointedly, Captain O'Connor also revealed that the officers at St. Ann's were faring little better than their men; these had established a garrison library for themselves as early as 1833, but it was "held on sufferance in an officer's quarter in the Stone Barracks; a confined and inconvenient make-

been set up for the Royal Artillery and Royal Engineers at stations both at home and abroad (pp. 55–56).

[13] "From Major Boothby, Local Inspector of Schools at Malta," 3 April 1861, Appendix II – No. 6 to *First Report by the Council of Military Education on Army Schools* (London: HMSO, 1862), p. 54.

[14] Henry Clayton, letter to his parents, 12 January [?] 1857, NAM 1996-11-53, 23.

shift for a reading room, and for which the regulated lodging-money has to be allowed to the individual, who would otherwise occupy it, when the barracks are full."[15]

Many of the libraries and reading rooms were in similar circumstances nearly 30 years later, and this prompted some commanding officers to be quite critical in the evidence that they gave to the various committees of enquiry that were established at this period. In response to the 1861 committee's question "Are they comfortable," for example, Colonel Norton in Limerick replied "Not so much as it ought to be"; Lieutenant-Colonel Allan of the 25th Regiment in Aldershot observed "As far as a hut will permit"; and Lieutenant-Colonel Russell of the 1st Battalion Rifle Brigade, also at Aldershot, simply answered "Certainly Not."[16] Some officers, such as Major Gamble, the Assistant Quarter-Master General at Shorncliffe, were pointed in their criticism of the army's miserly attitude when it came to matters such as heating and lighting, and suggested that it seriously detracted from the comfort—and reading experience—of soldiers. One of the "primary objects of importance to the welfare of a reading room," he remarked, was "a liberal allowance of fuel and light, and this without a liability to its being withdrawn or diminished suddenly on an early day in the year, which ... only [had] the effect of reducing the attraction and inflicting expense."[17] Colonel Cooper, of the 45th Regiment at Aldershot, for his part drew attention to the sometimes quixotic nature of the army's attitude to lighting; there were, he remarked, "10 candlesticks, but no candles issued," and "8 lamps would do."[18]

The army's growing interest in the physical condition of the libraries and reading rooms was the result of a number of (linked) factors, including the fact that several of those who were most interested in the institutions were hugely influenced by evolving notions of the importance of environment. As Felix Driver points out, mid-Victorian social scientists became increasingly convinced that the "critical problems" associated with the working classes—"pauperism, crime, ill-health, drunkenness, delinquency,

---

[15] "The Command in the Windward and Leeward Islands. By Captain L. Smyth O'Connor, 1st West India Regiment, Deputy Assistant Adjutant-General, West Indies," in *Colburn's United Service Magazine and Naval and Military Journal* (1843), Part II, pp. 95–96.

[16] "Table showing the principal Results contained in the Replies to Questions sent by the Committee to the undermentioned Stations," Appendix No. 3 to *Report of a Committee*, pp. 40, 34. Henceforth "Table (1862)."

[17] "Summary of Special Reports," Appendix No. 3 to *Report of a Committee*, p. 50.

[18] "Table (1862)," p. 34.

and degeneracy" —could be explained at least in part by the influence— both physical and moral—of the places and spaces where such individuals were housed and/or congregated. There were several consequences to this kind of thinking, including the fact that those who advocated institutional reform "saw institutional design as a mechanism in the production of reformed and healthy individuals."[19] Several of the most passionate advocates of the libraries, including Florence Nightingale, John Henry Lefroy, John Sutherland, and Douglas Galton, were firmly of this view, and worked hard to convince the army of the importance of the soldier's living and recreational environment. It was precisely in this context, for example, that Lefroy used his 1859 report to stress that a visit he had made to the Royal Barracks in Dublin two years previously had convinced him that any improvements made to libraries and reading rooms necessarily would have a regulatory effect upon the men. Upon first visiting the reading room at that barracks, he observed, he found it to be "entirely naked and deserted, its sole attraction the periodicals sent from the Stationery Office, and a few newspapers contributed by private individuals." The introduction of some furniture, games, and a wider selection of reading material had an immediate positive effect, and "during the ensuring winter the room was crowded, as many as sixty soldiers sometimes frequenting it in the course of the day, and … an average attendance of about twenty was secured even in the summer months." Significantly, according to Lefroy, most of the men who now used the reading room did so between six and nine in the evening, and "needless to add these are the hours at which it is most desirable to withdraw the young soldier from the temptations of the town."[20]

Lefroy also served on the 1861 committee, which similarly stressed that libraries and reading rooms could play a vital role in tempting soldiers away from what it described as "places of evil resort." In making this point, moreover, the committee made a crucial admission, and acknowledged that libraries and reading rooms faced a particular challenge when it came to trying to attract illiterate or barely literate soldiers: "It has been shown by experience that books alone are not sufficient to withdraw men from places of evil resort. A large proportion of the troops cannot read at all, many soldiers can read but imperfectly, and many more have little

[19] Felix Driver, "Moral Geographies: Social Science and the Urban Environment in Mid-Nineteenth Century England," *Transactions of the Institute of British Geographers*, New Series, Vol. 13, No. 3 (1988): pp. 277 and 282.

[20] Lefroy, *Report*, pp. 58–59.

relish for little amusement or instruction." This observation was an important one, for it was predicated upon the committee's conviction, firstly,
that the condition of the spaces in which the libraries and reading rooms
were housed hugely mattered to soldiers and, secondly, that this aspect of
the institutions had been previously overlooked. "The general appearance
of the room," they thus declared—

> its size, lighting, warming, and decoration, may be supposed to exercise
> some influence in bringing men to the library, or the reverse. This point,
> which is of more importance than might at first sight appear, has not hitherto
> been sufficiently considered. ... It must be remembered ... that the [reading]
> rooms have to compete not only with the canteen, but with public houses,
> dancing rooms, and other similar places outside barracks, which, from their
> being better lighted and warmed, and being of larger dimensions, prove
> much more attractive to the soldier than his uncomfortable reading room.[21]

Arguments like these were not new ones, but what was different was
that the committee was making them at a moment when a number of
other circumstances were combining to convince authorities of the need
to pay proper attention to the recreational environment of soldiers. In
late 1861, for example, Captain Pilkington Jackson visited Aldershot to
ascertain whether a Soldiers' Institute ought to be established there, and
subsequently produced a report that provided an alarming insight into
the activities of what one newspaper was to describe as the "vultures"
who preyed on the camp.[22] Aldershot, which was begun in 1854, had
been designed to be the "great new centre" for the army, but instead
quickly became symbolic of all of the ills that plagued it.[23] Around
1860, for instance, it was calculated that the nearby town "provided
one bar for every 34 of the average 13,350 men stationed there."[24]
Jackson commenced his enquiries by visiting "the various places to
which the men [were] generally in the habit of resorting for amusement
when off duty," and discovered that these consisted mainly of "can-

---

[21] *Report of a Committee*, p. 6.

[22] *London Standard*, 20 May 1864.

[23] H.J. Hanham, "Religion and Nationality in the Mid-Victorian Army," in M.R.D. Foot
(ed), *War and Society: Historical Essays in Honour and Memory of J.R. Western, 1928–1971*
(London: Paul Elek, 1973), p. 169.

[24] Kenneth Hendrickson, "Winning the Troops for Vital Religion: Female Evangelical
Missionaries to the British Army, 1857–1880," *Armed Forces and Society* 23, No. 4 (1997),
p. 617.

teens, public-houses, and beer houses, nearly all belonging to brewers."
The canteens, he remarked, were "the largest, most comfortable, and
cheerful huts in the camp," and many of the public houses had "large
halls attached, fitted up with great splendour." The proprietors and ten-
ants of these establishments, moreover, encouraged the presence of "gaily
dressed" prostitutes to tempt the men, and they also competed fiercely
with each other in terms of trying to make their premises attractive: "first,
in their appearance and comfort; secondly, in the varied character of the
entertainments; and thirdly, by an excitement of a highly demoralizing
and injurious tendency." Of the public houses and beer houses overall,
Jackson declared, "The most craftily devised plans are in full operation,
first to attract, and then to excite and gratify the sensuous passions of the
men." One result that "naturally" flowed from all of this, he gloomily
concluded, was that the "number of admissions to the hospital [in 1859]
for diseases incident to lust, at Aldershot, was in excess of the average of
all other stations in the United Kingdom."[25] Jackson's report came to the
attention of newspaper editors as well as the army, and so also reminded
the general public of the importance of providing soldiers with proper
facilities with which to fill their leisure hours. As *The Daily News* put it,
"The soldier must have virtuous comfort to save him from vicious luxury.
The thing must done; and it is for the people of England to see that it is
done. The Salvation of the Army is at stake; and the Salvation of the Army
may any day mean the Salvation of the Country." [26]

The rhetoric employed by the *Daily News* was clearly informed by
a determination to convince readers that the neglect of British soldiers
might have devastating consequences for Britain at some point in the
future, and this, of course, was a variation of the argument that soldiers
themselves frequently put forward: namely, that the great British public
thought of the condition of Britain's military only when their own lives or
interests were imperiled. The newspaper's observation, however, was also
reflective of a further influence that affected the army's changing attitude
to the accommodation of the libraries and reading rooms, and this was
that it had before it the example of evangelical missionaries who were
busily establishing "Soldiers' Homes" at this period. Charles Henry Kelly,

---

[25] "[Copies of] Captain Pilkington Jackson's Report to the Secretary of State for War, on
the Soldiers' Institutes at Aldershot and at Portsmouth" in *Army (Soldiers' Institutes), and
Army (Soldiers' Libraries, &c.)* (London: HMSO, 1862), p. 2.

[26] *The Daily News*, 3 May 1862.

a Wesleyan, set up the first of these at Chatham in 1861, and it functioned as "a little-club house in a basement, with a reading room, a chapel, and minimal sleeping quarters."[27] Louisa Daniell and Elise Sandes offered soldiers similar facilities in the homes that they established, as we have already observed, and explicitly celebrated the notion of the "home" as a peculiarly female space. Soldiers who visited the Sandes' homes, for example, were reportedly delighted to discover the "homely" touches with which the female volunteers decorated them, and one soldier supposedly asked a volunteer for permission to address her as "mother" despite the fact that she was several years younger than himself.[28] These two women were, with Kelly, pioneers in viewing soldiers as fit subjects for the efforts of Christian missionaries, but their examples were quickly followed by the Primitive Methodists, The Salvation Army, and the Church of England, among others.[29] Notwithstanding the several differences that existed between the homes or institutes that these respectively established, all were united by a common purpose: to facilitate the conversion of soldiers by tempting them into more "moral" social and recreational environments. Many of the men, it must be remarked, were hugely resentful of the proselytizing that they encountered when they visited such homes; as Horace Wyndham put it, "Should a fresh arrival enter the reading-room to have a look at the evening paper he will certainly be made welcome. He will also have a tract pressed upon him. The natural consequence is that he departs in wrath and straight way [sic] enters upon the broad path that leads to the nearest canteen." Other men, though, stayed, either because they were amenable to the efforts of the missionaries, or because, like Wyndham, they responded to them in a purely pragmatic fashion. "I must confess," he wrote,

> that I used to rather abuse the hospitality of 'Curragh Home' by surreptitiously taking a novel there and spending an hour or two in a comfortable armchair with my pipe. It was rather a nuisance certainly, until one got used to it, to hear in an adjoining room the strains of a wheezy harmonium, to the accompaniment of which a number of the chosen were lustily vociferating

---

[27] Hanham, "Religion and Nationality in the Mid-Victorian Army," p. 169.

[28] M. Helen Jeffrey, *The Trumpet Call Obey: The Story of the Homes for Servicemen founded a Century ago by Elise Sandes* (London: Marshall, Morgan, and Scott, 1968), pp. 62 and 50.

[29] Hanham, "Religion and Nationality in the Mid-Victorian Army," pp. 170–71.

their orthodoxy. My only excuse is that my barrack-room was so unpleasant at night and I had not yet become so inured to it as was the case later on.[30]

The army's efforts to improve the libraries and reading rooms in the last four decades of the nineteenth century must be situated against this backdrop, for it increasingly looked to them as a means of tempting soldiers in its own more masculine—and secular—recreational environments. In so doing, it hoped to lessen the men's tendency to look outside of their barracks for the purposes of relaxation and amusement, and to retain them in spaces that were explicitly designed to improve both morale and discipline. As such, the army's efforts in this regard were clearly reflective of what Miles Ogborn and Chris Philo have described as the "early expertise" that both the army and the navy developed "in the techniques and *spatial* practices of 'discipline' … They infiltrated the social worlds of their employees more deeply than did virtually any other nineteenth-century employer, and in the name of national morality and martial strength increasingly sought to extend control over all aspects of the lives of their officers and recruits" (my emphasis).[31] It was in this context, then, that the 1861 committee recommended that the garrison libraries be moved to the "centre" of the army's evolving "system of regimental Day, Reading, or Recreation rooms," and be used as the "source" from which supplies of books, newspapers, periodicals, and the "less portable sorts of games" would be supplied to the different regiments. The idea was that regimental reading, recreation, and day rooms together would function as a sort of soldiers' club, facilitating "the reception of books, … reading, writing, playing games, smoking, and refreshment." To add to the convivial atmosphere, it was recommended both that a "mixed committee of non-commissioned officers and men" be appointed to oversee the operation of the rooms, and that the soldiers who used them should enjoy "[a]bsence from restraint... as perfect as discipline and sense of propriety can admit. In dress, especially, the most perfect ease and comfort should be allowed, and everything should be made as much as possible to resem-

---

[30] Horace Wyndham, *The Queen's Service: Being the Experiences of a Private Soldier in the British Infantry at Home and Abroad* (London: William Heinemann, 1899), p. 85. Spiers and Alan Ramsay Skelley both remark that such homes were popular with soldiers, notwithstanding the proselytizing that they encountered there. See Spiers, *The Late Victorian Army*, p. 145, and Alan Ramsay Skelley, *The Victorian Army at Home: The Recruitment and Terms and Conditions of the British Regular, 1859–1899* (London: Croom Helm, 1977), pp. 61–64.

[31] Miles Ogborn and Chris Philo, "Soldiers, Sailors, and Moral Locations in Nineteenth-Century Portsmouth," *Area*, Vol. 26, Number 3 (September 1994), p. 221.

ble the freedom of a private club."[32] The model that was being advocated, in other words, was not very far removed from what some had
been calling for earlier in the century, and which was predicated upon an
explicitly masculine notion of socialization and conviviality. "We think it
would be an admirable arrangement," as one writer put it in 1848, "were
a comfortable apartment always to adjoin the library, in which the Soldier
might either digest quietly, or discuss with his comrade the contents of his
book or newspaper, over a red herring, or a cup of tea or coffee, a bit of
toasted cheese, or a glass of well-brewed beer."[33] The fact that the army
permitted the preparation and/or sale of refreshments in or adjacent to
rooms where reading was being carried on, incidentally, may be pointed to
as evidence of the differences that exist between nineteenth-century and
modern notions of book preservation.[34]

The relationship that developed between the garrison libraries and the
regimental libraries, reading, and recreation rooms was a close one, and to
some extent driven by an awareness of the preferences of soldiers. One of
the arguments that was often made about the garrison libraries and reading rooms, for example, was that they were not as popular with soldiers as
were their regimental counterparts; that men preferred to socialize within
their own regiments if they had a choice and were left to themselves. This
was something that was commented upon by the then Captain A.C. Gleig
in 1861, when he noted that the regimental rather than the garrison reading rooms were "much more in favour" with the men in his district. "From
all that I have seen and heard upon the subject," he declared,

> I am led to believe that a well-furnished reading-room of sufficient size for
> the barrack of a regiment has a great effect upon the *moral* [sic] of the men;
> and I think, considering the number of works in every garrison library which
> are now taken from the shelves, that it would be well to spend less money
> upon these establishments, and to make a small pecuniary grant to each
> regiment in aid of the funds of the reading-room.[35]

[32] *Report of a Committee*, pp. 7–8.

[33] Quotation from *Fraser's Magazine* in "Remarks on Certain Topics of the Day, By a Staff
Medical Officer," in *Colburn's United Service Magazine and Naval and Military Journal*
(1849), Part II, p. 80.

[34] Michael D. Calabria, "Florence Nightingale and the Libraries of the British Army," in
Libraries and Culture 29: 4 (Fall, 1994), p. 377.

[35] "Captain A.C. Gleig, Royal Artillery, Assistant Inspector of Army Schools in South
Britain, to the Secretary of the Council of Military Education," 22 May 1861, Appendix I –
No. 1 to *First Report by the Council of Military Education*, p. 3.

The recognition that many, if not most, soldiers preferred to fraternize within their own regiments helped shape the "complete system of libraries and recreation rooms" that developed in the army, and whose "general principle" was that, while libraries were "common to all the troops in a garrison, recreation rooms [were] regimental institutions, for the use of the men of each regiment separately."[36] The implementation of this model, though, was further informed by the recognition that it had the potential to broaden the reading tastes of soldiers, facilitating their introduction to works that would otherwise lie undisturbed on garrison libraries' shelves. As the by now Lieutenant-Colonel Gleig remarked in 1865: "The regimental subscribers have no means of knowing what books there are in the garrison library, and if they had, many of them would learn nothing of the character of a work merely from reading the title of it in a catalogue, who yet might be attracted by it, and find pleasure in reading it, if they had the opportunity of examining it in their regimental reading rooms."[37] It was as a result of all of these factors that garrison libraries were turned into "central depot[s]" for books by the mid-1860s; their function was to receive and store the works; facilitate their circulation among the reading and/or recreation rooms of the various regiments; and gather them back safely again when they were no longer required. Only in one very particular instance was a garrison library henceforth supposed to serve as a site of reading, and this was when soldiers wished to consult books of reference that could not be "circulated generally" among the men.[38]

Such a transformation, however, could not be accomplished overnight, and so more immediate measures were advocated and, in some cases, adopted, in the interests of improving the reading and recreational experiences of soldiers. The 1861 committee, for instance, recommended that the furniture provided for the libraries and reading rooms could not be "too unlike anything that the men can associate with a barrack room," and advocated the use of fireplaces instead of stoves to heat the rooms: "Stoves are much disliked by the men as

---

[36] *Second Report by the Council of Military Education on Army Schools, Libraries, and Recreation Rooms* (London: HMSO, 1865), p. xxxiv.

[37] *Third Report by the Council of Military Education on Army Schools, Libraries, and Recreation Rooms* (London: HMSO, 1866), p. xxxii.

[38] "Reprint of the Regulations for Garrison Libraries and Regimental Recreation Rooms," in Appendix XV – No. 1 to *Second Report by the Council of Military Education*, pp. 216–17.

affording warmth only, and not adding to the cheerful aspect of the room."[39] The committee's advocacy of fireplaces over stoves, though, was predicated upon a number of considerations, including their recognition of the significance that the open hearth had come to occupy in the British imagination by this period. As Leonore Davidoff and Catherine Hall observe, "the availability of cheap coal, combined with the imagery of the open fire and hearth, meant that the continental style 'close' stove was never popular. Ruskin was only one of the powerful coterie who saw the domestic hearth as the apogee of the domestic temple, the image which easily overrode arguments for efficiency in use of fuel or labour."[40] In part, the committee's preference for this form of heating obviously was the product of such sentiments and, as such, demonstrates once again the extent to which notions of "home" informed the (competing) models of socialization that dominated the British army until the First World War.

A further point must be made about the committee's preference for fireplaces over stoves, however, and this was that it was also reflective of their appreciation of the importance that was attached to the hearth as a communal reading space. "As a rule," they thus observed, "the grates should be large, and with a considerable frontage of fire, round which men can congregate, while one of them tells a story or reads aloud."[41] This image of soldiers gathered around cozy firesides is an important one, for it invites us to consider more closely how soldiers' reading was affected by the peculiarly communal nature of barrack life. One of the most obvious consequences of life in barracks, for instance, was negative: it meant that soldiers were frequently in competition with each other for the sometimes quite limited resources that the army provided. This was one of the reasons why soldiers often stressed in their letters home how little they had to read, and pleaded with relatives and friends to send them reading material. As Private Clarke put it in a letter from the 1890s, "tell Berty I have not received the book he said he would send me yet ... I shall be very pleased when I receive it as I can't get much to read here."[42] Some soldiers

[39] *Report of a Committee*, pp. 8–9.

[40] Leonore Davidoff and Catherine Hall, *Family Fortunes: Men and Women of the English Middle Class, 1780–1850* (London: Routledge, 1987), p. 380.

[41] *Report of a Committee*, p. 8.

[42] Private P.P. Clarke, Letter to his mother and siblings, not dated [1896?], NAM 1992-08-445.

were quite pointed in the letters that they sent home, and suggested that a shortage of reading was an inevitable aspect of army life. Writing from India in 1896, for instance, John Butterworth acknowledged that he had access to a library and reading room, but also remarked that he had to join in the general "struggle" to catch sight of "the weekly papers sent from England, which of course are always a month behind." More than this, he observed that there were always far more readers than there were books available, and emphasized that rank intruded into even this aspect of army life: "[T]he books in the library about 600 vols. [sic] are always out, there being 120 men in the battalion, and the sergeants always collar 4 or 5 to read before they come back. Rank is everything in the Army."[43] Horace Wyndham's recollection of a stint that he spent in hospital suggests that Butterworth was not alone in his sentiments, and that rank affected soldiers even in their hospital beds: "A generous supply of literature was despatched to the hospital every day from all the barracks in the command. As, however, it filtered through the hands of the orderlies first, the patients did not come off very well. The Sergeant-Major, too, appeared to think that a magazine less than a month old had a bad effect on us, and took care that we never saw one."[44]

Significantly, Butterworth not only appealed to his relatives to send him reading material, but also intimated that whatever he received would do the rounds: "We don't get much reading, but when a fellow gets some good poetry or reading matter, it is handed around among the reading set—for do you know even among the Rifles there are some."[45] Other soldiers' memoirs and letters reveal that Butterworth was not alone in sharing reading material with his comrades, and suggest that this was common practice among men who were used to pooling their resources. Private Ware, for instance, wrote to his parents from India to express his gratitude for some newspapers they had sent to him and his brother, and also stressed that they sent whatever they received back-and-forth between them at their different stations: "When I get a paper I send it down to Jack and when he gets one he sends it up here."[46] Henry Clayton for his part wrote to his mother from his barracks in Athlone in 1851, remarking, "What pleasure the receipt of your papers gave me and all my Comrades

---

[43] Corporal John Butterworth, Letter from July 1896, Mss Eur D900, 6.
[44] Horace Wyndham, *Following the Drum* (London: Andrew Melrose, 1912), p. 199.
[45] Corporal John Butterworth, Letter to his father, 28 July 1896, Mss Eur D900.
[46] Private W. Ware, Letter to his mother and father, 25 May 1895, NAM 2001-09-77.

I cannot tell."[47] Before we move on here, it should be pointed out that one letter, from a Private Joseph Reid, offers an intriguing possibility: namely, that some soldiers may have used their libraries to supply reading material *to* their relatives. Writing to his mother, brother, and sisters from Portsmouth in 1853, he observed, "I also received a newspaper which I am fond of and as soon as our Library arrives from Canterbury I shall send you some."[48] Reid's meaning, of course, is not entirely clear; he might simply have meant that he would send on the newspapers with which he was finished once he had something else to read himself.

There were, of course, positive aspects to barrack life as well, including the fact that it promoted a very social mode of living amongst soldiers and accustomed them to the fact that their resources would be shared. This meant that reading was, for many men, a communal activity rather than a private practice, and they were used to reading—or listening to the reading aloud of—a book or a newspaper together. We have already seen evidence of this in our previous chapters; most vividly, perhaps, in William Douglas' description of soldiers in a regimental library in India avidly listening to the reading aloud of newspaper accounts of events that were unfolding in the Crimea.[49] The fact that soldiers shared their reading material in this way had a number of consequences, including the fact that it played into the hands of those individuals who pleaded with authorities to provide the men with more and better resources. A piece that appeared in *The United Service Journal and Naval and Military Magazine* in 1842, for example, obviously wanted to impress two linked points upon its readers: that the books provided to soldiers' libraries could entertain several men at once and, thereby, improve several men simultaneously: "[M]any a barrack-room have we seen filled with attentive listeners to the reader of an amusing and instructive book, who, previous to the formation of the library, passed their long, tedious winter evenings in a public house for want of better employment."[50] Arguments like this were important, especially to an army that was increasingly concerned about the literacy of its troops.

---

[47] Henry Clayton, Letter to his mother, 3 June 1851, NAM 1996-11-53, 4.

[48] Joseph Reid, Letter to his mother, brothers, and sisters, 11 August 1853, NAM 1999-03-130, 13.

[49] See page 85.

[50] *The United Services Journal and Naval and Military Magazine* (1842), Part II, p. 169.

Probably the most important point that must be made about the communal nature of soldiers' reading, however, is demonstrated by a recollection of James Hawker, who enlisted in the militia in 1852 and, two years later, was sent to Dublin with the Northamptonshire regiment. In the memoirs that he penned in the early 1900s, Hawker reminisced about the time that he spent on garrison duty in the Irish capital, and conjured up a particularly colorful scene of military life. "One evening," he recalled,

> October 25—after reading the Charge of the Light Brigade, I was playing my concertina and the Men were Dancing when Captain Vivian came to the door.
> "Corporal Hawker," he shouted, 'where did you Get that Thing?'
> "I bought it, Sir," I told him.
> "Surely not out of your pay?" he said.
> "Yes, sir," I replied. "I bought it to keep the men out of the Canteen. It cost me ten shillings."
> He put five shillings in my Hand, a reward for setting the Men a Good Example.[51]

Hawker's recollection of this scene is hugely important, and invites us in the first instance to speculate to what extent it may have been shaped by him to facilitate both the expectations and sensibilities of his (notional) audience. Significantly, for instance, Hawker preceded his description of this scene with the observation that he made the "most" of his time in Dublin "by not drinking," thereby setting up a complex frame of reference wherein he simultaneously engaged with and challenged the stereotypical view of the drunken soldier. Like Captain Vivian, we may assume, most of Hawker's upper-class contemporaries would have been both surprised and delighted by the efforts that this lower-class man made to improve his comrades, and similarly have believed that such noble intentions should be rewarded.

[51] James Hawker, *James Hawker's Journal: A Victorian Poacher*, edited by Garth Christian (London: Oxford University Press, 1961), pp. 5–6. Hawker's military career was as colorful as was his life as a poacher, and included a later spell in the Leicestershire militia and in the Regular Army (from which he deserted). He wrote his memoirs, "seemingly in several versions," between 1904 and 1905, and these were edited by Christian for publication by Oxford University Press. See Robin P. Jenkins, "Hawker, James (1836–1921)," *Oxford Dictionary of National Biography*, Oxford University Press, 2004 [http://www.oxforddnb.com.remote.library.dcu.ie/view/article/74229, accessed 20 April 2015].

Hawker's recollection, however, is significant for a further reason: it throws into sharper relief the complex role that reading played in the social lives of soldiers. What Hawker's account of this scene demonstrates is that men like him did not privilege reading over any other activity; that they instead folded it into the variety of other diversions with which they tried to entertain and, sometimes, improve themselves. Hawker's rendering of this scene is therefore on the one hand a highly charged one, for it appears to describe a soldier who inspired himself and, possibly, his comrades, by reading Tennyson's celebrated poem on the anniversary of the Battle of Balaclava. On the other hand, though, his description of this moment in barrack life is curiously ambiguous; he is not explicit, for example, as to whether he read Tennyson's verses to himself or aloud to the men; he is not clear as to whether it directly inspired either the concertina playing or dancing that followed the reading of the poem. What his recollection does reveal, though, is that soldiers like him frequently read in a communal atmosphere, and in the midst of all of the other recreational activities with which they tried to divert themselves and each other. To put all of this another way, Hawker's recollection underlines the fact that for some men reading was but one of several ways through which they sought both to relax and deepen bonds with comrades; that it was only one part of the recreational life of the soldier.

The army's recognition of this fact obviously informed its decision to cultivate a close relationship between the garrison and regimental libraries and recreation rooms, and scenes such as the one that Acland-Troyte described below were probably replicated in many barracks:

The library [in Anglesea barracks in Portsmouth] is a good-sized room, where any could go, by subscribing a very small sum (about 4d a month) and see most of the London daily papers, various magazines, etc., and make use of the books kept there; or, if preferred, take away a volume to the barrack-room. ... The recreation room was adjoining the library. Here all sorts of games were provided draughts, chess, backgammon, cards, and two or three bagatelle tables. Of course, smoking is allowed, and usually coffee can be bought from the man in charge of the room, who also sometimes makes, for the satisfaction of the drummer-boys "plum-duff" or other luxury.[52]

---

[52] Anon. [John Edward Acland-Troyte], *Through the Ranks to a Commission* (London: Macmillan & Co., 1881), pp. 62–63.

Acland-Troyte's recollection of this scene from the 1870s both underlines the range of recreational activities with which soldiers sought to entertain themselves, individually and collectively, and also conjures up the image of men—and boys—united in their determination to make the very best of the circumstances in which they were placed. This compulsion also makes itself felt in Sergeant Greening's account of his time in late-nineteenth-century India, where he describes how he and his comrades tried to pass their time during the heat of the summer: "The soldiers while away the weary and long hot hours by knitting or reading and after 5 in the evening all make for the roads round the barracks and indulge in a good walk after the hot confinement of the day."[53] Soldiers' fondness for knitting, by the way, was also attested to by Private Ware, who both devoted considerable effort to producing four pairs of socks as a gift for his brother back home in England *and* revealed that the pastime was a great favorite with many of the men in his regiment: "There are about 1/3 of our Regt. [sic] that can knit and I can tell you anyone can learn a lot of fancy ways if he likes to put himself about it, I can knit about six different ways already."[54]

Libraries and reading rooms in India, it must be remarked, were viewed as something of a special case by the army, largely because it recognized that regimental libraries already were "common in regiments serving in the East."[55] Notwithstanding this fact, official reports began to carry some information on the system that was operational in India, suggesting that both regimental and garrison libraries were available to the men. Lieutenant-Colonel W.B. Laurie, who was the Superintendent of Army Schools in the Madras Presidency, for instance, used his report of May 1868 to stress that reading soldiers were particularly well served in the subcontinent. "All the regiments," he wrote,

> and nearly all the batteries of artillery that I have inspected in the Madras army, as well as depots, have their libraries, the accommodation for such varying according to circumstances. ... The officers I have generally found most liberal in affording aid to soldiers' libraries, if not by subscription, by means of books and periodicals, when no longer required. I have before recommended a more frequent change in the books of garrison libraries. Pensioners in particular feel this want in an age remarkable for its continual changes.

[53] Diary of W. Greening, 90th Regiment, Scottish Rifles, NAM 1983-07-121, p. 15a.
[54] Private W. Ware, Letter to his father and mother, 25 May 1895, NAM 2001-09-77.
[55] *Second Report by the Council of Military Education*, p. xxxvi.

Laurie also suggested that reading and recreation rooms were "very attractive in India, and may either be found in the same room as the library, or separate, which is by far the best, and is the most general plan."[56] Major H.L. Grove, however, succeeded Laurie in his post as superintendent, and was much more critical of the facilities that were available to the men. "For the recreation, library, and reading room" of the Artillery at Fort St. George, he thus observed, "a part of the bomb-proof ramparts is matted off, and all the light and air it receives is admitted through two low portals. The place is excessively hot, ill ventilated, and dark by day; and by night, I was told, the lights were found to be insufficient for the requirements of the few men who used the room. There were no games and refreshments."[57] Grove was even more pointed in his report for 1869: "All these institutions in India are I believe, in respect of comfort, &c., below those of England." He expressed the hope, though, that as the institutions became "self-supporting, which it is the wish of the commander-in-chief [sic] they should be, all improvements still wanting will be supplied from the regimental funds."[58]

The different conditions that readers continued to experience well into the nineteenth century illustrate another point about the rules and regulations that the army laid down in relation to the libraries and reading rooms, and this was that many of them were more often honored in the breach than in the observance. Acland-Troyte's description of the library in Portsmouth in the 1870s, for instance, reveals that some libraries continued to function as sites of reading despite orders to the contrary, and even the army's own reports acknowledged that many libraries, reading, and recreation rooms continued to find themselves in places that were unsuitable and/or unattractive. The 1865 report that proudly proclaimed the "general operation" of the "complete system," for instance, simultaneously acknowledged recreation rooms were still "confined to such spare barrack-rooms and huts as [could] be made available for the

---

[56] "Lieutenant-Colonel W.B. Laurie, Superintendent Amy Schools, Madras Presidency, to the Secretary to the Council of Military Education," 08 May 1868, Appendix II – No. 13 to *Fifth Report by the Council of Military Education on Army Schools, Libraries, and Recreation Rooms* (London: HMSO, 1868), p. 69.

[57] "Report for Major Grove for 1868," Appendix II – No. 14 to *Sixth Report by the Council of Military Education on Army Schools, Libraries, and Recreation Rooms* (London: HMSO, 1870), p. 107.

[58] "Report by Major Grove for 1869," Appendix II - No. 15 to *Sixth Report by the Council of Military Education*, p. 114.

purpose ... Many corps have only one recreation room; some have no place for reading and amusements beyond the garrison library, and at a few stations the library room is sufficiently large for the accommodation of the books only." This same report, however, confidently looked forward to the day when the army's ambitious plans would be carried to fruition, and "each regiment [would] possess a building 30 ft long and 33 ft broad, containing two commodious rooms for reading and games, as well as a bar for refreshments."[59]

The army did not commit itself to a sustained program of barrack building and renovation until the last decade of the nineteenth century, as we have already noted, and so this meant that some officers pursued various strategies in the intervening years in an attempt to improve soldiers' reading and recreational facilities at a local level. Colonel Maude, for example, proposed in both 1864 and 1865 that the two garrison libraries for the Infantry at Gibraltar should be amalgamated, observing that this would both enable the purchase of more books and also save on the expense of one of the librarian's posts. Maude's further point, though, was that the plan could not be carried out as things then stood because of the want of suitable accommodation, and suggested that the army sanction the building of a "library room, somewhere near the barrack-master's quarters, the present library rooms being both too small for the purpose." Maude also emphasized that the actual reading of the books presented the men with considerable difficulties because each of the Infantry regiments had only been able to establish a reading or recreation room for themselves "by temporarily appropriating a barrack or school room for this purpose." These were "well attended and worked well," he admitted, but the provision of "good sized recreation rooms ... would tend very much to increase their popularity."[60] The fact that Maude's pleas fell on deaf ears is demonstrated, firstly, by the fact that he was still trying to advance his plan in 1866 and, secondly, by the fact that his successor used his report of 1868 to point out he did not concur with the measures that had previously been proposed. "I am still of opinion," Colonel Smith stoutly declared, "that two garrison libraries are required in this garrison"; he did admit,

---

[59] *Second Report by the Council of Military Education*, p. xxxvi.

[60] "Annual Report on the Army Schools at Gibraltar, by Col. F.F. Maude, V.C. and C.B.," Appendix III—No. 4 to *Third Report by the Council of Military Education*, p. 18.

though, that "[t]he accommodation generally in the garrison [was] very indifferent for recreation rooms."[61]

Despite the fact that some libraries and reading rooms continued to find themselves in conditions that were far from ideal, they clearly assumed tremendous significance in the lives of both individual men and regiments. Many soldiers, for instance, obviously became hugely attached to their libraries and reading rooms on a personal level and reflected this in their memoirs and letters. John Pindar, we have seen, emphasized that librar- ies were crucial to soldiers in educational terms, but he also stressed that they were very significant recreational and social spaces. The Curragh in Ireland, he thus remarked, was "a good place to Soldier in during the summer, but ... extremely dull in the winter season. There is no gas in the camp, and candle affords but a poor light in the long winter evenings." Luckily, however, all of the regiments at the camp were "supplied with a good library and recreation room, which is a great boon to those who love to frequent such places."[62] Sergeant Greening, we saw above, painted a poignant picture in his letters of soldiers reading and knitting in the eve- nings on stations in India, but he also encoded therein his sense of the tre- mendous importance of the libraries and reading rooms to the social life of soldiers on the subcontinent. Describing Deolali, "the great central depot [sic] of India," for instance, he observed, "There are hundreds of tents and rows of great bungalows all full of soldiers, a great canteen where old friends and new faces meet to talk over their beer of doings past and to come. There is a beautiful library, reading and recreation room [and] also a good grocery and coffee bar, surrounded by a large garden prettily laid out where soldiers sit of an evening after the heat of the day is over." The barracks at Bareilly, he declared, were "large and comfortable, the library and recreation room being one of the finest in India."[63]

Soldiers' responses to the libraries that were provided for them were as varied as they were personal, and sometimes appear to have had little to do with the books that were on the shelves. One Sergeant Holmes, for instance, who had been a soldier for some 24 years before he came to the notice of the *Aldershot Military Gazette*, established and carefully tended

[61] "Annual Report on the Army Schools at Gibraltar, by Colonel Smith," Appendix II – No. 8 to *Fifth Report by the Council of Military Education*, pp. 48–49.

[62] John Pindar, *Autobiography of a Private Soldier* (Cupar-Fife: Printed in the "Fife News" Office, 1878), p. 87.

[63] Diary of W. Greening, 90th Regiment, Scottish Rifles, NAM 1983-07-121, pp. 10b–11 and 14b.

a garden in the midst of his other duties as a soldier and librarian: "It is, we believe, the only instance in which a yard or so of ground all round the buildings which serve the threefold purpose of library, gamesrooms, and reading rooms, has been enclosed. ... [T]he effect of vegetation in a spot where it is probable that not one in a hundred would expect to find it, is very pleasing to the eye."[64] Not all soldiers, however, appreciated the libraries that were provided for them, and some failed to recognize the importance that they had assumed for the men. In July of 1872, for example, *Freeman's Journal* reported that James Tooth, a private soldier at the Marine Barracks in Chatham, had "cut the throat of a drummer boy, named George Stook, in the privates' library"[65] and, in 1875, the *Chelmsford Chronicle* gave an account of an "Impudent Robbery by a Soldier." This latter case involved a Thomas Redmond, aged 20, who was charged with stealing "a time-piece from the Garrison Library, Royal Artillery Barracks, in the month of September. Prisoner took the time-piece in broad daylight, and was seen with it at a public house." Significantly, Redmond was caught when he was later being held in the guard room for a military offense: "He bragged about the robbery to some fellow prisoners, and the matter coming to the knowledge of the authorities, he was apprehended."[66] Implicit here, clearly, is recognition of the fact that some of the men objected to their comrade's actions, and decided to report what he had done.

Some libraries fulfilled several functions for soldiers and their regiments, some of which were practical and others again symbolic. The garrison library in Gibraltar, for example, served both as the space to which honored visitors were welcomed, and also preserved the book wherein those visits were carefully recorded. It was in this context, for example, that a piece in *Freeman's Journal* for April 21, 1876 commented upon a visit by the Prince of Wales to Gibraltar, and noted that he "visited the garrison library, where he inscribed his name in the visitors' book, as he did 17 years" before.[67] The fact that other artifacts of varying importance may have found their way into some libraries is suggested by another newspaper piece upon Gibraltar: the *Portsmouth Evening News* not only noted the death of "Fergusson, the largest monkey on the Rock" in late 1891, for instance, but also observed that the library held the skull of his pre-

[64] *Aldershot Military Gazette*, 17 February 1866.
[65] *Freeman's Journal*, 2 July 1872.
[66] *Chelmsford Chronicle*, 5 November 1875.
[67] *Freeman's Journal*, 21 April 1876.

decessor.[68] The absence of "an English Club" in Gibraltar was pointed to in another newspaper piece that same year, which also declared there was no "real necessity" for one. This was in the first case true because the "English element" on the rock was "almost all military," and most of their wants were catered for by the messes. For a "general meeting place," the writer continued, "there is the Garrison Library. This is a handsome building, containing two general reading-rooms, one reserved for the sterner sex, and one reserved for ladies; also billiard and smoking rooms."[69]

This library, it must be pointed out, was recognized as being an exceptionally fine affair, and most rank-and-file soldiers would not have enjoyed such facilities at this period. Horace Wyndham, indeed, stressed as much in his late-nineteenth-century memoir, where he intimated that the ability of soldiers to access facilities such as libraries or reading rooms depended largely upon where they were serving. Soldiers at home stations fared better than their overseas comrades, he seems to suggest, as there was in "all barracks" a room set apart for use as a library and recreation room:

> Here the men may come and read the newspapers and magazines, a plentiful supply of which is maintained. They can also write letters here, and profitably employ their leisure over the delights of draughts, backgammon, dominoes, and other exciting pastimes. Cards are allowed, but no gambling is permitted. Books may be borrowed from the regimental library and retained for a week at a time.[70]

Soldiers stationed overseas were far less fortunate, according to Wyndham, because the army appeared to adopt an "out-of-sight-out-of-mind" attitude to colonial troops. "One of the greatest of the many great wants in Cape town, from a military point of view," he thus declared, "was that there existed no place in town where a man could spend his leisure profitable [sic] and pleasantly." There was, he noted, "no Soldiers' Club, or Garrison Recreation-room, as there [was] in almost every other military station," and the Soldiers' Home at the Cape was housed in a "dingy barn-like building" whose outer walls "were painted [with] aggressive remarks about the future state of those who did not subscribe to their tenets.'" Having visited this home on one occasion to test "its hospitality," he came away convinced that—

[68] *Portsmouth Evening News*, 8 September 1891.
[69] *The Graphic*, 30 May 1891.
[70] Wyndham, *Queen's Service*, pp. 103–4.

The Salvation Army principles on which it was conducted [were] singularly unlikely to wean men from the rival attractions of the public-house and Canteen. Before I had been in the reading–room for five minutes I was anxiously asked "if I was saved," and on expressing with becoming diffidence my doubts as to whether either I or my questioner was fully qualified to give an authoritative opinion upon the matter, I was evidently regarded as a degraded being capable of almost any infamy imaginable.[71]

Wyndham was quite pointed in his criticism of the army's treatment of colonial soldiers, and stressed in general "the pressing need of the provision of rational recreation for the leisure hours of the rank-and-file." The men stationed in Malta were so poorly served in this regard, he emphasized, that they decided to establish a club for themselves as an alternative to "the low-class public houses with which [the island was] so liberally provided." This club, he observed, was an "excellent" one, "modelled apparently after the style of the Garrison Recreation-rooms in Gibraltar, and was a great boon to the troops serving there … A Canteen … a large concert hall[,] … billiard and reading rooms, with others for suppers, baths, and beds, were included in the premises." The army was not alone in its indifferent attitude to colonial troops, he further declared: "While well-meaning faddists in England are expending their energies in providing the troops with 'Soldiers' Homes,' and 'Associations for the supply of Pure Literature,' their brothers abroad, in tropical climates, and surrounded by every temptation, are in danger of being forgotten."[72]

Wyndham's analysis of the state of the state of the army's recreational facilities in the last decade of the nineteenth century is worth noting, because it suggests there were negative as well as positive outcomes to the proliferation of regimental libraries, reading, and recreation rooms in the late-Victorian period. In part, these were no doubt to do with issues of scale: it was no easy matter, after all, to facilitate the provision of such facilities to places that were scattered across the face of the globe, and the maintenance of them where there were few subscribers presented particular challenges. In relation to the latter point, for instance, it was noted as early as 1868 that some of the "very small libraries" were already facing "extinction" because "the subscriptions [were] insufficient to cover

---

[71] Wyndham, *Queen's Service*, pp. 140 and 142.
[72] Wyndham, *Queen's Service*, pp. 197–98 and 140.

the cost of repairs and renewals."[73] Some of the problems that emerged, though, were to do with the way in which the evolving system was managed, and the dangers that were necessarily attendant upon releasing garrison library books into regimental facilities that were overseen at a local level. The army itself quickly realized this, as the Council of Military Education stressed that "unless a more attentive supervision [of the garrison libraries] is exercised by the quarterly and other boards, the libraries will in the end be frittered away."[74] Ongoing concerns like these eventually prompted the army to put in place regulations that required regiments to make good any losses, and it at different times tried to make up for shortfalls in individual libraries by making special grants of books or funds.[75]

By the end of the nineteenth century, then, the British army had been providing libraries for rank-and-file soldiers for just over 60 years and, according to some of their most enthusiastic advocates, they had made a material contribution to both the literacy *and* discipline of the troops. As one commanding officer put it in 1869,"I cannot express myself too strongly in favour of all that gives relaxation to the soldier within his barrack, and tends to make it a respectable and comfortable home. The number of men who pass their evenings in the recreation rooms, or in reading a book in their barracks, instead of in public houses, increases steadily, and is a source of much gratification."[76] The observations of this officer appear to be borne out by the army's figures, which reveal that the circulation of books increased during the years for which details are available. The Council of Military Education's third report of 1866, for instance, drew upon quarterly reports to conclude that garrison, artillery, and engineer libraries held 196,511 volumes for the year ending 31 March, 1865, of which the "circulation among the men, during the year, [had] been 462,503 volumes."[77] The 1870 report noted that garrison libraries held 223,345 volumes on

[73] *Fifth Report by the Council of Military Education*, p. xxxii.

[74] The Council's sentiments were reported in "W. Paulet, Adjutant-General, Letter of 30 December 1865," in Appendix X – No. 2, to *Fourth Report by the Council of Military Education on Army Schools, Libraries, and Recreation Rooms* (London: HMSO, 1866), p. 118.

[75] See, for example, *Third Report by the Director General of Military Education on Army Schools and Libraries* (London: HMSO, 1877), p. xxiv.

[76] *Sixth Report by the Council of Military Education on Army Schools, Libraries, and Recreation Rooms* (London: HMSO, 1870), p. xxvii. This was the final report of this committee, as the Director-General of Military Education produced subsequent reports.

[77] *Third Report by the Council of Military Education*, p. xxx. These figures did not include India, as libraries there did not provide returns.

31 December, 1869, observing that the number in circulation on March 31ˢᵗ of that year "was 514,461 against 373, 895 in [the] preceding year." While these figures taken together demonstrate that the circulation of books among soldiers could go down as well as up, the overwhelming conviction of the writers of the 1870 report was that "There [was] no doubt that the benefit to be derived from the libraries [was] constantly becoming more widely appreciated by the troops."[78] This sentiment was echoed by E.H.F. Pocklington, the Director General of Military Education, in 1877, who calculated that "573,683 volumes were circulated in 1874, 603,780 in 1875, and 600,740 in 1876." These figures, which include both garrison and some regimental libraries, prompted Pocklington to remark: "Looking at the large and increasing number of books issued to the non-commissioned officers and men at the various stations, it may fairly be inferred that these libraries continue to be attractive and appreciated by the troops."[79]

It is, however, important to exercise caution when considering the praise that authorities tended to heap upon the libraries and reading rooms, and to remember that many of these individuals had a stake in stressing the beneficial effects of the institutions. In the first place, figures relating to reader usage and circulation reveal only part of the story, and give no indication of what actually happened to a book once it was taken back to barracks. As Alan Ramsay Skelley points out, "men were encouraged to read but Grenville Murray recalled of his military service that only 20 % of the rank and file at the most ever used the regimental library and that many borrowed books intending to read them but never actually did so."[80] Similarly, the claims that were made in relation to the effects of the libraries and reading rooms upon the men's behavior or attitudes were not always borne out by other statistics. After 1868, for instance, the army's ongoing concern about drunkenness among soldiers prompted it to empower officers to inflict fines for this offense, and statistics reveal that 16.1 % of the men were punished in this regard the following year. The figure, though, rose significantly to 28.1 % in 1872, before falling to 12.1 % in 1898.[81] These figures, although they themselves have to be treated with caution, demonstrate that the army's provision of facilities such as libraries to soldiers did not inevitably result in more sober men. Indeed, William Elliot

[78] *Sixth Report by the Council of Military Education*, p. xxv.
[79] *Third Report by the Director General*, pp. xxiv–xxv.
[80] Skelley, *The Victorian Army at Home*, p. 97.
[81] Skelley, *The Victorian Army at Home*, pp. 128 and 130.

Cairnes, who was a serving officer and wrote extensively on military matters, expressed his view of the supposed sobriety of soldiers by this period in the following terms: "[A]ll I can say is, … if it is seriously intended to argue that drunkenness is a thing now unknown in the army, all I can reply is 'Rats,' which may be vulgar, but is certainly expressive."[82] Similarly, Elise Sandes' experience when she was taken by a companion on a tour of the places frequented by soldiers in late-nineteenth-century Dublin appears to suggest that some men were beyond the influence of the libraries and reading rooms that had been established for the garrison: "Between 8 and 11 p.m. they went from music halls to dancing rooms to public houses and then lower still. … 'Hundreds of soldiers,' said her companion solemnly, 'every year are ruined and destroyed in Dublin, body and soul.'"[83]

There is a further point that must be borne in mind when considering the possible effects of the libraries, and the reading and recreation rooms, and this is that the army itself felt compelled from 1889 onwards to revise downwards its estimation of the literacy rate of soldiers. Prior to this date, as we saw in our introduction, authorities made some very ambitious claims about the ability of soldiers to read and write; after 1890, they suggested that the vast majority of the rank-and-file had only "elementary" skills at best. Figures like these, of course, do not in themselves provide a complete picture of the possible effects of the libraries, reading, and recreation rooms, but they certainly encourage us to be cautious about the claims that some commanding officers made in relation to the institutions. The officer above who could not express himself "too strongly in favour of all that gives relaxation to the soldier within his barrack," for example, also insisted that in his opinion the provision of "the reading and recreation rooms" and, by implication, libraries, had "a powerful influence in inducing men to avail themselves of the regimental schools."[84] Such an observation is obviously interesting, but sits somewhat uneasily along-

---

[82] The Author of "An Absent-Minded War" [William Elliot Cairnes], *The Army from Within* (London: Sands & Co., 1901), p. 9. Cairnes died in April of 1902, but is credited with having contributed through his writings to army reform during and after the Boer Wars and, thereby to the "quality" of the 1914 British expeditionary force. See Roger T. Stearn, "Cairnes, William Elliot (1862–1902)," *Oxford Dictionary of National Biography*, Oxford University Press, 2004; online edn, May 2006 [http://www.oxforddnb.com.remote.library. dcu.ie/view/article/32241, accessed 14 July 2015].

[83] Jeffrey, *The Trumpet Call Obey*, p. 71.

[84] *Sixth Report by the Council of Military Education*, p. xxvii.

side John Pindar's recollection of the cynical way in which some soldiers manipulated school attendance at this period.[85] And this, of course, leads us to our final point, which is that scrutiny of statistical data only provides a partial picture of the issue that is under discussion and, in our case at least, cannot do justice to the libraries and readers whose histories we have been exploring. For this reason, we will reserve judgment on the libraries until our conclusion, wherein we will finally consider the significance of the provision of these facilities to the nineteenth-century British soldier.

[85] See Introduction, page 21.

CHAPTER 6

Conclusion

The British army had gone through decades of "fitful" reform by the time the Victorian period drew to a close and enjoyed a degree of popularity that was greater than at any point during the 1800s.[1] The achievements of Generals such as Wolseley and Roberts were celebrated by an enthusiastic public, and the defeated and slain Gordon had been elevated to the annals of the martyrs and the saints. Even humble Tommy Atkins appeared to have risen in the estimation of his contemporaries, and to be viewed by (most of) them as a fellow human being.[2] In part, this was due to the efforts of writers such as Kipling, whose *Soldiers Three* (1890) and *Barrack-Room Ballads* (1892), for instance, hugely influenced—and softened—many late-Victorians' view of the private soldier[3]; it was also, though, a consequence of the army's own insistence that it had done, and

---

[1] Correlli Barnett, *Britain and her Army, 1509–1970: Military, Political, and Social Survey* (Harmondsworth: Penguin, 1970), pp. 291 and 313.

[2] Edward M. Spiers, *The Late Victorian Army, 1868–1902* (Manchester: Manchester University Press, 1992), p. 180. The use of "Tommy Atkins" as an affectionate nickname for the rank-and-file British soldier was first popularized by Rudyard Kipling in the 1890s, although the precise nature of its origins remain obscure (it may have been used on forms). See Byron Farwell, *The Encyclopedia of Nineteenth-Century Land Warfare: An Illustrated World View* (New York and London: W.W. Norton & Company, 2001), p. 817.

[3] Barnett, we saw in our introduction, also comments on the importance of Kipling to the British army (*Britain and her Army*, p. 314), and Spiers treats of the writer's influence on late-Victorian notions of the private soldier (*Late Victorian Army*, p. 200). I am indebted to both of their arguments here.

© The Editor(s) (if applicable) and The Author(s) 2016   157
S. Murphy, *The British Soldier and his Libraries, c. 1822–1901*,
DOI 10.1057/978-1-137-55083-5_6

was still doing, much to improve both the men themselves and the conditions in which they served.

Impressions, though, can be misleading, and many families still considered it a singular mark of disgrace to have a son go for a soldier.[4] The two Boer Wars; 1880–1881 and 1899–1902, moreover, prompted both authorities and the general public alike to ponder whether the British army really had been improved by the various reforms and educational initiatives that had been implemented at different points during the 1800s.[5] The *Report of His Majesty's Commissioners on the War in South Africa* (1903) that was produced in the immediate aftermath of the second war, for example, effectively damned every level of the army, and suggested that the British soldier "was inferior in intelligence ... both to the Boers and to British colonials who joined the war later," and to soldiers in countries such as Germany and France.[6] Findings like this were in one sense not too surprising, for the army continued to draw the majority of its rank-and-file from among the most deprived sections of the working classes. Men such as these were unlikely to have enjoyed the benefits of a superior level of education during their childhood and early youth, and it was unreasonable to expect that the army's schools—or libraries—could quickly rectify this deficiency. As Alan Ramsay Skelley puts it, "If the soldier was to make full use of his leisure time and of the facilities at his disposal, he needed not only to acquire a certain proficiency but to be taught to enjoy and to see the value in both reading and learning. These were habits best acquired when young, but to which few recruits can have been exposed before the last few years of the century."[7]

Success, though, is seldom judged by just one measure, and it is clear that the army's libraries—and reading and recreation rooms—were hugely appreciated by the soldiers who used them. This was a point that Horace Wyndham was keen to stress in his memoir, where he commented upon the proliferation of libraries and recreation rooms in the late 1800s:

[4] This is a point that Barnett also makes (p. 313).

[5] Again, nomenclature is an issue here: the wars were, for the Boers, Wars of Independence, and they are sometimes referred to as the Anglo-Boer Wars today.

[6] Barnett, *Britain and her Army*, pp. 341–43. Barnett also makes the point that this was largely due to deficiencies in soldiers' education, and I am indebted to his arguments both here and below.

[7] Alan Ramsay Skelley, *The Victorian Army at Home: the Recruitment and Terms and Conditions of the British Regular, 1859–1899* (London: Croom Helm, 1977), p. 98.

These recreation-rooms and libraries are greatly valued by the troops, and to a great extent ably fulfil the objects for which they are instituted. These are, according to the *Queen's Regulations*, 'To encourage soldiers to employ their leisure hours in a manner that shall combine amusement with the attainment of useful knowledge, and to teach them the value of sober, regular, and moral habits.'[8]

Wyndham's account of the libraries and recreation rooms, we saw previously, reminds us that some of the army's more ambitious plans were not carried through until the early 1900s, but it also underlines the importance that the facilities assumed by the time the nineteenth century drew to a close. In part, of course, the *army's* attitude to the libraries and recreation rooms in the last decade of the century may be pointed to as a somewhat cynical one, for it is clear that authorities believed that the provision of such facilities affected—or could affect—its ability to attract and retain recruits. It was in this context that recruitment posters at this time stressed the superior quality of life in the army, and it was also why pamphlets emphasized that the use of libraries and recreation rooms was one of the "general advantages" enjoyed by soldiers.[9] The general tenor of the army's recruitment efforts in the late nineteenth century was as clear as it was pointed, and intimated that men who enlisted enjoyed better living conditions—and better recreational facilities—than did their working class brethren. This, indeed, was something that William Elliot Cairnes was keen to stress in his consideration of the army "from within" in 1901, where he emphasized unmarried soldiers were particularly fortunate in this regard:

So long ... as Tommy is a bachelor, his existence will compare very favourably with that of the working man in the large majority of civilian occupations. He is well lodged, well fed, well clothed. He is not by any means hard worked, in fact, I think he would probably be happier if given more work—of an interesting nature—to occupy his time. And he has at his disposal a fine club with its library, its billiard tables, most of the daily and weekly newspapers, and a refreshment department where everything is of the cheapest and of excellent quality.[10]

[8] Horace Wyndham, *The Queen's Service: Being the Experiences of a Private Soldier in the British Infantry at Home and Abroad* (London: William Heinemann, 1899), p. 104.

[9] *Army and Militia: Pamphlets showing the Conditions of Service in the Army and Militia respectively* (London: HMSO, 1898), p. 9. The use of a gymnasium is mentioned alongside that of libraries and recreation rooms.

[10] "The Author of 'An Absent-Minded War'" [William Elliot Cairnes], *The Army from Within* (London: Sands & Co., 1901), p. 113.

The amount of time that soldiers had on their hands, then, remained an issue at the turn of the century, but it was also one of the factors that helped to inspire what was surely one of the most important library initiatives of the 1800s; or two of the most important, strictly speaking. The East India Company's decision to provide garrison libraries for men serving on military stations in India clearly was the more remarkable of the two, for it was a truly pioneering measure that was implemented at a very early point in the century. The Court of Directors was obviously influenced by a number of factors when it decided to establish the libraries, but chief among them seems to have been the recognition that the life of a soldier in India was particularly difficult. This was in part due to the huge amounts of leisure time that soldiers in India had on their hands, but it was also because of the particularly harsh nature of the Indian environment. As Robert Edmondson put it in the early twentieth century, "[I]f soldiering in England is purgatory, soldiering in India is hell. The troopship that carried me out to India took a load of fine, healthy young fellows; the ship that brought me back was crowded with human wrecks."[11] The provision of books and other types of reading material to the men who served in this "hell" in the early nineteenth century was obviously never going to be sufficient in itself to ameliorate their condition, especially given the particularly primitive nature of the military stations or cantonments at this period. That said, the establishment of the libraries was one of the most significant measures that the Company introduced at this time, and demonstrated that authorities were at least thinking about the welfare and, in particular, the recreational needs of the soldiers who protected—and furthered—their interests on the subcontinent.

The Regular Army was later than the East India Company in providing similar facilities for its soldiers, which can be pointed to as evidence that there was a marked difference in the attitude to literacy between the two forces. In truth, this was not too remarkable, for John Company's army was actually a private army, and served a concern whose very existence was predicated upon a desire to extract as much profit as possible from India and other parts of Asia. This fact alone probably meant that those who controlled or served in the Company's army were likely to have a more enlightened attitude to literacy than did their Regular Army counterparts; at the very least, it could be argued, they might have been more disposed to view

[11] Robert Edmondson, *John Bull's Army from Within: Facts, Figures, and a Human Document from one who has been "Through the Mill"* (London: Francis Griffiths, 1907), p. 140.

it pragmatically. It is important, though, not to overstress this point, especially as there were some within the Regular Army who advocated the need for literate soldiers from quite early in the 1700s. What is finally at issue here, perhaps, is a point to do with nomenclature: specifically, the fact that the word "army" may blind us to the fact that the force we are discussing was both complex and large. One of the things that is most clearly demonstrated by study of the East India Company and the Regular Army libraries, for example, is the degree to which both were hugely dependent on the efforts of individuals; to put this another way, it shows that there were men in *both* forces who were convinced that the provision of such institutions was a positive measure, and did everything possible to advance it at either a "central" or a local level. The crucial role that individual officers played in both the establishment and subsequent operation of solders' libraries during the nineteenth century is therefore a striking feature of their history, but so, too, is the part that was played by concerned civilians and/or charitable and/or religious societies, organizations, and institutions. This, of course, remained true well into the twentieth century and was particularly demonstrated in times of war. Edmund G.C. King, for instance, notes that "unprecedented" efforts were made to get books to soldiers during World War I, and Donald Mesham observes that the project that was designed to provide army standard unit libraries to British soldiers during the Second World War was driven by "seven-soldier librarians (and one civilian)".[12] It must be remarked, though, that "*none* of the close-to-a-million books" that were ordered in relation to the latter by February 1945 were distributed "until after the war in Europe was over," which is clearly reflective of another aspect of the history of the libraries that we have been examining: namely, authorities were often (but not always) quick to issue orders, instructions, and regulations, but frequently these were very slowly (and sometimes never) implemented on the ground.[13]

There are, therefore, points of comparison as well as difference to be traced between the histories of the East India Company and the Regular Army libraries, and probably one of the most interesting examples of the latter relates to the issue of discipline. What we have seen is that, while

[12] Edmund G.C. King, "E.W. Hornung's unpublished 'Diary,' the YMCA, and the Reading Soldier in the First World War," *English Literature in Transition*, vol. 57, no. 3 (2014), p. 365, and, Donald Mesham, "A Forgotten Book Collection: The Army Standard Unit Library" *Publishing History*, vol. 69 (2011), p. 85.

[13] Mesham, "Forgotten Book Collection," p. 89.

both forces clearly hoped that the provision of libraries would "improve" soldiers, the Regular Army from the very first took a distinctly utilitarian view of the contribution that the institutions could make to the regulation of men's attitudes and behavior. Again, it might be argued here that the only difference was one of degree, and that Sir Charles Colville, for instance, was very clear what he was thinking of when he expressed the hope that the East India Company's provision of libraries would lessen what he described as the "licentious propensities" of soldiers serving on the subcontinent.[14] Notwithstanding this, the evidence suggests that the discipline issue was of particular importance to the evolution of the Regular Army's libraries, and that a major factor behind their establishment was the perception that they could be used to "punish" or "reward" troops. The East India Company, of course, also increasingly looked to the libraries as a means of facilitating the regulation of soldiers' behavior as the years went by; the point is, though, that the primary impulse behind the Court of Directors' decision to establish the institutions seems to have been their recognition that it was essential to ameliorate the conditions in which the men were serving. In other words, and to emphasize the point made earlier, the provision of libraries to soldiers in India was peculiarly linked to the nature of the subcontinent itself, and the realization that failure to consider the welfare and, in particular, the recreational needs of men serving there had the potential to imperil the power and interests of the Company and, by implication, those of Britain.

This leads us to our next point, which is that the East India Company and the Regular Army imbued soldier' libraries with increasing significance as the years went by, and some of the individuals mostly closely involved with their oversight and/or operation made some very ambitious claims for the institutions. E.A. Vicars, the Assistant Inspector of Army Schools for Ireland, for example, was particularly eloquent when he expressed what he thought was at stake in 1867: "Military schools, libraries, reading and recreation rooms, and lectures rightly viewed, will be regarded as forming parts of one great system designed to civilize and domesticate the soldier, to win him from what is low and degrading, and to attach him to all that is pure and elevating and of good report."[15] Vicars' comments are

[14] See Chap. 2, pp. 36–37.

[15] "From E.A. Vicars, Esq., Assistant Inspector of Army Schools for Ireland," February 1867, Appendix II—No. 5 to *Fifth Report by the Council of Military Education on Army Schools, Libraries, and Recreation Rooms* (London: HMSO, 1868), p. 35.

particularly interesting, made, as they were, at a very particular moment in the history of Ireland. This was the period, after all, when members of the Irish Republican Brotherhood were busily fomenting rebellion; when John Devoy, for instance, was working hard to entice Irish soldiers in Irish garrisons into the Brotherhood.[16] As Vicars had it, the different parts of the army's "great system" proved more than capable of meeting the challenges with which they were faced at this time, and the libraries and reading rooms effectively functioned as sites wherein soldiers' loyalty to the Crown could be proven. "The library system continues to be popular and successful," he thus declared. "The papers, periodicals, and books purchased are chosen with taste and discrimination. Publications of an objectionable nature, either in religion or politics, are not to be found in the reading rooms with which I am acquainted."[17] Vicars was even more pointed in his report for 1866: "At a time when attempts have been made to seduce some of her Majesty's troops from their allegiance and loyalty," he wrote, "it is gratifying to put on record the fact, that the newspapers and periodicals to be found on their reading room tables, and chosen by their own body, are entirely free from any taint or suspicion of sympathy with disaffection."[18]

Vicars' comments obviously were highly partial ones, and ignored the fact that the material that made its way into the army's reading rooms was by *regulation* subject to the prior scrutiny and approval of commanding officers. His remarks also failed to register that not every soldier in Ireland was proving his loyalty to the crown at this period, and that contemporary newspapers were regularly carrying accounts of men charged with involvement in the Fenian "conspiracy." Many of the courts martial that were subsequently convened in relation to such charges, moreover, were held in the Victoria library in the Royal Barracks in Dublin, which, no doubt, was an irony that Vicars preferred to avoid.[19] Notwithstanding both of

---

[16] F.S.L. Lyons, *Ireland Since the Famine* (London: Fontana Press, 1971), p. 134. For an interesting account of Fenian activity at the Curragh Camp, see Con Costello, *A Most Delightful Station: The British Army on the Curragh of Kildare, Ireland, 1855–1922* (Cork: The Collins Press, 1996), pp. 108–110.

[17] "From E.A. Vicars," Appendix II—No. 5 to *Fifth Report by the Council of Military Education*, p. 35.

[18] "From E.A. Vicars, Esq , Assistant Inspector of Army Schools for Ireland," February 1866, Appendix II—No. 3 to *Fourth Report by the Council of Military Education on Army Schools, Libraries, and Recreation Rooms* (London: HMSO, 1866), p. 30.

[19] See, for example, the account of the General Court Martial of Private William Curry, of the 87th Regiment, in *Freeman's Journal*, 28 August 1866.

these qualifications, however, Vicars' comments remain extremely interesting, for they are reflective of the greater significance that many in authority attached to soldiers' libraries—and reading rooms—during the 1800s. Put simply, few of those who were most closely implicated in either the establishment or operation of the libraries saw them as mere collections of books, or as the spaces where books were read or housed; they viewed them, instead, as tools that would contribute to the education and improvement of soldiers and, by implication, to the progress of civilization itself. In this context, some of the more ambitious claims that were made by commanding officers—or, indeed, by army chaplains—become much more understandable: these men were, in the final analysis, articulating nothing less than their conviction of the superiority of the culture that the libraries—and they themselves—represented.

The non-commissioned officers and men, of course, also responded in a complex fashion to the libraries, and many were similarly convinced of the cultural and symbolic significance of the institutions (although they may not have expressed this explicitly). We have seen, for instance, that Sergeant Greening commented upon the different libraries that he encountered during the time that he spent in India, and underlined his conviction of the importance of the institutions to soldiers' lives on the subcontinent. In so doing, though, he also revealed both the tremendous pride that he clearly felt as a result of the very presence of the libraries in India, and his appreciation of the fact that it was the British and, in particular, the British military who were bringing these symbols of culture and civilization to far-flung and otherwise "primitive" places. The fact that books were, for Greening, peculiarly potent symbols of civilization is expertly illustrated by a later entry in his diary, where he recorded his response to a scene of devastation that he witnessed on the Veldt during the second Boer War: "Passed more ruined farms, one very pretty one amidst some big trees, with wood pigeons cooing and it was a pity to see such wanton damage, little children's things, books &c [sic] all destroyed and laying about on the ground. I felt like shooting the first Boer I met after seeing all the damage done."[20] Greening's reaction to this scene was clearly complicated, and most likely informed in the first instance by what he had himself gone through with his family shortly after returning home from service in India. "The effects of the deadly Indian summer," he wrote, "made havoc with the health of my wife and little ones, for after arriving

[20] Diary of W. Greening, 90th Regiment, Scottish Rifles, NAM 1983-07-121, p. 45.

home, the wife was bad for three months with fever and ague, and the eldest girl also, and after ... going to Aldershot in 1899, I lost the eldest girl and my little son of 18 months."[21] Greening's response to the devastated farm therefore was on one hand that of a recently bereaved father; of a man who was probably in a peculiarly vulnerable state when he came across the destruction of "little children's things." On the other hand, however, his reaction to the scene was also patently that of an individual for whom books were symbols of civilization as well as material objects and, as such, it was the response of a soldier who saw such "wanton" destruction as further evidence of the uncivilized nature of the enemy that he was fighting. It was perhaps because of this that Greening afforded the books a specificity within his description that he denied everything else; it must be acknowledged, though, that the exact nature of the "little children's things" were, perhaps, something that he was incapable either of recording or expressing.

Greening was not the only nineteenth-century soldier to register an intense response either to the libraries or the works that they contained, as we have seen, and many men treasured the ability to get their hands on reading material. The reading—or listening to the reading aloud of—such material, we have also seen, fulfilled several complex functions for soldiers, sometimes simultaneously. Yorkshire man Richard Hardcastle, for example, suggested that his (solitary) reading of anything by (or about) Charlotte Brontë both satisfied his desire for good literature *and* transported him to distant but much-loved places. William Douglas intimated that the reading aloud in India of newspaper accounts of events in the Crimea kept the men informed *and* reduced them to a state of rapt attention and stillness. James Hawker revealed that his reading of Tennyson's *Charge of the Light Brigade* in a Dublin barracks in the mid-1800s was immediately followed by concertina playing and soldiers capering. What all of these men were actually demonstrating, of course, was that books or newspapers were rarely just material objects for soldiers; that they were, instead, vehicles that facilitated their (sometimes competing) desires for entertainment, instruction, information, comfort and, sometimes, sociability *or* mental privacy. Books and newspapers also served as something else for soldiers, and this was as the hugely important symbols of the people, places, *and* culture that they both missed and represented. In this context, the libraries and reading rooms that the East India Company and Regular Army

[21] Diary of W. Greening, NAM 1983-07-121, p. 37.

established signified a truly remarkable cultural achievement on the part of both forces, functioning as sites where British culture was preserved and celebrated and, potentially, shaped and interrogated as well. This point, obviously, was of huge significance in relation to all of the libraries and reading rooms, but it was particularly so when the institutions in question were located outside of Britain. Put simply, the very existence of soldiers' libraries and reading rooms in places such as India, Ceylon, South Africa, or New Zealand symbolized not only a desire to facilitate the men's reading and recreation: it also represented British power and culture and, in particular, the ability of Britain's military to convey (or impose) the fruits of this "civilization" to (or on) remote parts of the world.

This, of course, leads us to an important question, which is whether it is possible to estimate the degree to which the provision of the libraries and reading rooms may have facilitated the colonial and imperial projects in which Britain was engaged. Many of those in authority in both John Company and the Regular Army certainly suggested that they did, in the sense that they insisted the provision of the facilities improved men's attitudes and behavior. The arguments of such individuals, however, must be treated with caution, especially as many of these were closely involved with the establishment and/or operation of the institutions and therefore had a stake in proving that their effects were beneficial. That said, it must be remarked that some ordinary soldiers also commented upon the positive influence of the libraries and reading rooms, thereby also suggesting that their provision contributed to the discipline, morale and, *ipso facto*, workings of the military. Then again, it has to be remembered that soldiers such as these did not speak for all of the rank-and-file, the greater part of whose opinions went largely unrecorded. It must also be borne in mind that some contemporary newspaper commentary either flatly contradicted the claims that were made in relation to the effects of the libraries and reading rooms, or suggested that they were overstated. Some newspapers in India, we saw, for instance, continued to comment upon the disgraceful condition of British soldiers on the subcontinent long after the East India Company's libraries had been established.

There is a further point that must be acknowledged when contemplating the possible effects of the libraries, and this is that individuals are seldom affected by just one influence; to suggest otherwise, as Carolyn Steedman might put it, is to adopt a position of tremendous "arrogance" and assume "that people 'get' their ideas from somewhere, that social and political analysis is *always* taken from above" (*emphasis added*).[22] Recognition of this fact means that we have to acknowledge not only that several measures were put in place by both forces to improve soldiers during the course of the nineteenth century, but also that the men in question were the "products" of *everything* that they read and *all* of their experiences. Each of these points is obviously important, but the former is especially so given that we are thinking about the possible effects of library provision. One of the things that becomes particularly clear from the study of either force's libraries, for example, is that the institutions were frequently unable to keep up with soldiers' hunger for reading material: this meant, firstly, that some men worked their way repeatedly through *everything* that the libraries contained; and, secondly, many purchased books and other types of reading material themselves and/or obtained it from charitable or religious organizations and/or their friends and relatives. In this context, it is clearly not possible to state either that the contents of the libraries alone shaped the intellectual development and, hence, attitudes, opinions, and behavior of soldiers, or that any such development was influenced by just one type of reading material. All of the evidence certainly suggests, for instance, that most men preferred reading works of fiction, but this was not true of every soldier who took books from the libraries' shelves. It also must be acknowledged, as we noted above, that evidence relating to soldiers' preference for fiction is complicated by the fact that many frustrated readers worked their way again and again through all of the reading material that was available.

A further point must be made here, and this relates to the difficulties of trying to estimate the effects of the libraries on either illiterate soldiers or soldiers who left no record of their reading experiences. In relation to the former point, for instance, we have seen that authorities responsible for the operation of the East India Company's libraries gradually modified their attitude to the "where" of soldiers' reading as the years went by, and that this modification was partly informed by the recognition that it would facilitate the reading aloud of books and, thereby, benefit less literate or illiterate soldiers. The Regular Army, too, registered its awareness of the fact that soldiers sometimes listened to works being read aloud, and allowed men to take reading material back with them to their barracks. The degree to which semi literate or illiterate soldiers may have

[22] Carolyn Steedman, *The Radical Soldier's Tale: John Pearman, 1819–1908* (London and New York: Routledge, 1988), p. 102.

been affected by the libraries is difficult to gauge, especially as much of the evidence relating to the subject is mediated in the testimony of the men's commanding officers and/or literate comrades. This means that all we can say with confidence is that many of the former individuals stoutly declared that semi-literate or illiterate soldiers hugely benefitted from the libraries, and some of the latter supported this assertion.

Not every literate soldier, moreover, commented upon reading in his memoirs or letters, but this does not necessarily mean that he did not read (or that he failed to benefit from the libraries with which he was provided). In the first place, the very nature of a soldier's life was challenging, and men often had a great deal more on their minds than issues relating to reading, books, libraries, or literacy. Surviving letters of John Pine that were examined for the purposes of this study, for example, contain one reference each in relation to his attendance at school and writing of letters, and two concerning newspapers that he either wanted or had received. The soldier falls silent on all of these matters in his letters from the Crimea, where he at one point observes that men "are dying like rotten sheep. ... I heartily wish this affair was settled and we could get out of this accursed country. ... I am heartily sick of this kind of work."[23] Private Duggan's long-distance efforts to patch up his relationship with Miss Sarah Powell remind us of another reason why some soldiers may have failed to comment upon reading in their letters: they were preoccupied with issues of a more pressing and personal nature. Writing from South Africa to a sweetheart who was obviously miffed because a promised letter and gift had failed to arrive, he protested, "I know you had no Letter. Because the Boat went Down with the mails on Board but that was not my Fault[.] [T]here was a lot of things went Down by that Boat[,] especially Chocolate Boxes."[24]

The mention of survival brings us to another issue, which is that much material relating to nineteenth-century soldiers' libraries, reading preferences or habits probably has been lost. A substantial amount remains, though, and, while this volume is based upon empirical research, only a portion of what is available has been examined. For example, this study focused for methodological reasons primarily on the garrison libraries that

[23] John Pine, Letter of 8 January 1855, NAM 1996-05-4, 19. The reference to his attendance at school is in letter 2 and to writing is in letter 6; his references to newspapers are in letters 3 and 7.

[24] Private M. Duggan, Letter of 26 May 1899, NAM 1998-03-13, 5.

were established for British soldiers during the 1800s; this seemed to be a logical approach to take, especially as these were the types of libraries that both the East India Company and the Regular Army first chose to provide for their rank-and-file. Regimental libraries assumed increasing significance as each system evolved, however, and, while this study tried to take some account of this fact, more work obviously needs to be done here for the purposes of comparison. It would also, clearly, be useful to examine surviving evidence in relation to the reading that was carried on in officers' messes, and the libraries that were provided for soldiers on board of the ships of the East India Company and Her Majesty's navy also deserve consideration (as, indeed, do those provided for Her Majesty's sailors and merchant seamen).[25] It is hoped, though, that the work that has been done here will directly illuminate areas of possible enquiry and, in particular, facilitate the drawing of useful comparisons between soldiers and other types of readers and libraries at this period. One of the things this study has shown, for example, is that many of those responsible for the soldiers' libraries were greatly preoccupied by the role that the provision of fiction could or should play within the institutions and, in the case of the East India Company in particular, from a very early moment in the 1800s. It might therefore be useful to conduct a detailed consideration of the holdings of both a soldiers' library and one of the free public libraries in Britain, and explore whether any appreciable differences can be discerned in terms either of contents or readers' preferences and usage (where such records exist). More immediately, of course, further work is also calling out to be done on the soldiers' libraries themselves, particularly in relation to those institutions whose records are more detailed and complete. Literary critics preoccupied with perceptions of genre during the nineteenth century would find much to interest them here, for instance, as, indeed, would those who are concerned with exploring the role that fiction played (or may have played) in facilitating the imperial project both within and beyond Britain. It was curiosity about this latter point that inspired the line of research that has led to the production of this volume and, while all of the questions originally contemplated have not been answered, other ways of thinking about them have at least been suggested.

---

[25] On the provision of books to soldiers on ships and to merchant seamen in the nineteenth century, see K.A. Manley "Engines of Literature: Libraries in an Era of Expansion and Transition," in Giles Mandelbrote and K.A. Manley (eds), *The Cambridge History of Libraries in Britain and Ireland, Vol. II, 1640–1850* (Cambridge: Cambridge University Press, 2006), pp. 519–521 and 524.

In the final analysis, then, the writing of this book was predicated upon a desire to ponder soldiers' reading in places such as India; to contemplate the types of works that the men might have read, and the places where they read them. It was also, though, informed by a wish to let soldiers' speak for themselves wherever possible and, in this context, it seems right to conclude here by recalling some of the soldiers whom we have met in the course of the previous chapters and, in particular, to remember the delight that so many took in being able to obtain reading material. We might think, therefore, of individuals such as Sergeant John Ramsbottom, who expressed his happiness at being able to read all night in a library in India, or of Thomas Quinney, who climbed to the foretop of the ship taking him to the subcontinent so that he could read in greater seclusion. Or, we might remember Sergeant Greening, and his fond account of soldiers passing their evenings together reading or knitting, or John Mercier MacMullen, and his description of the howls of laughter that accompanied some men's reading of the exploits of Mickey Free. Or we might think, perhaps, of John Pindar, and his insistence that reading poetry in his barracks afforded him more pleasure than he could have experienced in all the gin palaces of the world. Pindar's observation, clearly, was not a very "scholarly" one, and was no doubt viewed with distaste by many of those who labored to prove that drink was not the primary preoccupation—or cultural marker—of the British soldier. It is, though, a good place for us to conclude our study because is suggestive of a crucial point about the libraries whose histories we have been examining: namely, their contents gave many nineteenth-century British soldiers the greatest earthly happiness that they were capable either of imagining or expressing.

SELECT BIBLIOGRAPHY

PRIMARY SOURCES:

Oriental and India Office Collections of the British Library:

In the interests of brevity, the lists below give full citations for all sources quoted in the text and footnotes, but do not include all sources that were consulted for the purposes of this study.

L/Mil/3/1162, Military Letter from Madras [Board's copy], 5 August 1834.

L/Mil/3/1331, No. 262, Copy of a Letter from the Adjutant-General of the Army, 17 March 1840, [containing] Extracts from the Annual Reports for 1839.

L/Mil/3/1457, No. 480, Adjutant-General's Letter of 4th June, 1847, forwarding Extracts from the Annual Reports for 1845.

L/Mil/3/1506 [1850], No. 98, From Lieutenant-Colonel R.I.H. Vivian, Adjutant-General of the Army, to Col. C.A. Browne, Secretary to Government, Military Department: "Return of Books in the Lending Library at Fort St George for 1849."

L/Mil/3/1555, Fort Saint George, Military Cons. of August 1856, Nos. 131 & 132 [comprised of] "Extracts from the Annual Reports of 1855 upon the Soldiers' Lending Libraries of this Army."

L/Mil/5/384, Collection 85A, Reply to the communication from the Court on the subject of a supply of Books for the use of the European Soldiers.

"Larger List of Books for the four principal stations viz, Bombay, Poonab, Kauria, and Maloonga to be applied for the Court of Directors."

"List A, Books which may be obtained from the Bombay District Committee of the Society for Promoting Christian Knowledge."

© The Editor(s) (if applicable) and The Author(s) 2016
S. Murphy, *The British Soldier and his Libraries, c. 1822–1901*,
DOI 10.1057/978-1-137-55083-5

171

"List B, Additional Books to be obtained from the Court of Directors."

"List of Books sent to Bengal."

Military letter to Bombay [extract], 27 February 1822.

Military letter from Bombay [extract], 29 January 1823.

"Rules for Stationery Libraries" [sic].

L/Mil/5/391, Collections 134-138.

F/4/1243/40911:

Extract from Fort St. George Military Correspondence, 18th August 1829.

"General Order," Madras Presidency.

F/4/1272/51087:

"List of Books in the Lending Library established by the S.P.C.K. at Bangalore on the 08th [sic] October 1829."

Military Letter from Fort St George [extract], 15 June 1830.

"Proceedings of Committee assembled ... to value books ... at Bellary Lending Library ... 26th September 1829."

"Proceedings of Station Committee assembled at St. Thomas Court on Tuesday the 8th September 1829 for the valuation of Books to be purchased ...[.]"

"Proceedings of the Station Committee assembled ... at Trichinopoly for the purpose of balancing the Books intended to be purchased for the use of the Station Library."

"... Proceedings of Committee assembled at Vizagapatam ... [18 November 1829]."

F/4/1428/56391, Madras Military, Collection No. 1, Report on Soldiers Libraries and Indent for Books.

F/4/1486/58611, Collection No. 4, Report upon the Soldiers Libraries, and recommendation that they should be formed into Regimental, instead of Station, Libraries, and that the number of Books be increased.

"Western Library, State[ment] shewing the number of works and volumes in that Library, as also the number of times each has been taken out for the purpose of being read since the 1st March 1832, [dated] Cawnpore 6th November 1832."

F/4/1701/68730, Collection No. 20—Books for Soldiers' Libraries. "Extracts from Annual Reports for 1836 [Madras]."

F4/1949/84727, Extract from a Military Letter from Bengal, 30 September 1841, Bengal Military Collection No. 12, Reports Relating to Soldiers' Libraries.

E/4/753, "General Order Modifying System of Establishment and Regulations approved" in Letter dated 30th Jan. 1837 (No. 10).

E/4/759, India Ecclesiastical 2 July 1839, Bengal Despatches.

E/4/764, Court's Letters to Bengal on 23 December 1840 and 21 April 1858, Bengal Despatches.

E/4/765, Extract from letter from Bengal, reproduced in Court's Letter of 3 February 1841 to Bengal.

E/4/839, 8 October 1856, Bengal Despatches.

E/4/851, 21 April 1858, Bengal Despatches.

E/4/943, Court's letters to Madras on 5 June 1833 and 26 June 1833, Madras Despatches.

Papers of:
John Butterworth, Mss Eur D900.
William Hurd Eggleston, Photo Eur 257.
Richard Hardcastle, Photo Eur C332, 96.
Sergeant John Ramsbottom, Ms. Add 59876.

National Army Museum, London:

Again, the list below gives full citations for all sources quoted in the text and foot-notes, but does not include all sources that were consulted for the purposes of this study.

Papers of:
P.P. Clarke, 1992-08-445.
Henry Clayton, 1996-11-53-23.
W. Greening, 1983-07-121.
William Pattison, 1967-02-66.
John Pine, 1996-05-4.
Joseph Reid, 1999-03-130.
Charles Henry Smith, 2004-01-39.
W. Ware, 2001-09-77.

Official Publications:

Army Orders, Regulations, Pamphlets

Abstract of General Orders from 1817 to 1840. Compiled by Captain David Thompson. Delhi: Printed at the Gazette Press, 1840.
Addenda to the General Regulations and Orders for the Army. From 1836 to 1839, Inclusive. London: William Clowes & Sons, 1840.
Addenda to the Queen's Regulations and Orders for the Army. From the First of July, 1844, to the Thirty First of March, 1854. London: HMSO, 1854.
Army and Militia: Pamphlets showing the Conditions of Service in the Army and Militia respectively. London: HMSO, 1898.
General Orders Issued to the Army of the East, from April 30 1854 to December 31 1855. London: HMSO, 1856.
Queen's Regulations and Orders for the Army. 1844. Third Edition. London: HMSO, 1854.

Army Reports

Many of the reports below include extensive appendices, which contain valuable material relating to the libraries (e.g., officers' letters/reports, responses to committees' enquiries, lists of libraries, etc.). In the interests of brevity, full citations for such materials are confined to the footnotes.

Report on the Regimental and Garrison Schools of the Army, and on Military Libraries and Reading Rooms. By Brevet-Colonel J.H. Lefroy, Royal Artillery, Inspector-General of Army Schools. London: HMSO, 1859.

"[Copies of] Captain Pilkington Jackson's Report, to the Secretary of State for War, on the Soldiers' Institutes at Aldershot and at Portsmouth," in *Army (Soldiers' Institutes), and Army (Soldiers' Libraries, &c).* London: HMSO, 1862.

Report of a Committee appointed by the Secretary of State for War to inquire into and report on the present state and on the improvement of Libraries, Reading Rooms, and Day Rooms. London: HMSO, 1862.

First Report by the Council of Military Education on Army Schools, Libraries, and Reading Rooms. London: HMSO, 1862.

Second Report by the Council of Military Education on Army Schools, Libraries, and Recreation Rooms. London: HMSO, 1865.

Third Report by the Council of Military Education on Army Schools, Libraries, and Recreation Rooms. London: HMSO, 1865.

Fourth Report by the Council of Military Education on Army Schools, Libraries, and Recreation Rooms. London: HMSO, 1866.

Fifth Report by the Council of Military Education on Army Schools, Libraries, and Recreation Rooms. London: HMSO, 1868.

Sixth Report by the Council of Military Education on Army Schools, Libraries, and Recreation Rooms. London: HMSO, 1870.

First Report by the Director-General of Military Education on Army Schools, Libraries, and Recreation Rooms. London: HMSO, 1872.

Second Report by the Director-General of Military Education on Army Schools, Libraries, and Recreation Rooms. London: HMSO, 1874.

Third Report by the Director-General of Military Education on Army Schools, Libraries, and Recreation Rooms. London: HMSO, 1877.

Other Reports

Inspectors of Prisons, Great Britain: Second Report. London: HMSO, 1837.

Report of the Commissioners appointed to inquire into the Regulations affecting the sanitary condition of the Army, the organization of Military Hospitals, and the treatment of the Sick and Wounded, with Evidence and Appendix. London: HMSO, 1857.

General Report of the Commission appointed for improving the sanitary condition of Barracks and Hospitals. London: HMSO, 1861.

Military Memoirs and Letters:

"A Late Staff Sergeant of the 13th Light Infantry" [John Mercier MacMullen or McMullen]. *Camp and Barrack Room; or, the British Army as it is.* London: Chapman and Hall, 1846.

"A Soldier" [Joseph Donaldson]. *Recollections of an Eventful Life: Chiefly Passed in the Army.* Glasgow: W.R. McPhun, 1824.

Anon. [John Edward Acland-Troyte]. *Through the Ranks to a Commission.* London: Macmillan & Co., 1881.

Bancroft, N.W. *From Recruit to Staff Sergeant.* Introduction and Epilogue by Major-General B.P. Hughes. N.P. [Essex]: Ian Henry Publications, 1979.

Corneille, John. *Journal of My Service in India.* Ed. Michael Edwardes. London: The Folio Society, 1966.

Douglas, William. *Soldiering in Sunshine and Storm.* Edinburgh: Adam and Charles Black, 1865.

Edmondson, Robert. *John Bull's Army from Within: Facts, Figures, and a Human Document from One who has been "Through the Mill."* London: Francis Griffiths, 1907.

Fraser, John. *Sixty Years in Uniform.* London: Stanley Paul & Co., 1939.

Gordon, Iain (ed). *Soldier of the Raj: The Life of Richard Purvis, 1789–1868. Soldier, Sailor, and Parson.* Barnsley, Sth. Yorkshire: Leo Cooper, 2001.

Gowing, Thomas. *Voice from the Ranks: A Personal Narrative of the Crimean Campaign by a Sergeant of the Royal Fusiliers.* Ed. Kenneth Fenwick. London: Folio Society, 1954.

Gowing, Timothy. A *Soldier's Experience; Things not generally known, showing the Price of War in Blood and Treasure.* Colchester: Benham & Co., 1883.

Green, John. *The Vicissitudes of a Soldier's Life, or a Series of Occurences from 1806 to 1815, together with an Introductory and a Concluding Chapter: the whole containing with some other matters, a concise account of the War in the Peninsula, from its commencement to its final close.* Louth and London: J. & J. Jackson and Simpkin and Marshall, 1827.

Hall, William. *The Diary of Sergeant William Hall, of Penzance, Cornwall, Late of Her Majesty's Forty-First Regiment: Containing the Incidents connected with Two Years' Campaign in Scinde and Affghanistan During the Late War: to which is Also Added the Sermon Preached to the Troops on the Sunday After the Battle by the Rev. J.N. Allen, B.A. ... Also the Particulars of Numerous Shooting Excursions in India After Game of All Descriptions, Including the Lion and Other Wild Beast of the Jungle.* Penryn: Printed for the Author, n.d. [1848?].

Hawker, James. *James Hawker's Journal: A Victorian Poacher.* Ed. Garth Christian. London: Oxford University Press, 1961

Hervey, Captain Albert. *A Soldier of the Company: Life of an Indian Ensign, 1833–43.* Ed. Charles Allen. London: Michael Joseph, 1988.

Hodson, William Stephen Raikes. *Twelves Years of A Soldier's Life in India: Being Extracts from the Letters of the Late Major W.S.R. Hodson, B.A. Trinity College, Cambridge; First Bengal European Fusiliers, Commandant of Hodson's Horse, Including a Personal Narrative of the Siege of Delhi and Capture of the King and Princes, Edited by his Brother, the Rev. George H. Hodson, M.A.* 2nd edition. London: John W. Parker & Son, 1859.

Jowett, William. *Memoir and Diary of Sergeant W. Jowett, Seventh Royal Fusiliers.* London and Beeston, Nottinghamshire: W. Kent & Co. and B. Porter, 1856.

Lawrence, William. *A Dorset Soldier: The Autobiography of Sergeant William Lawrence.* Ed. Eileen Hathaway. Tunbridge Wells: Spellmount, 1993.

Liddell Hart, Captain B.H. (ed). *The Letters of Private Wheeler, 1809–1828.* Adlestrop, Gloucestershire: Windrush Press, 1951.

Palmer, Roy (ed). *The Rambling Soldier: Life in the Lower Ranks, 1750–1900, through Soldiers' Songs and Writings.* Gloucester: Alan Sutton Publications, 1985.

Pindar, John. *Autobiography of a Private Soldier.* Cupar-Fife: Printed in the "Fife News" Office, 1878.

Quinney, Thomas. *Sketches of A Soldier's Life in India by Staff Sergeant Thomas Quinney, Honorable East India Company's Service.* Glasgow: David Robertson and Edinburgh: Oliver & Boyd, 1853.

Shipp, John. *The Military Bijou: or, the Contents of a Soldier's Knapsack: Being the Gleanings of Thirty-Three Years Active Service.* London: Whitaker, Treacher, and Co., 1831.

Small, E. Milton (ed). *Told from the Ranks: Recollections of Service during the Queen's Reign by Privates and Non-Commissioned Officers of the British Army.* London: Andrew Melrose, 1897.

Somerville, Alexander. *The Autobiography of a Working Man, By One Who Whistled at the Plough.* London: Charles Gilpin, 1848.

Taylor, William. *Life in the Ranks.* 2nd edition. London: T.C. Newby; Parry, Blenkarn Co., 1847.

"The Author of 'An Absent-Minded War'" [William Elliot Cairnes]. *The Army from Within.* London: Sands & Co., 1901.

Tuker, Francis. *The Yellow Scarf: The Story of the Life of Thuggee Sleeman or Major-General Sir William Henry Sleeman, K.C.B. 1788–1856 of the Bengal Army and the Indian Political Service.* London: White Lion, 1961.

Waterfield, Robert. *The Memoirs of Private Waterfield, Soldier in Her Majesty's 32nd Regiment of Foot, (Duke of Cornwall's Light Infantry) 1842–57.* Arthur Swinson and Donald Scott (eds). London: Cassell & Co., 1968.

"Written by Himself." *Narrative of a Private Soldier in His Majesty's 92nd Regiment of Foot. Written by Himself. Detailing many Circumstances relative to the Insurrection in Ireland in 1798; the Expedition to Holland in 1799; and the Expedition to Egypt in 1801; and Giving a particular Account of his Religious History and Experience. With a Preface by the Rev. Ralph Wardlaw, D.D.* 2nd edition. Glasgow: University Press, 1820.

Wyndham, Horace. *The Queen's Service: Being the Experiences of a Private Soldier in the British Infantry at Home and Abroad*. London: William Heinemann, 1899.
Wyndham, Horace. *Following the Drum*. London: Andrew Melrose, 1912.

Contemporary Publications:

Works on Military Matters

Carter, Thomas. *Curiosities of War and Military Studies: Anecdotal, Descriptive, and Statistical*. 2nd edn. Illustrated. London: Groombridge & Sons, 1871.
Marshall, Henry. *Military Miscellany, Comprehending A History of the Recruiting of the Army, Military Punishments*, &c. &c. London: John Murray, 1846.
Stocqueler, Joachim Hayward. *The British Soldier: An Anecdotal History of the British Army, from its earliest formation to the present time*. London: Wm. S. Orr & Co., 1857.

Newspapers, Journals, and Periodicals

Bengal Hurkuru (August 1822-January 1823 and July 1840)
Calcutta Weekly Gazette (January to May 1840)
Delhi Gazette (1837 and January-June 1848)
Government [Calcutta] Gazette (October 1818-January 1819)

Aldershot Military Gazette
Chelmsford Chronicle
Colburn's United Service Magazine and Naval and Military Journal
Freeman's Journal
Portsmouth Evening News
The Buck's Herald
The Burnley Free Press
The Cork Examiner
The Daily News
The Dundee Courier
The Graphic
The Standard
London Standard
The United Service Journal and Naval and Military Magazine

SECONDARY SOURCES:

Arabian Nights' Entertainments: Consisting of One Thousand and One Stories. 4 vols. 10th ed. Dublin: W. Whitestone, 1776.
Allan, David. *A Nation of Readers: The Lending Library in Georgian England*. London: British Library, 2008.

Allen, Walter. *The English Novel: A Short Critical History*. Harmondsworth: Penguin, 1954.

Altick, Richard D. *The English Common Reader: A Social History of the Mass Reading Public, 1800–1900*. 2nd edn. Columbus: Ohio State University, 1998.

Baggs, Chris. "Radical Reading? Working-Class Libraries in the Nineteenth and Early Twentieth Century," in Alistair Black and Peter Hoare (eds), *The Cambridge History of Libraries in Britain and Ireland. Vol. III. 1850–2000*. Cambridge: Cambridge University Press, 2006.

Ballaster, Ros. *Fabulous Orients: Fictions of the East in England, 1662–1784*. Oxford: Oxford University Press, 2005.

Barnett, Correlli, *Britain and her Army, 1507–1970: Military, Political, and Social Survey*. Harmondsworth: Penguin, 1970.

Bayly, C.A. "Elphinstone, Mountstuart (1779–1859)." *Oxford Dictionary of National Biography*. Oxford University Press, 2004; online edn, Jan 2008 [http://www.oxforddnb.com.remote.library.dcu.ie/view/article/8752, accessed 17 Oct 2015].

Belchem, John and Richard Price (eds). *The Penguin Dictionary of Nineteenth-Century History*. London: Penguin, 1994.

Black, Alistair and Peter Hoare. "Libraries and the Modern World" in Black and Hoare eds. *The Cambridge History of Libraries in Britain and Ireland. Vol. III. 1850–2000*.

Bourne, J.M. "The East India Company's Military Seminary, Addiscombe, 1809–1858," *Journal of the Society for Army Historical Research* LVII Winter (1979): 206–22.

Bowyer-Bower, T.A. "The Development of Educational Ideas and Curricula in the Army during the Eighteenth and Nineteenth Centuries." Master's Thesis, University of Nottingham, 1954.

Brereton, John M. *The British Soldier: A Social History from 1661 to the Present Day*. London: Bodley Head, 1986.

British Newspaper Archive in partnership with the British Library (www.british-newspaperarchive.co.uk).

Browne, Douglas G. *Private Thomas Atkins: A History of the British Soldier from 1840 to 1940*. London and Melbourne: Hutchinson & Co., [1940?].

Bryant, Gerald James. "The East India Company and its Army, 1660–1778." Ph.D. thesis. University of London, 1975.

Burroughs, Peter. "Crime and Punishment in the British Army, 1845–1870" *English Historical Review* 100: 396 (July, 1985): 545–71.

Burroughs, Peter. "An Unreformed Army? 1815–1868" in David Chandler (General ed) and Ian Beckett (Associate ed), *The Oxford History of the British Army*. Oxford and New York: Oxford University Press, 1996.

Calabria, Michael D. "Florence Nightingale and the Libraries of the British Army," *Libraries and Culture*, 29, No. 4 (Fall, 1994): 367–88.

Callahan, Raymond. *The East India Company and Army Reform, 1783–1798.* Cambridge, Massachusetts: Harvard University Press, 1972.

Colclough, Stephen. "Readers: Books and Biography" in Simon Eliot and Jonathan Rose (eds), *A Companion to the History of the Book.* Malden, Massachusetts, Oxford, England, and Carlton, Australia: Blackwell, 2007.

Colley, Linda. *Captives.* New York: Pantheon Books, 2002.

Concise History of the British Newspaper in the Nineteenth Century. Available at [www.bl.uk/.../findhelprestype/news/conscisehistbritnews/britnews19th].

Costello, Con. *A Most Delightful Station: The British Army on the Curragh of Kildare, Ireland, 1855–1922.* Cork: The Collins Press, 1996.

Dalrymple, William. *White Mughals: Love and Betrayal in Eighteenth-Century India.* London: HarperCollins, 2002.

Darnton, Robert. *The Kiss of Lamourette: Reflections in Cultural History.* London and Boston, Faber and Faber, 1990.

Das Gupta, Anil Chandra (ed). *The Days of John Company: Selections from Calcutta Gazette, 1824–1832.* Calcutta: Government Printing, 1959.

Davidoff, Leonore and Catherine Hall. *Family Fortunes: Men and Women of the English Middle Class, 1780–1850.* London: Routledge, 1987.

Dawood, N.J. Introduction to *Tales from the Thousand and One Nights,* trans. N.J. Dawood. 1954. London: Penguin, 1973.

Defoe, Daniel. *The Life and Adventures of Robinson Crusoe.* London: Penguin, 1965.

Delafield, Catherine. *Serialization and the Novel in Mid-Victorian Magazines.* Farnham: Ashgate, 2015.

Driver, Felix. "Moral Geographies: Social Science and the Urban Environment in Mid-Nineteenth-Century England" *Transactions of the Institute of British Geographers* New Series, Vol. 13, No. 3 (1988): 275–87.

Duncan, Ian. *Modern Romance and Transformations of the Novel: The Gothic, Scott, Dickens.* Cambridge: Cambridge University Press, 1992.

Eden, Emily. *Up the Country: Letters to her Sister from the Upper Provinces of India* 1930. London and Dublin: Curzon Press, 1978.

Edgeworth, Maria. *Popular Tales.* 3rd edition. London: J. Johnson, 1807.

Edgeworth, Richard Lovell Edgeworth and Maria Edgeworth. *Practical Education.* 2 vols. London: J. Johnson, 1798.

Edgeworth, Richard Lovell. *Memoirs of Richard Lovell Edgeworth, esq. Begun by himself and concluded by his Daughter, Maria Edgeworth,* 2 vols. London: R. Hunter, 1820.

Eliot, Simon and Jonathan Rose. Introduction to *A Companion to the History of the Book,* eds. Eliot and Rose.

Farwell, Byron. *The Encyclopedia of Nineteenth-Century Land Warfare: An Illustrated World View.* New York and London: W.W. Norton & Co., 2001.

Feather, John. "The Book Trade and Libraries" in Giles Mandelbrote and K.A. Manley (eds), *The Cambridge History of Libraries in Britain and Ireland. Vol. II. 1640–1850.* Cambridge: Cambridge University Press, 2006.

Ferris, Ina. *The Achievement of Literary Authority: Gender, History, and the Waverley Novels.* Cornell and London: Cornell University Press, 1991.

Finkelstein, David, and Alistair McCleery. *An Introduction to Book History.* New York: Routledge, 2005.

Fish, Stanley. *Is there a Text in this Class? The Authority of Interpretive Communities.* Cambridge, Massachusetts, and London: Harvard University Press, 1980.

Foucault, Michel. *Discipline and Punish: The Birth of the Prison.* Trs. from the French by Alan Sheridan. 1975. London: Allen Lane, 1977.

Garside, P.D. J.E. Belanger, and S.A. Ragaz, *British Fiction, 1800–1829: A Database of Production, Circulation & Reception,* University of Cardiff, designer A.A. Mandal http://www.british-fiction.cf.ac.uk

Garside, Peter. "The English Novel in the Romantic Era: Consolidation and Dispersal" in Peter Garside, James Raven, and Rainer Schöwerling (eds), *The English Novel 1770–1829: A Bibliographical Survey of Prose Fiction Published in the British Isles, Vol. II. 1800–1829.* Oxford: Oxford University Press, 2000.

Green, Martin. *Dreams of Adventure, Deeds of Empire.* 1979. London and Henley: Routledge & Kegan Paul, 1980.

Guha, Ranajit and Gayatri Chakravorty Spivak (eds). *Selected Subaltern Studies.* New York and Oxford: Oxford University Press, 1988.

Guy, Alan J. "'People who will stick at nothing to make money?': Officers, Income, and Expectations in the Service of John Company, 1750–1840," in Alan Guy and Peter B Boyden (eds), assisted by Marian Harding, *Soldiers of the Raj: The Indian Army, 1600–1947.* London: National Army Museum, 1997.

Hanham, H.J. "Religion and Nationality in the Mid-Victorian Army" in M.R.D. Foot (ed), *War and Society: Historical Essays in Memory of J.R. Western.* London: Elek, 1973.

Harries-Jenkins, Gwyn. *The Army in Victorian Society.* Hull: University Of Hull Press, 1993.

Harris, R.G. and Chris Warner, *Bengal Cavalry Regiments, 1857–1914.* Men-at-Arms Series. 1979. Botley, Oxford: Osprey, 2000.

Hendrickson, Kenneth. "Winning the Troops for Vital Religion: Female Evangelical Missionaries to the British Army, 1857–1880" *Armed Forces and Society,* Vol 23, No. 4 (1997): 615–34.

Holmes, Richard. *Redcoat: The British Soldier in the Age of Horse and Musket.* Hammersmith: HarperCollins, 2001.

Holmes, Richard. *Sahib: The British Soldier in India, 1750–1914.* London: HarperCollins, 2005.

Hook, Andrew. Introduction to *Waverley* by Walter Scott. London: Penguin, 1972.

Innes, Joanna. "Libraries in Context: Social, Cultural and Intellectual Background," in Mandelbrote and Manley (eds), *The Cambridge History of Libraries in Britain and Ireland. Vol. II, 1640–1850.*

Iser, Wolfgang. *The Implied Reader: Patterns of Communication in Prose Fiction from Bunyan to Beckett*. Baltimore and London: Johns Hopkins, 1974.

Iser, Wolfgang. *The Act of Reading: A Theory of Aesthetic Response*. Baltimore, Maryland and London: Johns Hopkins, 1978.

James, Lawrence. *Raj: The Making and Unmaking of British India*. London: Abacus, 1998.

James, Louis. *Fiction for the Working Man, 1830–1850: A Study of the Literature produced for the Working Classes in early Victorian urban England*. London, New York, and Toronto: Oxford University Press, 1963.

Jeffrey, M. Helen. *The Trumpet Call Obey: The Story of the Homes for Servicemen founded a Century Ago by Elise Sandes*. London: Marshall, Morgan, and Scott, 1968.

Jenkins, Robin P. "Hawker , James (1836–1921)." *Oxford Dictionary of National Biography*, Oxford University Press, 2004. [http://www.oxforddnb.com. remote.library.dcu.ie/view/article/74229, accessed 20 April 2015].

Johns, Adrian. *The Nature of the Book: Print and Knowledge in the Making*. Chicago and London: University of Chicago Press, 1998.

Kabir, Abulfazal M. Fazle. *The Libraries of Bengal, 1700–1947*. London: Mansell Publications, 1987.

Kaestle, Carl F. "Studying the History of Literacy" in Shafquat Towheed, Rosalind Crone, and Kate Halsey (eds), *The History of Reading: A Reader*. London and New York: Routledge, 2011.

Kaser, David. *Books and Libraries in Camp and Battle: The Civil War Experience*. Westport, Connecticut and London: Green Wood Press, 1984.

Keay, John. *The Honourable Company: A History of the English East India Company*. London: HarperCollins, 1995.

Kelly, Gary. *Women, Writing, and Revolution, 1790–1827*. Oxford: Clarendon, 1993.

Kelly, Gary. "Romantic Fiction" in Stuart Curran (ed), *The Cambridge Companion to British Romanticism*. Cambridge: Cambridge University Press, 1993.

Kennedy, Grace. *Father Clement: A Roman Catholic Story*. Edinburgh: William Oliphant, 1824.

Kincaid, Denis. *British Social Life in India, 1608–1937*. 2nd edition. London and Boston: Routledge and Kegan Paul, 1973.

King, Edmund G.C. "E.W Hornung's unpublished 'Diary,' the YMCA, and the Reading Soldier in the First World War" *English Literature in Transition*, vol. 57, no. 3 (2014): 361–87.

King, Edmund G.C. "E.W. 'Books are more to me than Food': British Prisoners of War as Readers, 1914–1918" *Book History*, vol. 16 (2013): 246–71.

Klancher, Jon P. *The Making of English Reading Audiences, 1790–1832*. Madison, Wisconsin and London: The University of Wisconsin Press, 1987.

Laugesen, Amanda. "*Boredom is the Enemy*": *The Intellectual and Imaginative Lives of Australian Soldiers in the Great War and Beyond*. Farnham: Ashgate, 2012.

Lawson, Philip. *The East India Company: A History*. London and New York: Longman, 1993.

Leadbetter, Mary. *Cottage Dialogues among the Irish Peasantry*, Part II. Dublin: John Cumming, 1813.

Lockyer, Dora. "The Provision of Books and Libraries by the East India Company in India, 1611–1858." Thesis submitted for Fellowship of the Library Association, 1977.

Makepeace, Margaret. *The East India Company's London Workers: Management of the Warehouse Labourers, 1800–1858*. Woodbridge: The Boydell Press, 2010.

Manley, K.A. "Engines of Literature: Libraries in an Era of Expansion and Transition," in Mandelbrote and Manley (eds), *The Cambridge History of Libraries in Britain and Ireland. Vol. II, 1640–1850*.

Manning, Molly Guptill. *When Books went to War: The Stories that helped us win World War II*. Boston and New York: Houghton Mifflin Harcourt, 2014.

Martin, Carol A. "Mary Howitt," in Janet Todd (ed), *Dictionary of British Women Writers*. 1989. London: Routledge, 1991.

Mesham, Donald. "A Forgotten Book Collection: The Army Standard Unit Library" *Publishing History*, vol. 69 (2011): 85–111.

Murphy, David. *Ireland and the Crimean War*. Dublin: Four Courts, 2002.

Murphy, Sharon. *Maria Edgeworth and Romance*. Dublin: Four Courts, 2004.

Neuburg, Victor. *Gone for a Soldier: A History of Life in the British Ranks from . 1642*. London: Castell Publishers, 1989.

Nix, Jonathan. "Landscape, Space, and Social Practice: Moral Geographies in and beyond the Warehouses of the Nottingham Lace Market." Research Papers General Series no. 2. London: Royal Holloway University of London, 1995.

Ogborn, Miles and Chris Philo. "Soldiers, Sailors and Moral Locations in Nineteenth-Century Portsmouth *Area*," Vol. 26, No. 3 (September, 1994): 221–31.

Oxford Dictionary of National Biography Online (http://www.oxforddnb.com/).

Oxford English Dictionary Online (http://www.OED.com/).

Paltock, Robert. *The Life and Adventures of Peter Wilkins*. Oxford: Oxford University Press, 1973.

Perera, Suvendrini. *Reaches of Empire: The English Novel from Edgeworth to Dickens*. New York: Columbia University Press, 1991.

Plumb, J.H. "The New World of Children in Eighteenth-Century England" *Past and Present* 67 (1975).

Pope, Stephen (ed). *The Cassell Dictionary of the Napoleonic Wars*. London: Cassell, 1999.

Ramsey, Neil. *The Military Memoir and Romantic Literary Culture, 1780–1835*. The Nineteenth Century Series. Farnham: Ashgate, 2011.

Ramsey, Neil. "'A Real English Soldier': Suffering, Manliness and Class in the Mid-Nineteenth-Century Soldier's Tale," in Catriona Kennedy and Matthew McCormack (eds), *Soldiering in Britain and Ireland, 1750–1850*. Houndsmills, Basingstoke: Palgrave Macmillan, 2013.

Raspe, Rudolf Erich. *The Travels and Surprising Adventures of Baron Munchausen.* 1785. Sawtry, Cambridge: Dedalus, 1993.

Raven, James. "From Promotion to Proscription: Arrangements for Reading and Eighteenth-Century Libraries," in James Raven, Helen Small, and Naomi Tadmor (eds), *The Practice and Representation of Reading in England.* Cambridge: Cambridge University Press, 1996.

Raven, James and Helen Small and Naomi Tadmor. Introduction to *The Practice and Representation of Reading in England.*

Richardson, Alan. *Literature, Education, and Romanticism: Reading as Social Practice, 1780–1832.* Cambridge: Cambridge University Press, 1994.

Richardson, Alan. and Sonia Hofkosh. Introduction to *Romanticism, Race, and Imperial Culture, 1780–1834.* Eds. Alan Richardson and Sonia Hofkosh. Bloomington and Indianapolis: Indiana University Press, 1996.

Riddick, John F. *Who Was Who in British India.* Westport, CT and London: Greenwood, 1998.

Rose, Jonathan. *The Intellectual Life of the British Working Classes.* New Haven and London: Yale University Press, 2001.

Said, Edward. *Orientalism.* 1978. London: Penguin, 2003.

Said, Edward. Foreword to *Selected Subaltern Studies.* Eds. Guha and Spivak.

Said, Edward. *Culture and Imperialism.* London: Chatto and Windus, 1993.

Schofield, Roger S. "Dimension of Illiteracy in England, 1740–1850," in Towheed, Crone, and Halsey (eds), *The History of Reading.*

Scott, Walter. *The Journal of Sir Walter Scott.* Ed. W.E.K. Anderson. Oxford: Clarendon Press, 1972.

Scott, Walter. *Waverley.* London: Penguin, 1972.

Scott, Walter. *Rob Roy.* London: Penguin, 1995.

Sherwood, Mary Martha. *Memoirs of Sergeant Dale, His Daughter, and the Orphan Mary.* 3rd edn. London: F. Houlston and Son, 1816.

Skelley, Alan Ramsay. *The Victorian Army at Home: Recruitment and Terms and Conditions of the British Regular, 1859–1899.* London: Croom Helm, 1977.

Snape, Robert. *Leisure and the Rise of the Public Library.* London: Library Association Publishing, 1995.

Snape, Robert. "Libraries for Leisure Time," in Black and Hoare (eds), *The Cambridge History of Libraries in Britain and Ireland. Vol. III, 1850–2000.*

Spiers, Edward M. *The Army and Society, 1815–1914.* London and New York: Longman, 1980.

Spiers, Edward M. *The Late Victorian Army, 1868–1902.* Manchester: Manchester University Press, 1992.

St. Clair, William. *The Reading Nation in the Romantic Period.* Cambridge: Cambridge University Press, 2004.

Stanley, Peter. *White Mutiny: British Military Culture in India, 1825–1875.* London: Hurst and Company, 1998.

Stearn, Roger T. "Cairnes, William Elliot (1862–1902)." *Oxford Dictionary of National Biography*. Oxford University Press, 2004; online edn, May 2006. [http://www.oxforddnb.com.remote.library.dcu.ie/view/article/32241, accessed 14 July 2015].

Steedman, Carolyn. *The Radical Soldier's Tale: John Pearman, 1819–1908*. London and New York: Routledge, 1988.

Stephens, H.M. "Frederick, Prince, Duke of York and Albany (1763–1827)." Rev. John Van der Kiste. *Oxford Dictionary of National Biography*. Oxford University Press, 2004; online edn, Oct 2007 [http://www.oxforddnb.com.remote.library.dcu.ie/view/article/10139, accessed 10 July 2015].

Stephens, H.M. "Colville, Sir Charles (1770–1843)." Rev. Roger T. Stearn. *Oxford Dictionary of National Biography*. Oxford University Press, 2004 [http://www.oxforddnb.com.remote.library.dcu.ie/view/article/6008, accessed 17 Oct 2015].

Stone, Lawrence. *The Family, Sex, and Marriage in England, 1500-1800*. Abridged Edition. London: Penguin, 1979.

Tales from the Thousand and One Nights. Trans. N.J. Dawood.

Thorne, Roland. "Hastings, Francis Rawdon, first marquess of Hastings and second earl of Moira (1754–1826)." *Oxford Dictionary of National Biography*. Oxford University Press, 2004; online edn, Jan 2008 [http://www.oxforddnb.com.remote.library.dcu.ie/view/article/12568, accessed 13 Oct 2015].

Todd, Janet (ed). *Dictionary of British Women Writers*. 1989. London: Routledge, 1991.

Tosh, John. *Manliness and Masculinities in Nineteenth-Century Britain: Essays on Gender, Family, and Empire*. Harlow: Pearson Longman, 2005.

Trumpener, Katie. *Bardic Nationalism: The Romantic Novel and the British Empire*. Princeton, New Jersy and Chicester, West Sussex: Princeton University Press, 1997.

Vincent, David. "Reading and Writing," in Towheed, Crone, and Halsey (eds), *The History of Reading*.

Viswanathan, Gauri. *Masks of Conquest: Literary Study and British Rule in India*. London: Faber and Faber, 1990.

Welsh, Alexander. *The Hero of the Waverley Novels*. New Haven and London: Yale University Press, 1963.

Yule, Henry and A.C. Burnell, *Hobson-Jobson: The Anglo-Indian Dictionary*. 1886. Ware, Hertfordshire, 1996.

INDEX

References to footnotes consist of the page number followed by the letter 'n' followed by the number of the note, e.g. 37n24 refers to footnote no. 24 on page 37. Regiments and other military units are listed under East India Company's army or Regular Army, as appropriate.

© The Editor(s) (if applicable) and The Author(s) 2016
S. Murphy, *The British Soldier and his Libraries, c. 1822-1901*,
DOI 10.1057/978-1-137-55083-5